Nelson

Thomas Nelson and Sons Ltd
Nelson House   Mayfield Road
Walton-on-Thames   Surrey KT12 5PL

51 York Place
Edinburgh EH1 3JD

Thomas Nelson (Hong Kong) Ltd
Toppan Building 10/F
22A Westlands Road
Quarry Bay   Hong Kong

First published by Thomas Nelson and Sons Ltd 1985
ISBN 0-17-555609-1
NPN 9 8 7 6

Designed by The New Book Factory, London
Phototypeset by Parkway Illustrated Press Ltd, Abingdon
Printed in Hong Kong

Contents

General Introduction

New Proficiency English

New Proficiency English is a four-book course, planned as a replacement of *Proficiency English*, published in 1976–8, and as a logical continuation of the approaches adopted in *New First Certificate English*, published in 1984. In effect, it is the result of several years' experience of using the previous course and gradually adapting materials to the needs of students taught at earlier stages in the learning process by different methods from those current in the early 1970s. As in the case of *New First Certificate English*, my co-authors, John Pidcock and Robin Rycroft, and I have preferred to write a new course, taking this experience into account, rather than rewrite the original. While some elements that have proved particularly successful have been retained – above all in *Book 3, Use of English*, where the revised Cambridge syllabus of 1984 for the paper shows no innovations – over 80% of the material in the course is new.

By this time, it will be evident that the examination as such has not changed to a noticeable extent, either in level of difficulty or in form, except in the design of the aural/oral tests (covered in this course by *Book 4*). The main change in our approach, especially in *Book 1*, has been to shift the emphasis away from the reliance on structures and towards the acquisition of skills, while retaining the overall coverage of necessary grammatical revision through an extensive reference section for students in *Book 1* and a wide variety of remedial exercises in *Book 3*. This change, however, was not influenced by changes in syllabus but by the continuing research and pretesting we have undertaken in recent years.

The main problem for teachers at advanced level and for students attempting the Proficiency examination is that the former are inclined to relax the pressure once students have passed First Certificate because the Proficiency examination is still a long way ahead, while the latter underestimate the difference in standard. This course has been written for students likely to attempt the examination two years after First Certificate if they attend classes five hours a week (300 hours) or three years afterwards if they attend three times a week (270 hours). The material has been pretested and graded through use with students at each stage to allow for the time span envisaged, but it is above all important to point out that the language-learning process should be continuous. Our experience leads us to believe that it is necessary to develop skills methodically throughout the period and that it is unwise to imagine that students can be left largely to their own devices for a year or so before making a systematic approach to the examination.

The design of the course

The four books comprising the new course can be used independently in order to concentrate on a specific paper in the examination, but they have been written in such a way that they complement each other. *Book 1, Language and Composition*, consists of 28 units, the last four forming a separate section intended for those students who wish to attempt the Prescribed Books option in composition. The units of the other three books have been written in parallel to the basic 24 teaching units of *Book 1* so that every unit of that book is supported by two out of three possible units devoted to the skills required for Reading Comprehension, Use of English and Listening Comprehension/Interview. The chart at the back of this *Teacher's Guide* shows the relationship. In this way, the themes of units in *Book 1* are frequently reflected in the choice of reading passages in *Book 2* so that there is an opportunity for revising and expanding vocabulary; the structures necessary for the composition tasks in *Book 1* are revised and practised in *Book 3*, and the topics for summary in *Book 3* also have a thematic relationship in the majority of cases with parallel units in *Book 1*; the opportunities for free discussion and the listening material provided in *Book 4* are also related to themes and group-work activities presented in *Book 1*. The design of the course, comprising 24 basic units for study in *Book 1*, permits teachers to make a convenient break either after Unit 8, if students are studying three hours a week, or after Unit 12, if they are studying for five.

A skills approach at advanced level

The problems of students at advanced level are not primarily grammatical, even though mistakes persist both in speech and writing. In both areas, but particularly in writing, they stem in our experience from the following causes:

1   inadequate training in English (and probably in

their own language) in the techniques of discourse, with the consequent inability to organise their thoughts in a convincing manner, uncertainty of the basic premises behind paragraphing, linking ideas together through the use of connectors and modifiers, etc.;

2 a limited vocabulary which makes it difficult for them to express themselves fluently except in general terms on a small number of subjects;

3 a growing awareness that the English of real life is much more subtle and varied than a diet of text books may suggest, which may cause them to become disillusioned, although it can be channelled into a new source of interest in the language;

4 a failure to perceive until too late that the demands of the Proficiency examination are not necessarily much more demanding linguistically than those of First Certificate, except in the range of vocabulary that students are expected to understand, but are intellectually much more demanding because of the nature of the tasks they are asked to perform.

The ways in which we have attempted to combat these potential weaknesses are explained in detail in the separate introductions to the books in the course and the notes that follow. Methodologically, there is nothing revolutionary in an approach that first presents a wide variety of materials appropriate to the level; secondly, enables students by means of examples to analyse not only its content in terms of structure and lexis but also the techniques of discourse employed to make it effective for its purpose; and finally permits them, first through activities in pairs and groups in class and afterwards through individual composition tasks etc. to use everything they have learnt for themselves. What we believe we have achieved, nevertheless, is a method in which the necessary components of such a system are thoroughly integrated in a logical manner that takes into account the relative length of a Proficiency course.

The stages in a Proficiency course

As indicated above, we designed this course for students with from 270–300 hours' tuition between passing the First Certificate examination and reaching the level of Proficiency. In our view, again as already indicated, the problem for teachers is to avoid introducing examination materials too soon in such a course but at the same time to avoid a long, easy-going period preceding intensive work for the examination. For students, too, the problem presents itself in similar terms; on the one hand, they must not imagine that the level of Proficiency is not much higher than that of First Certificate and overestimate their chances, while on the other, they cannot be allowed to think that the skills, and in particular the range of vocabulary they need, can be learnt in a hurry at the last minute.

For this reason, the skills to be learnt in terms of writing in *Book 1* of this course have been presented in a cyclical form of six stages, allowing for their gradual acquisition at the appropriate time; the passages for comprehension and the lexis taught, practised and tested in *Book 2* have been carefully graded; the structural items introduced and practised in *Book 3* have been graded in the same way; the tasks for listening comprehension and oral practice in *Book 4* have also been planned to relate to the basic stages in *Book 1*.

Pretesting

As in the case of *New First Certificate English*, we have been fortunate in being able to count on the help of the teachers and students of schools in Barcelona with over a thousand students between them in three levels of post-First Certificate classes and with good pass rates in previous Proficiency examinations. Consequently, every lexical or structural item in the progress tests and test papers in these books has been thoroughly pretested and assigned to an appropriate stage in the course. The teacher's notes for *Book 2* and *Book 3* in this *Teacher's Guide* contain detailed analysis of the results in all cases and provide accurate data from which teachers can measure the progress of their own classes.

Acknowledgements

We have acknowledged the help given to us by the staff and students as a whole and by a number of individuals in particular in the relevant students' books of the course, but we take the opportunity here of thanking them once again. Without their help, the organisation of this course in a logical, systematic manner would not have been possible.

WILL FOWLER, Barcelona,
October, 1984

NEW PROFICIENCY ENGLISH
Book 1
Language and Composition

Introduction

The organisation of units

As indicated in the chart at the back of this *Teacher's Guide*, *Book 1* of the course consists of 28 units. The first 24 units are divided into six stages of four units each, reflecting the different kinds of composition students may be asked to write – description, narrative, discussion and types of directed writing, more accurately defined as rewriting; the last was a task formerly set in the last section of the Use of English paper. The stages have been designed so that students can make progress towards more sophisticated techniques in self-expression and in the later stages there is an emphasis on the need to blend techniques (for example, of description and narrative) in order to handle certain topics. The last four units form an optional section on prescribed books for those students who are reading a book in order to take advantage of the fifth question in the composition paper. The design of the stages is such that teachers can make a convenient break either at the end of Unit 8 and Unit 16 in a three-year course of three hours a week, or at the end of Unit 12 in a two-year course of five hours a week.

In the notes that follow we have indicated throughout:

1 the aims of the unit and its components in terms of developing skills;
2 structures that will be required by students in order to complete the composition tasks and which may need to be revised, either with exercises appearing in this book or with the help of exercises in *Book 3*;
3 advice on presentation and on the activities, together with suggested answers for those activities where students are asked to analyse texts either for their style and content or for the techniques employed;
4 relevant links between the texts and activities in this book, related texts in *Book 2* and exercises in *Book 3*.

Teaching the skills

Although the persistence of elementary mistakes may at times suggest that the problems of students at advanced level resemble those of the intermediate student preparing for First Certificate, they are essentially different. The main difference lies in the fact that students who have passed First Certificate have sufficient knowledge of structure to write accurately and the structures they have learnt already are quite sufficient for them to achieve fluency if they know how to use them. Consequently, we regard grammatical revision (see below) as something that teachers should use with great discretion to avoid demotivating students; we also consider that the few structures students may not have encountered before are for the most part seldom used in good modern English and are best dealt with as items for structural conversion (*Book 3*), a matter of recognition rather than use.

On the other hand, primarily because the majority of students do not read widely enough in English and do not analyse the techniques of discourse employed in what they read, they are often incapable of developing their writing skills towards fluency without considerable instruction in technique. The difference between writing a satisfactory composition for First Certificate and for Proficiency is not one of employing more complex forms of expression, as many students imagine, but of having a much greater variety of technical resources and the correspondingly wider and more precise vocabulary in order to deal with more sophisticated topics. We have therefore provided a large number of texts aimed at helping students to identify techniques used in writing of different kinds, and in the accompanying activities have given students the opportunity to develop their command of these techniques for themselves, largely through pair and group work, so that they will be able to use them naturally in individual compositions.

Taken together, the texts and activities have the following general aims:
1 to introduce the theme of a unit (and potential source of composition topics) in an interesting way so as to help students to clarify their ideas;
2 to help students to analyse the construction, development and linkage of paragraphs;
3 to help them to analyse the style and content of passages written for a specific purpose, either in isolation or by means of comparison;
4 to aid the analysis of the techniques employed in these passages so that they can employ them for themselves;
5 to use information retrieval techniques as a basis for exercises enabling students to reorder and rewrite information in a different form, and to indicate what changes may be required in terms of structure, register, etc.;
6 in some cases, to revise grammatical points essential for specific composition tasks.

We have placed considerable emphasis on the use of pair work and group work in the classroom even though many of the tasks could be equally well completed by individuals. This is largely because tasks at this level require considerable powers of intellectual concentration and can easily be time-consuming but not very productive if too much weight is placed on individual performance.

At the same time, we have generally preferred pairs to larger groups as the best way of dealing with activities, since our experience in pretesting indicates that if too many people are involved in the same task, much time is taken up with needless details in discussion, or else the entire responsibility can easily fall on an outstanding student.

We expect individuals to demonstrate the progress they are making in the compositions they write at the end of each unit, which we would normally require to be done at home. It is also very important, for the activities to function effectively in the classroom and time not to be wasted, that students should contribute to this by reading texts before coming to class when asked to do so.

We have indicated what we have found to be the most effective way of handling each activity throughout the book, but we would stress that such suggestions are meant to be flexible and to be adapted to teachers' individual circumstances.

Grammatical revision

Whereas at First Certificate level, in the course preceding this one, *New First Certificate English*, we provided a checklist of grammatical items at the beginning of each unit which had to be thoroughly understood before the unit could be started, it seemed to us discouraging to students at advanced level to adopt the same approach. What we have done instead is to provide a thorough Reference Section at the end of the book for students to refer to.

This decision was based on practical experience; in common with the vast majority of teachers of advanced classes we have consulted on the subject, we are convinced that long-standing structural problems – as distinct from students' ability to develop writing skills and clear up points of vocabulary and usage by asking the teacher – can only be cured by the students making the effort to check such things for themselves. This is not to say that remedial practice is discounted. There is an ample section devoted to problems commonly found among advanced students at the beginning of *Book 3*, but this is primarily intended for revision of points that affect the majority of a class, not as an essential part of the initial presentation.

The units therefore form not so much a grammatical progression, although this feature is incorporated

within them, as a gradual approach to handling more and more complex topics in a more sophisticated manner. In such circumstances, it is not the teacher's role to introduce structures as if they were being presented for the first time, but only to remind students of those they will need to complete the tasks. In this connection, we have attempted to foresee students' needs and to provide the necessary cross-referencing so that remedial exercises can be done whenever they prove necessary.

Composition

In all cases, the composition task at the end of the unit is meant to measure the extent to which students have absorbed the content of the unit and are capable of putting what they have learnt into practice. While writing is therefore the ultimate aim of the unit, however, this does not mean that it should be the main activity in class. Above all, students should learn to deal with the activities in terms of making notes from which they can speak, rather than writing out long answers unless specifically required to do so.

The ideal from the teacher's point of view in dealing with each unit is to ensure that students read the texts beforehand so that most of the time in class can be spent on analysing them and discussing their content, appropriateness for their purpose and the techniques employed; in the same way, if the final composition task is set as homework, students have the opportunity to demonstrate their individual progress and should also take more time over their work, consulting the Reference Section whenever they need to do so. In this way, the classroom work is concentrated almost entirely on skills and the exchange of ideas.

Two further points need to be made in connection with composition. One is that in our experience the progress made by students almost always has a close correlation with the amount of written work they do at home and the consistency with which they produce it. It should be impressed on all students from the beginning of the course that if they are seriously interested in passing the Proficiency examination eventually, even though it may seem a long way away in terms of time and hours of study, they will hardly ever achieve this aim unless they are prepared to practise and improve their skills in written English throughout the period, and not as a last-minute form of preparation.

The second point is that compositions at advanced level are notoriously difficult to assess for a number of reasons. For the benefit of teachers inexperienced at this level, we have included a section on composition marking and assessment as a guide to what might reasonably be expected at the different stages in what is inevitably a long course.

Composition marking

Teachers new to advanced classes leading up to the Cambridge Proficiency examination may be unsure of what standards to apply and what method of marking to adopt. The examples given below are intended as a guide to standards. The system used, an impression mark out of 20, is similar to that used by Cambridge, with one notable difference. Cambridge indicate that they award 8/20 (40%) as a pass level and subsequently correlate scores with those in other parts of the examination (e.g. multiple-choice questions) where, although no pass mark is given, it must be of the order of 60%–65%. We consider it to be fatal to suggest to students at any time that 40% could be considered a pass mark, when nothing less than 60% would achieve a pass level elsewhere in the Proficiency examination. We have therefore adopted a pass mark of 12/20 (60%) for all the compositions assessed here. It is obviously necessary at the same time to realise that in long courses such as Proficiency, there is a considerable difference in what can reasonably be expected of students at different stages; as a rough guide, we would calculate that composition deserving a pass mark of 12/20 soon after the student has passed First Certificate would only be awarded 8/20 if he or she was in a Proficiency class approaching the examination.

We would not wish to convey that it is essential to give students marks in this way; it is a matter of opinion whether students benefit from receiving what can at best be an honest, but subjective, evaluation of their work in the form of numbers or letters. We ourselves do not give marks for students to see, except in examinations, but we note our assessments in a book for our own guidance on their progress. What is essential is that students should receive the maximum amount of advice (see 'Correction', below) but should be encouraged to analyse their own mistakes and realise that detailed correction involves a great deal of hard work, which will be wasted if they do not study the corrections afterwards. In this connection, giving a mark may be counter-productive, since it may lead students to become either over-confident or disillusioned.

Assessment

It is considerably more difficult to assess compositions at Proficiency level than at First Certificate because form and content and choice of subject play a much more important part. It is also necessary to bear in mind the comparative length of Proficiency courses and to recognise that what may appear a reasonable attempt not long after passing First Certificate is unlikely to be adequate later on. In all the examples given below, the mark given is an impression mark out of 20, where CPE level is 12, but in the first group of examples, taken from students with only 50 hours' tuition after First Certificate, the compositions would have received four marks less if they had been in a Proficiency class, so that none would have come close to passing. They have been chosen as illustrations of the main problems teachers are likely to encounter.

1. Organisation and Accuracy

Compare the two compositions on the same subject, which was to write a story beginning: 'There were six of us, and I was the only one who understood a word of English . . .' Note that the second, in fact, continued for a further fifteen lines within the single paragraph that constituted the whole composition. Make up your own mind about a mark for each before reading our comments below:

I   CLARA

There were six of us, and I was the only one who understood a word of English. Nobody else had any knowledge of the language and it was quite difficult to me to remember or pronounce correctly the few words I learned in a mounth course I took before going to this trip. As you can imagine we can explain a lot of funny and confused situations that happened to us.

You ask for a room and don't understand the number of it and they have to repeat it, or you ask for a place before having repeated the sentence to yourself twice or three times you say it correctly but you don't understand the answer. Mainwhile your friends are waiting for you. They believe in you! Anyhow, sooner or later you find the way to be understood.

The problem is the things that you loose because you don't know a language. You don't have the possibility to meet native people and you can't know anything about the way of life, how they live, what are their problems etc. You see things in your point of view.

Although we spent a good time all together it was as we had gone to some place in our country. That's why I don't want to go to another country if I don't know the language or they speak on English.

---

2   NURIA

There were six of us, and I was the only one who understood a
word of English. I had never been in such a situation before but
anyway it didn't sound very exciting to me. At first I was scared
but after a few days I decided that even if my English wasn't good
enough it wasn't that important; so finaly my friends convinced me
and there we went... We were going to spend our holidays in England,
there were a short holidays but realy good ones. A sunny Sunday
August morning we were leaving Barcelona by plane we arrive to
Gatwick on time the flight wasn't delay that was a great succed for
Iberia, I still remember that as soon as Montse trade English earth
told me 'these chaps are improving!' We took the bus to London and
as soon as we arrive at Victoria Coach Station I asked where was the
nearest information office, we easily found a bed and breakfast
house for one week, the house wasn't very far from there but we
didn't feel like carrying them so we took two taxis, I sent the
first group in a taxi to the right adress and the other three
followed them in another one.....

Assessment

Almost certainly, you awarded a higher mark to Clara
than to Nuria. In fact, the standard of English is not
very different, and Nuria has a more idiomatic
vocabulary ('scared', 'these chaps are improving', even
when she cannot quite remember the correct phrase –
'as soon as Montse trade (for 'trod') English earth'.
Nevertheless, Clara is at all times understandable
simply because she has organised the composition into
four simple paragraphs and punctuated the sentences.
Nuria has no idea of paragraphing at all and after a
reasonable start, punctuation also disappears, so that it
is virtually impossible to understand the last two
sentences here without re-reading them two or three
times. We consider that Clara merits a safe pass (13)
but Nuria cannot be awarded more than 10, even
though the story she is telling is quite lively.

2.   Theme

As in Cambridge Proficiency examinations, students in
the same class as Clara and Nuria were given a choice
of subject. Rather than attempt the narrative option
shown above, the next two chose a discussion topic:
'Marriage is the attraction of opposites'. Before looking
at our assessment, decide on an impression mark for
these compositions, using the same criteria as for Clara
and Nuria. The second, Barbara, represents only the
first half of the composition, and this should be taken
into account.

3   NEUS

To say that marriage is the attraction of opposites is so
easy that I can accept it.
It is sort of difficult to know the causes of marriage
but we know that humans have invented it. Specially our society
has adopted marriage as an institution which is the engine of
a great deal of people's life. In the past the family chose
the right person to be married with. So it was not a problem
of opposites but a resolution of conveniences.
Nowadays, fortunatelly, these ideas have changed quite a
bit. The vast majority of people do not believe in marriage.
Then, I can consider that there are lots of attractions for losts
of different people and of course, attraction of opposites can
be a possibility but not the only one. It is more complicated
than we think.

4   BARBARA

It is said that marriage is the attraction of opposites.
In my opinion, this is a conventional way to explain the attraction
between the two sexes, or a justification of marriage itself.
I understand the attraction of opposites, but opposites don't
necessary have to be a man and a woman.
What opposites are is a personal question. Anyway marriage
means or makes legal at society's eyes an attraction.
I think only religion or tradition makes people at the
necessity to get married.
At the nature state, the attraction borned between opposites
doesn't need any civil or religious justification. In fact
attraction can easy be satisfied by living together.
It's strange to notice that now young people are inclined to
get married even if tradition is more flexible. That makes me
think a lot that many people feels now secure when they get
married. I think people are afraid of loneliness........

Assessment

The level of English of these two students is not
markedly inferior to that of Clara and Nuria, and Neus,
in terms of accuracy, is perhaps a little better than
Nuria. The trouble is that Neus has very little to say
about the subject and never suggests that she really
understands what is involved in the title.
Unfortunately, in our experience, students do not seem
to regard composition topics in examinations as a
means of showing how much English they know but,
unless otherwise advised, seem to pick on them at
random. It is very common for the students whose
linguistic and intellectual equipment for the task is
most limited to choose the most abstract subjects. Neus

could not be awarded more than 9 out of 20 on our scale, but if she had written about something familiar to her she might well have passed.

Barbara, on the other hand, has plenty of ideas, because the complete composition contained four more of her 'paragraphs'. The ideas are expressed, however, without any continuity and her 'paragraphing' demonstrates it. It is likely that the tendency to basic errors would have shown itself in a composition on a simpler topic, but the result would surely not have been meaningless to the reader, as this is. The score awarded was 7, but in fact all that is clear is that the composition is a long way below the standard demanded.

Comment

In general terms, the only solutions we can offer to these problems are the specific training in techniques for different kinds of composition that we have included in *New Proficiency English, Book 1*, but it is evident that students should be warned from the beginning of the importance of organisation, as well as accuracy, and should learn that in examinations it is unwise to attempt subjects beyond their linguistic capacity, however interesting they may appear to be in themselves.

3. Proficiency-level compositions

The following compositions were written by students in Proficiency classes some 50 hours of tuition time before attempting the examination. For reasons already given, the marking scale adopted is different from that used by Cambridge, and assessment is based on a scale where Cambridge A = 17 or more, B = 15–16, C = 12–14, D = 11, and E = 10 or less.

In all cases, the subject is the same: 'What improvements do you think should be made in your town or village?'. As in the case of previous examples, you may like to decide on your own impression mark out of 20 before reading our assessment.

5   LEANDRO

In the last few years speculation of the soil has made Barcelona a not very comfortable town to live in. Dreadful high-rise blocks cluster on the outskirts of the town, leaving no place for parks and green areas. People need places where they can practise sports, let their children play or just walk safely without looking out for cars.

Traffic congestion is a problem which worries many people in Barcelona. One way out would be to build new motorways round the town so that cars do not have to go through Barcelona to get to the other end of town. It would make the town less noisy, saving energy at the same time. Perhaps cars should be banned from the centre of town but I think this is a point that needs further discussion. Attached to this there should be an improvement in public transport. We just cannot tell people not to take the car if there is no bus or subway that goes to the place they want to get to. Public transport should also be cheaper.

Another thing which must be taken into account is pollution. Decreasing the number of cars, we reduce pollution but there are other ways to overcome this problem. For example, factories should be taken out of the town and people working in them should be given homes nearby.

Last but not least is the problem of educating people. We must built a town where people can walk in the streets at any time without fear of being robbed or hurt. We must teach the new generations to behave rightly and respect not only other people but also their own town. This is perhaps the most important thing for there is no point in building a wonderful town with all the commodities you may dream of if you cannot walk safely along the streets.

Assessment

There is no doubt that this composition clearly merits a pass at Proficiency level, and the only question is whether it qualifies for A or B level. It is well organised in logical paragraphs that (a) introduce the subject; (b) answer the question, giving examples; (c) reach a sensible conclusion. It is accurate, using a variety of tenses and forms correctly, and the only obvious mistake, 'built' for 'build' early in the last paragraph, may be a slip of the pen. The lexical range is considerable, with the choice of the correct phrase in most cases clearly evident – 'high-rise blocks', 'traffic congestion' – though not in all – 'speculation of the soil'. The student uses connectors correctly – 'last but not least', though not to the extent that a native speaker would. Our mark was 16, on the grounds that the composition is of a high standard but would not suggest to us for more than a sentence or two that it had been written by a native speaker.

6 BLANCA

Barcelona is settled in a privileged natural area. In point of fact, its bounds are the sea and two hills, Tibidabo (in the north part) and Montjuich (in the south-west). At the beginning of the present century, there was an architect called Sardà who presented to the major of the Catalan capital a map where it appeared a beautiful planification of the town. He planned the city with lots of parks and small, independant houses, each one with its own garden. Nevertheless, as industrialism was growing speedily at that time, the authorities yielded to material profit and to greediness and they therefore didn't allow Sardà's plan to come into being.

Nowadays, Barcelona is suffering from that narrow-minded decision as it has become an enormous town not because it extends a lot but because of its overpopulation - its density represents one of its most striking problems. At the same time, as Barcelona is one of the craddles of industry in Spain, it particularly suffers from pollution too.

Bearing in mind all these outstanding problems, life for the citizens of Barcelona could be improved by taking special care of the environment of the town. That is, by creating a lot of green spaces and therefore by limiting the building of houses. There should also be a strict control of the factories near the town so that they wouldn't throw their waste into a river or into the sea. At the same time, people (especially young people) should be stimmulated to use a bicycle as their way of transport instead of going by motorbike or by car, not only to lessen pollution in general but also to avoid disturbing noises.

To sum up, Barcelona should follow the example of the most civilised countries, such as Germany, Sweden, where the respect of nature can even be called the worship of nature. In fact, the authorities and the citizens of Barcelona should react positively so that the well-spread sentence 'Let's hope it will rain so that we can breathe and we can see the sun' should never be uttered again.

Assessment

The composition is well organised. While it devotes more space to explaining the reasons for the city's problems than the solution to them, it provides an intelligent historical perspective and in the third paragraph concentrates on the major difficulties to be overcome. There are few serious errors – 'a map where it appeared a beautiful planification' – and the use of connectors throughout gives the composition a sense of continuity which makes it easy to read. The student's main weakness is inadequate vocabulary, with some confusions prompted by the first language – e.g. 'major' for 'mayor', 'planification'. Our mark was 13, influenced by the control of the argument and use of connectors.

7 MARTA

Barcelona is a big city and has all the common problems of a city of its size. The fact is that a great number of cities grew in a very disordered manner and without a rational planning. Nowadays, we are faced to the problem of improving things and trying to solve mistakes but in most cases we have very few possibilities. We cannot for instance destroy a building or a certain area completely and then built it up again, and that is what is necessary in a lot of cases.

The only thing we can do is try to solve the initial mistakes the best we can and also assume that the life in a big city has a series of disadvantages that we have to accept.

The most important of these disadvantages is pollution, the importance of traffic makes the city air dirty and we have very few solutions to that because it is difficult to decide which traffic is essential and which is not. One solution is to try to locate factories as far from the city as possible and then we will have to stand only the fumes of the cars. But the solution is not at all perfect because trying to protect Barcelona we are now destroying the countryside around.

Related to all the problems of traffic I would consider a good idea to try to reduce it in the commercial areas, so that people would be able to do their shopping in a more pleasant way. But if we reduce traffic in the commercial areas we have to be sure that the public transport is good enough to suply the necessities of the people.

Another point which I consider very important is the problem of the delincuence. I think that local government should improve their measures to fight against it.

Assessment

The composition is relevant to the question and an honest attempt to answer it. At first sight, the standard of English may appear to be approximately the same as Blanca (number 6), but the overall first impression is by no means as good because of the lack of organisation, inadequate paragraphing and a much less consistent and convincing use of connectors. The second paragraph is really an adjunct to the first, and the last is not a conclusion, but an afterthought, so that the composition has no real end. The vocabulary is accurate, though limited, and this is also true of the structural control displayed; it does not break down to the point where we are unlikely to misunderstand the meaning, but a second reading reveals weakness and uncertainty in some areas: – 'without a rational planning', 'the best we can', 'I would consider a good idea'. Our mark was 11, not quite enough for a pass, but if Marta had organised the composition as well as Blanca, she would have passed.

8 ANA

```
     Many of us consider Barcelona as a great city.  That's to say
full of daily entertainments, cultural activities, or just the
politic and economic centre of Catalonia.  Unfortunately we
counsciously forget the hide side of the city.
     Take for instance La Trina or La Prosperitat.  They are two
suburbs in the outskirts of Barcelona, where their problems such
as unemployement, different ethnic backgrounds, lack of teachers
who really are able to deal with those problems, bilinguism -
children are teached a new pair of language without knowing their
mother tonge properly - and so on.
     In spite of these the townhall has already done a great deal
of improvements.  However, many more are needed.  The Council
provided these areas of sport facilities, libraries, medical
assistance, as well as organized a set of rock concerts during
the last season.
     Why is it so difficult to integrate them?  Which is the
best way to improve life?  We should live there to understand
their daily problems: blocks of flats, drugs, no open spaces -
a completely new world for most of us.  Most citizens, the
afortunately ones, usually associate peripherical suburbs with
vandalism (which becomes true most of the time) but we should
consider that when  children and youngs play in an sport area
they are wearing the same shoes they use all the day, and many
teacher will explain you how many days off their students are,
because they work in an street market, trying to help their
families.  I only would suggest something:  try to get to know
them.
```

Assessment

A good example, in our view, of a student who is carried away by a theme which is not quite the same as that of the question, and whose enthusiasm leads her into linguistic difficulties beyond the capacity of her English. The second paragraph, for example, contains fluent phrases – 'different ethnic backgrounds', 'lack of teachers who really are able to deal with those problems', but even in the second phrase the definite article is missing and the position of 'really' is questionable; above all, the long relative clause beginning with 'where' never reaches an end because it has no verb or complement. The same problems occur in the long penultimate sentence of the composition, where the intention is clear but the English breaks down under the strain of the parenthetical ideas – 'the afortunately ones', 'which becomes true most of the time', 'youngs', 'many teacher will explain you', etc. Our mark was 8, but we would regard Ana as a student capable of reaching Proficiency standard if she was able to learn the techniques emphasised throughout this book.

Correction

The mass of corrections frequently required for compositions at advanced level demands a system that students can understand, since we are convinced that it is not helpful for compositions to be marked unless every mistake is indicated clearly.

It is a great advantage if students write their compositions on alternate lines; otherwise, there will be no room for the corrections. They should also use an exercise book so that they, and you, can compare their work with their previous efforts, and note repeated errors. In examinations they should always write on alternate lines, because they may wish to change things neatly, and many waste time producing rough copies and then hurriedly copying them out again.

The composition corrected below (9. Laura) is reproduced exactly as we would have corrected it ourselves. The symbols used can be replaced by any that are convenient to you. What is important about them is their intention. The main difficulties for the teacher are indicated by the scope of the corrections that must be made. To a considerable extent, errors tend increasingly to fall into the area of those that are not English usage ($\sim\sim\sim$) rather than those that are grammatically unacceptable (_____). The decision to 'improve' students' English is inevitably subjective – e.g. replacing 'possible' with 'feasible' in the last paragraph. What matters is to instil into students' minds the idea that they should learn by analysing their own mistakes; otherwise, the effort the teacher makes in correcting compositions in depth is wasted.

In our view, it is important to follow up the correction of pieces of written work with useful suggestions, and students are too often unwilling or too shy to ask about points they do not fully understand. We therefore make a point of raising issues (See me – ? – Ask me) that can be dealt with in class. In the first case, we would want to draw attention to the unnatural form of the sentence picked out and recommend the active construction: 'The state should give grants to the university, as well as to schools . . .' In the second, while we imagine 'motorways' is intended, the student may mean 'through-ways', 'clearways' or 'ring roads', and this is an opportunity to clear up the lexical problems involved; in many cases, we would be forced to put a question mark in this way, because we would genuinely not understand what the student was trying to say.

9 LAURA

Barcelona is the town where I was born and where I have
been living for twenty years, a town that I sometimes love and
~~others~~ *sometimes* hate. If it was in my hand [*power*], I would make lots of changes
in order to create a more agreable [*agreeable* (S)], beautiful,~~(and)~~ humanitarian
city.

Barcelona has some beautiful areas, which should be ~~arranged~~ *looked after*.
Buildings should be cleaned and painted, and there should be green
areas, even ~~small~~ *if they were small*, spurrounding [*surrounding* (S)] them, where children would play
freely and old people could ~~seat~~ *sit* and talk. But this seems quite
impossible ~~due to~~ *because of* the speculation ~~of soil~~ *in land*, something that would
have to disappear ~~in~~ *from* the ideal city.

SEE ME → Monetary ~~helps~~ *Grants* to the university ⌐should be given by the
state⌐ as well as to schools, in order to improve the quality
of teaching. New schools should be created, specially [*especially* e] in the
suburbs, where the need ~~of~~ *for* them is biger [*bigger* (S)] [*greater*].

ASK ME Barcelona is a hectic town, and during the day *the* traffic is
impossible. Some houses might be demolished and new motor rails [*ways?*]
might be created so that the traffic was fluid [*could move freely*]. Metro *The underground* lines
might be increased so as to have the possibility [*that people would be able to travel*] of travelling
underground and reach ⌐quickly⌐ different zones [*areas*] of the town, some
of which are ~~inconected~~ *not connected* nowadays.

The major [*mayor*] should tackle the problem of pollution, sometimes
imbereable [*unbearable*] in the town, as well as the one of security [*safety on the streets*], which
~~ocupies~~ *occupies (S) fills* the pages of the papers every day. Many other
improvements could be made, such as increasing the number of
librraies [*libraries* (S)] and parks, making special fees [*instituting rates*] for students in
theatres, cinemas and museums, creating public sport zones [*sports areas*],
and many others.

Some of these suggestions may seem possible [*feasible*], others may be
~~consider as uthopies~~ *considered idealistic*, but the capacity ~~of~~ *for* dreaming will ever [*always*]
exist.

Key to symbols used

✕   Serious mistake (i.e. beginners' error). No correct answer given.

—   Normal mistake at this level. Correct answer given at first.

〰   Not English usage, though not grammatically wrong. Always corrected.

⋀   Word omitted. Given until it becomes a consistent error.

( )   Word(s) to be omitted. Always indicated.

⌐⌐   Transpose word(s) indicated. Always indicated.

(S)   Spelling mistake. Correct version given until it becomes recurrent.

Description: People

Components	Aims	Grammatical revision
1 Who's who?	Introduction	
2 Appearance and personality	Grammatical revision	Book 3, Exs. 1, 2A–D, 70
3 Portrait of the Artist	Analysis – style and content	
4 Linking description	Analysis – writing techniques	
	Paragraphing	
5 Pen pictures	Directed writing	
6 Annoying characters	Analysis – writing techniques	Exs. 3, 4
	Grammatical revision	

Related texts: *Book 2*, Unit 1, passages 1 and 2.
Further grammatical practice: *Book 3*, Exs. 67 A–F.

Presentation and grammatical revision

As a general rule, we do not believe that it is essential in all cases to re-present familiar structures as part of the presentation of the unit. All references to grammatical revision made in the scheme above are included only to indicate where the emphasis on certain structures in the content is heavy or where a sound knowledge of them is required for subsequent tasks, *except in cases where grammatical revision is listed as one of the aims of a component.* In such cases, we suggest in the following notes where a revision exercise will almost certainly be necessary, in the light of our experience, and at what point it can be most conveniently introduced.

In this unit, it is essential for students to be able to:

1 use comparative forms of all kinds;
2 be aware of the rules governing the word order of adjectives;
3 differentiate between the different kinds of relative clauses, including co-ordinate relative clauses.

The last-named skill is not required until p. 7, and should be re-presented separately, if necessary.

Page 1 Who's who?

Before looking at the list of adjectives given in q. 1, ask students to look at the computer portrait and supply adjectives of their own to describe the face. Link their suggestions together in two ways: He's **thin and dark**/He's **a thin, dark man**. Ensure that students do not say: '*He's a thin* and *dark man*'. Then see how many of the adjectives listed are already known and teach the rest by reference to the computer portrait and photographs. Ask students to name well-known figures they would describe as 'bald', 'bearded', etc. Ask for connected descriptions of well-known people:

He's old, bald and hawk-nosed and again, make sure that the order of the adjectives is natural.

Move on to q. 2, ask students to decide which photograph fits the computer portrait, and in listening to the reasons given, note their control over comparative forms with a view to using *Book 3*, Ex. 2, particularly 2A (comparative and superlative forms) and 2D (**the same as, different from**, etc.) for revision, if necessary. Introduce q. 3 by mentioning the relationship between face and voice (not necessarily reliable) but stressing the more accurate clues given by age and personality.

Play the cassette twice, first straight through and then after a pause, allowing students to form ideas, play each voice at a time and ask students for reactions without giving the answers. Ask pairs to justify their choices.

Use *Book 3*, Exs. 2A and 2D for revision of comparatives, if necessary.

Page 2 Appearance and personality

Remind students of the basic rules of using more than one adjective in a description, and ask them to study 'Adjectives: word order' in the Reference Section, p. 170. This would best be done before the class begins.

Activity 1

1　This simply confirms the point just made, but if the class show doubt, use *Book 3*, Ex. 1 before proceeding.
2　Treat this as a first step towards recognition of style and technique, which will be most important later. Ask students to justify each adjective used, or reject it as irrelevant.

Activity 2

This is a grammatical exercise, to be done in pairs, to see if students can put into practice the rules given in the Reference Section. It is hard for native speakers to justify choices in all cases in such combinations and not always clear to say that 'the more precise adjective comes closest to the noun'. However, it can be considered a success if students can overcome such errors as: '*He was an old* and *tall man*'.

Page 3 Portrait of the Artist

Activity 3

The aim here is to show students how a good writer builds up an impression of a person which makes a rounded picture. Further practice of the same kind is available with the two passages in Unit 1 of *Book 2* mentioned above. Suggested answers:

1　He is 43; he is thin, fair-haired and wears small gold glasses; he is wearing a dark-blue baseball cap . . . trousers; he studied art at Bradford Art School and later at the Royal College of Art; he is designing scenery for a ballet and two operas at the New York Metropolitan.
2　a) he is dressed in a rather eccentric way; b) he mentions it himself, and the author places this statement immediately after describing his clothes.
3　By his hobbies, through falling asleep in the train, and through having a violent argument on his way to a march for peace.
4　'He became younger by the minute'. By conveying the impression of a youthful, active person, who waltzes from enthusiasm or for fun.
5　Cf. the waltzing, but also Hockney's comments on light and shade, and the effect of drawing.
6　Yes, because it is a rounded impression of a man who is in fact an artist.

Page 4 Linking description

As a first step in teaching students to write rounded descriptions, we draw their attention to the value of connectors and modifiers and interesting detail. The passage also indicates the importance of paragraphing.

Activity 4

This should not take long, but is necessary. Emphasise to students at this early stage in the course that good writing in English is not a matter of complicated structures and long sentences, but of organisation – when and why do you start a new paragraph (usually because you are dealing with a new topic, or the same one from a different angle)? – and providing the reader with links to help him follow the argument and details to make the picture clearer. Discuss these points in the course of dealing with the questions.

Note that the first version here is an example of a composition that would be marked highly at First Certificate level, the level the students have just passed, because it is accurate, but is not the way to future progress towards fluency.

Page 5 Pen pictures

Students must now put into practice in the classroom what they have learnt so far. Effectively, this is a trial run for the compositions they will write individually for homework.

Allow not more than half an hour for the writing, so that time can be spent on comparing results. As an alternative, to speed up the process, this can be done with groups of five, each member writing one paragraph. In that case, the first and last paragraphs should be discussed by the group for five minutes to decide on content, while the middle three can be left to individuals.

Comment on the results, noting in particular how far students have managed to link items of information together in complex sentences and whether they have provided any connectors between sentences and paragraphs. Suggest improvements of this kind, where relevant.

Page 6 Annoying characters

The emphasis here is on the use of subordinate clauses to expand description. It will almost certainly be necessary to remind students of the forms of defining and non-defining relative clauses and the differences between them, and also to explain how co-ordinate relative clauses are used (but see 'Relative clauses', Activity 7, q. 2). All the basic information is contained in the Reference Section, p. 179, but Exs. 3 and 4, particularly the latter, in *Book 3*, may be necessary for further practice.

A good class can be relied on to know the content of Exs. 3A–C and these could be omitted, but very few students have any idea of punctuation. Revision of the basic differences in purpose and form of relative clauses could in such cases be limited to study of the Reference Section, followed by the first, and if necessary, second part of Ex. 3D (Use of the comma).

Activity 6

Note that the passage can be read straight through for the meaning without any of the details added. Tell students to do this first and then work in pairs to supply the missing phrases.

Activity 7, p. 7

Check that they have chosen the correct phrases and deal with any questions about lexis and content before asking students to do q. 1. The second question is a matter of comprehension with a grammatical end. As an alternative to presenting all the relative clauses together, you could

reserve Ex. 4 from *Book 3* as consolidation of this point until after students have done this question.

Activity 8

A revision exercise on non-defining relative and co-ordinate relative clauses. To avoid confusion, point out at the start that **with** is used with the meaning of 'considering that' (see the last two sentences).

Composition

These topics arise naturally out of the work that has been done. This book contains a section on assessment and correction of compositions (pages 10–15) and teachers new to teaching these levels may find it helpful to consult it. In this first composition what should be most encouraged in students is the attempt to produce rounded pictures of the people they are describing, using subordinate clauses, more than one adjective in a phrase, etc., and the extent to which they have paragraphed sensibly and used connectors and modifiers in a logical way.

2

Narrative: Work

Components	Aims	Grammatical revision
8 What's his/her line?	Introduction	*Book 3*, Exs. 5, 9
9 A life in the day of . . .	Comparison – style and content	
10 A typical day	Information retrieval,	Exs. 6, 7
	Grammatical revision	
11 An eventful day	Analysis – writing techniques	
	Directed writing	

Related texts: *Book 2*, Unit 2, passages 1–3.
Further grammatical practice: *Book 3*, Exs. 8, 71–2.

Presentation and grammatical revision

In this unit, it is essential for students to:

1 differentiate between the uses of the Present Simple and Continuous tenses;
2 understand the use of the Past Simple and Continuous tenses and Past Perfect Simple and Continuous tenses in narrative.

The use of some impersonal structures, of the gerund form in general statements, **there is/have**, and the distinction between **as** and **like** are covered in follow-up exercises in *Book 3* which would also be of use to students before they write their final compositions for the unit.

In terms of presentation, however, students at this level should not really need to revise the Present tenses but are likely to need some reminders with regard to Past-tense combinations in narrative.

Page 8 What's his/her line?

As in Unit 1, pictures and recorded voices are used to introduce the topic. When students have looked at the pictures (q. 1) ask them what each person is doing and what they think his/her job is. Make sure that in questions and answers there is no confusion between **What is he/she doing?** and **What does he/she do?** If there is, it will be necessary to do Exercise 5 from *Book 3* (but see notes to p. 9, below). In q. 2, the same kind of

problem is presented aurally. Play the cassette in four sections, repeating any where students are unable to decide on a person's job from the information given after listening once. Ask students to give reasons for their decision and if necessary help with questions:
What time does he go out? Why does he go out so late? etc.

The third part of the introduction should be attempted if it conveniently rounds off the class. In large classes, divide students into four or five groups. Each group must provide a person to mime, and must also guess one of the mimes from the other groups. Further language practice of the Present tenses can be provided if you suggest that students ask questions while the actor is doing the mime first of all:
Are you opening a door?/Are you mending something?
and then ask general questions:
Do you work at night?/Do you travel in your work?
At the end of the game, students should have decided what the person *does* and what he/she *was doing* in the mime.

Page 9 A life in the day of . . .

The main purpose of this page and Activity 1 (printed on p. 8) is to compare the style and content of the two passages. Emphasise, however, in introducing them, that they are unusual in using Present tenses to describe a recreation of a typical day. This adds immediacy and dramatic effect, but students should not

19

be encouraged to use these tenses in straightforward narratives of past events, a common technique in some other languages.

Exercise 5 in *Book 3* is in fact based on the content of the second passage. If there has been persistent confusion over the uses of the Present tenses, it would be logical to revise them here, when you have completed Activity 1.

Ask students if they can guess who the person interviewed in the second passage is. She plays in a group with her husband, Paul (McCartney).

Page 10 A typical day

The passage here resembles the previous days except that it describes yesterday in someone's life.

Activity 2 contains questions to discover whether students are aware of the relationship of tenses in narrative. Allow them to complete the first two parts of the activity before drawing their attention to the grammatical implications. Then see if they can answer q. 3 successfully for themselves before deciding whether revision of these tenses is required. If it is, do Exercises 6 and 7 from *Book 3* before proceeding.

Page 11 An eventful day

Activity 3

The aim here is for students to realise that narrative normally requires highlighting of some kind or another to make it interesting. Ask them to do the activity, and then to explain to you why the account differs from the one on the opposite page. What different purposes have the two writers in mind? If necessary, draw students' attention to the use of dialogue or direct speech in such accounts and emphasise the importance in most narrative compositions of concentrating the reader's attention on important events or moments.

Activity 4, p. 12

Before dividing the class up into pairs to work on this directed writing exercise, make sure that they understand all the lexis used in the prompts. The task is in effect a reverse process to the preparation of timetables on the previous two pages. Point out that while some details of a normal day (on the left) must be included to set the scene some can be omitted, and they should pay most attention to dramatising the events (on the right). Allow not more than half an hour for the completion of the task, and then ask different pairs to read out their accounts. Judge them, apart from their accuracy, on their ability to create atmosphere and highlight the main events.

Composition

The topics give students the opportunity to employ the techniques used on pp. 10, 11 and 12 respectively. If the task is set for homework, remind them to study the relevant page again and base their compositions on the format presented.

3

Discussion: The British

Components	Aims	Grammatical revision
13 How much do you know about Britain?	Introduction	
14 Writing a paragraph	Paragraphing	
15 National and regional characteristics	Paragraph analysis	
16 Developing paragraphs	Paragraphing	
17 The English	Analysis – writing techniques	
	Clarifying ideas	
	Discussion	

Related texts: *Book 2*, Unit 3, Passages 1 and 2A–C, although not directly relevant, refer to English country houses and the work of the National Trust.
Further grammatical practice: *Book 3*, Exs. 10, 11, 76A–B, 77.

Presentation and grammatical revision

Although most teachers regard this sort of composition topic as the most difficult, this has much more to do with students' problems in organising their arguments than with any structural difficulties, since most topics can be covered almost entirely in the Present Simple tense. No grammatical presentation is required here, therefore, but the exercises listed above will be useful reminders for students before they attempt their final compositions. The importance of the relationship between Present Perfect and Past tenses here is that students are invited to discuss the British in terms of their experience of them, where personal reminiscence should be employed as well as general statements – a good rule to follow in any case for almost all discussion topics, since the greatest single fault of the majority of students is their inability to reinforce the abstract with the concrete.

Page 13 How much do you know about Britain?

This quiz is intended as a starting point for a much wider discussion based on students' previous experience of Britain and British people, whether it has been gained through travel, reading or meeting people in their own country. The answers are deliberately intended to be beyond the range of most native-speaking teachers! The correct answers are given at the back of the students' book.

Page 14 Writing a paragraph

Many students enter advanced classes hardly aware that such a thing as a paragraph exists. While paragraphing is a relatively easy task in descriptive (see Unit 1, Activity 5) and narrative compositions, where it is possible to deal with a subject by separating the topic into different aspects or according to a time scheme, for the discussion topic, similar to a formal essay, the order of paragraphs and the development of an argument within each paragraph is essential not only in order to present ideas clearly but also in order to construct a convincing, related argument. We have therefore concentrated on paragraphing in this first discussion unit, prior to looking at techniques used in such compositions.

Activities I and 2

The texts here are a means of demonstrating the internal organisation of a paragraph and the way in which paragraphs must link to those that follow. Students are being asked to work these things out for themselves. Ask them to read the page before coming to class and then to spend the first ten minutes working in pairs on the questions, so that most of the lesson can be devoted to page 15.

The technical terms which students should carry away from reading the first paragraph are *topic sentence, development by exposition, example, comparison and contrast, transitional sentence, concluding sentence*. The sentences themselves illustrate their name and purpose (q. 5).

The two paragraphs for Activity 2 contain the most useful advice and the most necessary warning we can provide for students at this stage. Insist that all discussion compositions written in class or for homework are preceded by a plan, and indicate as often as is necessary that the English language does not lend itself to vague generalisations in the abstract, which are probably uncongenial to the English temperament and certainly anathema to most examiners.

Page 15 National and regional characteristics

This is an initial model of a general essay, where we have attempted to put our principles into practice. Students should be encouraged not merely to read it but to analyse its construction carefully in handling Activity 3.

Activity 3

Students should reach the following conclusions:

1   The topic sentence is the first in each case, except in the last paragraph (printed out of order) where it will become the first, but is printed last.
2   The first paragraph is developed by example (two sentences); the second by contrast (two sentences); the third by further exposition and example of this (one and two sentences respectively); the last by further exposition (one sentence).
3   The order of the sentences should be 3, 2, 4, 1 and once re-established their purpose is 1) topic; 2) further exposition; 3) transition (from the topic of national and regional characteristics to that of steroetypes of people); 4) conclusion, which is the same for both topics.

Before moving on to further paragraph work on page 16, which has to do with ways of developing paragraphs, ask students to see if they can see any relationship between the concluding sentence of each paragraph here and the topic sentence of the next, and comment on the techniques employed. They should realise that:

1   topic sentence 2 is an example of concluding sentence 1. Draw attention to the use of 'for instance' (lines 19–20);
2   topic sentence 3 further develops concluding sentence 2. Draw attention to '*these* characteristics' (line 40);
3   topic sentence 4 summarises the advice given in concluding sentence 3. Draw attention to 'The fact is that . . .' (line 75).

Because this unit contains a series of pages of the same kind, it is obviously a good idea to break it up at this point, either by having a general discussion on national and regional characteristics in the students' own country or countries, or by using reading material from *Book 2*, where the passages are related to British life.

Page 16 Developing paragraphs

Activity 4

Students must now take their study of the paragraph further by developing and concluding paragraphs themselves along the lines of the guidance so far given.

The three paragraphs presented all begin with the same sentence but develop differently: a) is developed by contrast – '*however*', . . . and '*On the contrary*' should be mentioned; b) by examples; c) by comparison developing out of a second sentence which offers further exposition of the topic.

The relationship in q. 2 is a) iii; b) i; c) ii. All three are transitional, clarifying or developing what has previously been said in preparation for the conclusion.

Suggested answers for q. 3:

i)   . . . led to the differences in the way they are played today.
ii)   . . . public schools took the lead in organising games, they cannot claim credit for their popularity, importance in modern life, etc.
iii) . . . claimed that the enormous popularity of these contests today has its origin in the emphasis on sport in English schools over a hundred years ago.

Page 17 The English

Activity 5

It is now time for students to analyse the equivalent of a discussion essay, as practised by the ideal model for them to aspire to, George Orwell. This analysis is best done in groups of three or four, with one student appointed as 'secretary' to note down the conclusions of the group as a whole. The first five questions are to aid comprehension, but most time will need to be spent on the last.

Suggested answers:

1   (c). They 'don't matter in themselves', but that is not the same as saying they are of no importance.
2   The answer is not in the passage, but Orwell surely refers to the English habit of eating so much cake, chocolate, etc.
3   Literature. He refers to this exclusion later in the same article.
4   All the examples in the last sentence of paragraph 2. In fact the system of weights and measures has officially

changed, but is still resisted; methods of town planning and water supply have improved on the whole, the first considerably: their innate conservatism and affection for tradition, the 'way things have always been done', is the most probable answer.

5 This is open-ended.

6 Paragraph 1: example (2nd sentence); Paragraph 2: example and comparison (3rd sentence), further exposition and contrast (5th and 6th sentences) leading to a concluding sentence which is a series of examples: Paragraph 3: examples (2nd and 3rd sentences).

Further to what has already been said about students' love of the abstract in this kind of composition, this can be rubbed in by reference to Orwell's remark that the English 'have a horror of abstract thought'. The other thing that should be emphasised is the way in which he always gives examples for every general statement he makes, and these are straightforward, clear and based on everyday observation.

Activity 6, p. 18

The same groups can be used for this activity. The aim is to prepare students for the discussion that follows so that they have had time to think out what they are going to say and have reasons for saying it. Too often, lack of preparation for topics like this leads to a series of unsupported statements with little relation to one another.

Composition

The preparation for the discussion is good preparation for the composition topic, too, since the majority of first attempts students make at this sort of thing read like an unstructured debate. We have deliberately indicated to students that they should write in such a way that they include plenty of examples of their own experience. Insist that students provide a plan of what they are going to do.

The exercises from *Book 3* at the beginning of this unit, dealing with the Present Perfect and Past tenses, word order of adverbs of frequency, clauses of concession and **because/because of** are all useful revision for the kind of composition that is to be attempted.

Rewriting: Telegrams and notes

Components	Aims	Grammatical revision
19 Telegrams	Information retrieval	
20 Expanding notes	Directed writing	
21 Newspaper reports	Directing writing	

Further grammatical practice: *Book 3*, Exs. 14A–E.
Students should also refer to the Appendix: Connectors and modifiers (p. 164) and to the Reference Section:
Prepositions (p. 171) for further help.

Presentation and grammatical revision

In common with the other final units in each stage of four units in the book, this deals with transformation of information from one form to another. It therefore resembles guided composition but in all cases the form is different from the original and therefore different techniques are required. The tasks here are deceptively easy. Especially for students outside Britain they are difficult for two reasons; one, because they are unaware of the social norms governing them; two, because such tasks require confident handling of linking words such as prepositions, the need for modals in many cases, and an understanding of the appropriate use of connectors. Little formal work on this can be usefully done in presentation, but the errors that emerge from students' attempts at the tasks must be noted and corrected.

Page 19 Telegrams

The introduction here, instead of being thematic, sets the scene for the tasks. Students should work in pairs to decipher the context of the first four telegrams and fill them out into a story, but there is no need for everyone to do them all, and time can be saved by allotting a separate telegram to each pair.

The second group form a complete story. In this case, all pairs should work on it, and different versions should be asked for.

Students should not produce carefully written versions for these tasks. It is much better training for them to explain the stories in their own words, using a few notes if necessary.

Page 20 Expanding notes

The transformation from telegrams to letter is exemplified.

Activity 1

As in the first part of the task on page 19, pairs should be given only one of the telegrams to work on. Fifteen minutes should be enough for the four written versions to be produced. Emphasise the last sentence of the instructions and monitor pairs, helping them where necessary with suggestions for 'a suitable tone'. Ask each pair about the probable feelings of the person writing the letter in each case and what effect he or she wishes to convey to the recipient. Compare the versions produced, and note from the results obtained whether remedial work needs to be done on modals (Exs. 14A–E in *Book 3*) and whether there are persistent errors with prepositions and connectors. Show by reference to the Reference Section how letters could be improved by the inclusion of appropriate connectors.

Page 21 Newspaper reports

Activity 2, p. 22

This is a very similar task to the previous one, to be handled in the same way. The only difference is that students must be aware of the need to engage a reader's interest in a newspaper. The techniques already practised in Unit 2, Activity 4, are important here.

Activity 3

Here the aspects of information retrieval, expanding notes and writing an interesting newspaper article, are all combined. The connectors given are an aid to students and a reminder. In comparing the different versions groups produce, pay special attention both to the incorrect use of these connectors, and also to their omission. For this task, it is best to form groups of four or five. Students should agree

on the approach to be adopted in each paragraph, and either write one paragraph each, or if time permits, one should act as 'secretary', advised by the other three or four. The task is likely to take 20–25 minutes to complete by the first method but over half an hour by the second.

Composition

The topics are a recasting of the tasks already done in class.

5

Description: Processes

Components	Aims	Grammatical revision
23 Looking good, feeling fit	Introduction	*Book 3*, Ex. 15
24 Games	Paragraph analysis	Exs. 16A–C
	Analysis – writing techniques	
	Directed writing	
26 Saga of a film script	Rewriting	
28 Active and passive	Grammatical revision	

Related texts: *Book 2*, Unit 4, parallel with this unit, deals with 'Health'.
Further grammatical practice: *Book 3*, Exs. 17 and 82.

Presentation and grammatical revision

Unlike Units 1–3, this one has no common theme with corresponding lexis. The first topic requires some knowledge of medical vocabulary, though its main emphasis is on the forms of giving advice. *Book 3*, Ex. 15, revising **should** and **had better**, might be used when the task has been explained as a reminder. A number of technical terms for golf and tennis are needed for the second task, and for the third some vocabulary connected with films. Unit 6 in *Book 2* is devoted to 'The Cinema', but this is an area where students' vocabulary is already likely to be extensive. The main structural requirements for this kind of composition are the use of the passive voice, highlighted on page 28 in preparation for students' own compositions, and the different forms of purpose clause, practised in *Book 3*, Exercises 16A–C. It will probably be necessary to remind students of these before beginning the directed writing exercise on page 25.

Page 23 Looking good, feeling fit

This introductory exercise is in the first place a matter of information retrieval. Form five groups to hunt for the information needed, which consists first of discovering which diet is appropriate for the five people concerned, and then which foods in the chart given contain the proteins, vitamins and minerals in appropriate quantities. Allot one character to each group and allow the groups to be as large as possible.

The information should be assembled in note form so that a representative can summarise the conclusions on the lines of: 'We recommend this person to eat . . . because . . .' 'He/She could also find these necessary vitamins in . . .' 'People in his/her situation need . . .'

What is rather a pedestrian exercise can be made much more interesting if you give the characters names and one of the group volunteers to play the part of the patient and another that of the doctor. In that case, what has appeared up to now in the Present Simple tense must be adapted to the conversational situation and students will need to be reminded of **should** for general advice and **had better** for immediate advice (see *Book 3*, Ex. 15).

Page 24 Games

The article on golf continues work on paragraphing from Unit 3 in indicating the development of paragraphs in three further ways and also serves as a model for the directed writing exercise on the opposite page. As indicated above, it may be necessary to remind students of purpose clauses so that they can complete the second paragraph satisfactorily, and this reminder, using Exs. 16A–C, can be given either at the beginning of Activity 1 or before Activity 2.

Activity 1

Note that golf clubs are not called 'sticks', and also draw the class's attention to polo mallets, cricket bats, etc. Ask the class to work on the questions in pairs. Questions 1 and 3 are analytical and short, but q. 2 demands more thought and preparation. If anyone in the class plays golf, ask him/her to enlarge on the difficulties of completing holes in the standard four strokes. This will also be helpful to answer questions like: *What would you do if the ball went into a bunker, a wood, etc?*

The answer to q. 3 is that the game is cheap in the country of origin, but expensive elsewhere.

Activity 2, p. 25

Most students will be far more familiar with the rules of tennis, though not necessarily with the history of the game. Form groups of four to deal with one topic each, breaking the equivalent to the third paragraph of the golf article into two. Advise by suggesting ways of building up the paragraphs through classification, description of the process, and space and time relationships, and also by clarifying any technical points. Students may like to enlarge on the third and fourth paragraphs with information more appropriate to the development of the game in their own countries.

Page 26 Saga of a film script

Activity 3, p. 27

The previous tasks have primarily depended on describing processes in the Present tense. Here, students must transform comic-strip dialogue into an account written in the Past tenses. Indicate once again (see Notes to p. 9) that the Present tense used in picture-to-picture narrative is inappropriate for a written account. Students should work on this task individually, and then compare notes with a partner before answering your questions as a pair. Most of the sentences that emerge will need to be written in the passive voice, since the script, not the screen writer, is the focus of the questions. If necessary, based on experience with the previous task, refer students beforehand to the Reference Section (Active and passive, p. 177) and/or do Exercise 82 from *Book 3*.

The final question, on which students should work at the same time as the rest, differs in that they are being asked to look behind the story at the pressures, attitudes, etc. which led to it taking the course it did. It can best be handled as an exercise in deduction, and Ex. 17, on the past forms of **must**, may also be necessary as a reminder before students attempt it.

Page 28 Active and passive

Activity 4 and Composition

The text here has been converted from the scientific passive into an active form, and students are asked to convert it back to the original. The passive voice, as used in scientific accounts, is important for the composition topics. Depending on whether you have already found it necessary to do Exercise 82 from *Book 3*, this exercise is either a final reminder of passive forms before students write their compositions or becomes an optional additional confirmation of them.

6

Discussion: The Press

Components		Aims	Grammatical revision
29	News shorthand	Introduction	
30	Headlines	Comparing style and content	
32	Editorials	Comparing style and content	
34	Main news	Comparing style and content	
35	Sports news	Comparing style and content	
36	Composition	Directed writing	

Related texts: *Book 2*, Unit 5 (parallel with this), passages 1 and 2A–C.

Presentation

No grammatical revision is required here that has a direct relationship with the content.

The unit appears out of order (i.e. before the second unit dealing with narrative compositions) because in that unit we want to develop students' ability to recognise nuances of style as well as technical approaches and it is useful for them to have previous experience of the much more blatant differences to be found when comparing, for example, the approach to the same news story of the *Guardian* and the *Sun*.

As a discussion unit, its aim is primarily to introduce students to the ways in which information is slanted by journalists to express the point of view of the newspaper they work for; this has the double purpose of making them more aware than they are likely to be of English written to win an argument and of teaching them the techniques that are employed.

On this occasion, because students may not be familiar with the way in which newspapers operate and the technical terms in English, it would be useful for them to do the introductory exercise and to read the first passage from *Book 2*, Unit 5, before attempting the first task here. The second series of passages from the same book are a more subtle, demanding version of the comparisons that form most of this unit, and can be used as follow-up material afterwards.

Page 29 News shorthand

The task here is relatively simple. Divide the class into five groups, and ask them to imagine what sort of news interests the readers of each newspaper or magazine. On the basis of that decision, they should be able to see which stories they would give prominence to.

The items themselves may cause some lexical difficulties for students who are not used to reading newspapers in English. Ask groups to summarise what each news item says in two or three simple sentences of their own as a way of clearing up such difficulties.

Page 30 Headlines

The next seven pages of the unit compare three newspapers and the way in which they handled a number of stories on two days in November, 1983. The aims of these newspapers and their readership are indicated to students on this page.

We have often seen headlines used in ELT texts for students and are convinced that outside Britain they are a meaningless guessing game unless they are accompanied by text. The purpose of headlines in British newspapers is quite different from their purpose in most European countries; they are meant to intrigue or excite, not to inform. We have therefore aimed to show students that in fact the first paragraph or so in the newspaper usually paraphrases the headline and indicates the topic that is to follow.

Activity 1

Ask students to match headlines with accompanying stories. Because of the topics, the only doubts should concern those where the story is duplicated. In fact, the phrase 'retreats to his last base' is echoed by 'pushed back to their final stronghold', while 'Besieged Arafat is defiant' relates to the paragraph beginning 'Both the United States and Israel . . .'. 'Turks reject generals' clearly relates to the paragraph where mention is again made of this point, which is not mentioned in the first sentence of the other article.

These stories are obviously those that were covered both by the *Daily Telegraph* and the *Guardian* (q. 2), the Arafat story being placed first in both cases.

Question 3 is important as an introduction to the unit as a whole in indicating the importance of readership, and the fact that the *Sun* clearly has a quite different concept of what makes news from the other two. In order of importance, the three stories from the *Sun* concerned Joan Collins, package holidays, and Arthur Scargill. Draw students' attention to the fact that in the package holiday story, each sentence forms a new paragraph, and to the word 'FORCE' in capital letters.

Page 32 Editorials

The previous comparison was concerned with introducing students to the three newspapers' concept of what makes news. This one demands an analysis of style and content. Students should at the same time recognise the obvious differences in the construction of sentences and paragraphs, but also realise that the views expressed meet the demands of the respective readership.

Activity 2

Let's open Buck House (the *Sun*). The use of one-sentence paragraphs, capital letters in bold type with black dots, sentences in bold type that are underlined, indicates the source straightaway.

Contrary to what is sometimes believed in Britain, students often find newspapers like the *Sun* much more difficult to understand than the 'quality' papers. This is because of phrases like 'palaces galore', 'the super-rich royals' 'the royal coffers', etc. Explain these, and also explain that 'Buck House' began by being upper-class slang for Buckingham Palace, but the phrase is now used more generally.
Suggested answers:

1 Partly because it emphasises the royal family's wealth and suggests they can afford to raise their own income; more importantly, perhaps, because it puts the palace, the royal yacht, etc. on a level with the reader's house and car, so that the ideas can be understood in the context of a domestic budget.

2 and 3 are clear from the first paragraph above.
4 Clearly, the advice to students is: follow our advice and don't imitate the *Sun*. The second half of the question is open to different interpretations, but we think that it is (a) intended to catch the eye; (b) written for people who find reading a comparatively difficult task, since they have not been well-educated. Consequently, it is thought that their interest would flag if they had to face a paragraph like those in the 'quality' papers.

The newest profession (the *Daily Telegraph*). Note that in differentiating from the *Guardian*, the views of the newspaper are the determining factor.

1 Its belief that jobs are being deliberately created by left-wing councils for their friends, and that socialism has become a financially rewarding career in itself. The phrases are 'left-wing activists' and 'professional revolutionaries'.
2 Posts created and paid for which do not in fact involve any work.
3 Because the newspaper does not believe these organisations are 'voluntary'. Voluntary service involves the person offering to do work without being paid, whereas the paper argues that these organisations are created to provide jobs.
4 Socialism as a career with financial rewards.
5 The old type began by aiming at reforming society and found that through the development of bureaucracy, there were certain personal advantages to be enjoyed; the new aims at obtaining these advantages at the expense of society as a whole. Obviously, the people concerned would say that they were doing essential work on behalf of the community.
6 It works by example.
7 The first sentence of the last paragraph suggests that there is nothing unusual in the developments already mentioned, but uses this as a way of comparing the past to the present in a very unfavourable way. Note the use of **might**, which indicates that the argument will not be sustained, compared to **can**, which would give it a fair hearing. The destruction is a statement of opinion, despite the reference to Michels' book, but it poses as evidence because of the word **demonstrated** (scientific truth) instead of **said**, **claimed**, etc.

An Oxbridge hurdle goes (the *Guardian*). Note that in differentiating from the *Daily Telegraph*, the views of the newspaper are the determining factor.
Suggested answers:

1 The newspaper regards Oxford and Cambridge as outposts of privilege – 'Oxford has at last struck a blow for egalitarianism'. Their examinations favoured candidates from public schools (i.e. private schools from the students' point of view). The last paragraph refers to 'Oxbridge élites'.

2   In brief, it is looking forward to the day when it disappears. If the research it quotes is correct, parents will no longer think it worth while to send their children to private schools. 'This . . . would represent a considerable advance' in the interests of social justice and ensuring that the best, not the richest, students reach universities.

3   It has apparently shown that comprehensive students do better than public-school students in GCE examinations at 'A' and 'O' level, and so they would obtain far more places at Oxford and Cambridge if the university's own examinations were abolished.
    NOTE: Cambridge, at the time of writing, has not abolished its own entrance examination. The research done by Mayer and Collier was based on the results of one faculty at one university, so no one is likely to regard it as conclusive unless, like the author of this editorial, he was already convinced.

4   The second paragraph explains 'the point', which is that on the whole Oxford may be changing its attitude not because it is less élitist than before but because it is frightened of losing the best students and suffering a fall in standards.

To get the most out of these passages within a reasonable time, students must read all of them, but answer questions on one passage in groups. The best plan is to ask students to read all three before coming to class, clear up any lexical or cultural points – e.g. 'Buck House', etc. in the first; 'rate-rebate system', 'race-relations advisers', 'quangos' in the second; 'public schools', 'O' and 'A' levels in the third – and then choose groups to concentrate on one set of questions.

Page 34 Main news

Activity 3

The previous comparisons are extended here to show clearly the differing political and social views of the three newspapers by comparing the way in which they reported the same main news story. As in the previous activity, students should read all three tests, and groups should be formed to deal with the questions relating to each one. Each group should define 'its' newspaper's attitude to the four parts of q. 2, and then these answers should be pooled to show the differences.

Maggie in new blast at Reagan (the *Sun* – type used, reference to Mrs Thatcher as 'Maggie', etc.). The *Sun* wants to make the Prime Minister seem a familiar figure like the woman next door, so it calls her 'Maggie'. It pictures her dealing with the United States representative like an angry working-class housewife berating a man from a shop who has not mended her TV properly: 'waded into', 'she sent him away with a flea in his ear'. The idea behind this is that Great Britain can order the United States to do what it

thinks right in world affairs; the 'DON'T' is not merely imperative but printed in capital letters.

Envoy at Chequers (the *Daily Telegraph* – headline is impersonal, where the third suggests a defeat for the Prime Minister). The paper reports everything from Mrs Thatcher's point of view and says nothing about the American reaction, other than indicating that there is a risk of further disagreement. Britain is shown to be concerned about American policy in the Lebanon, but no mention is made of Grenada or Argentina, both more directly relevant to British interests and national pride (Grenada being a former British colony, and Argentina not having formally ended hostilities after the Falklands war). Mrs Thatcher is presented as a serious politician, supported by the Foreign Minister, dealing formally with the representative of an ally.

PM is snubbed over US retaliation (the *Guardian* – emphasis on the humiliation of the Prime Minister, 'failed yesterday', 'seems to have been equally unsuccessful'). The newspaper reports what the American envoy said about the Lebanon, but has clearly not been in touch with the Prime Minister herself – 'seems to have been . . . unsuccessful', 'apparently left no doubt'. The impression is the complete opposite of the *Sun*, showing Mrs Thatcher as being unable to affect American policy in any way and suggesting that the envoy 'snubbed' her, like an important person refusing to take any notice of someone lower down the social or political scale.

Page 35 Sports news

Activity 4

The last two stories appear on p. 36. The approach in the classroom is the same.

1   *McEnroe return ordeal for Lloyd* (the *Guardian*); *Supermac won't frighten the new Lloyd* (the *Sun*); *Lloyd to meet McEnroe* (the *Daily Telegraph*).

2   The *Guardian* sees Lloyd's situation as hopeless ('ordeal', 'hopes . . . were dashed'); the *Sun* almost predicts a victory ('*Supermac won't frighten . . . Lloyd*', 'hoping for a supersonic performance'); the *Daily Telegraph* clearly expects Lloyd to lose but makes out the most optimistic case it can ('Lloyd has shown distinct signs . . . of rediscovering world-class form'). This repeats the attitudes of the three newspapers on the opposite page, where the *Guardian* sees the Prime Minister as humiliated and expects Lloyd to be, the *Sun* sees British representatives as aggressive and dominating, the *Daily Telegraph* puts on the best face it can in view of probable British failure. Note the stylistic point that the *Sun* calls McEnroe 'Supermac' just as it calls the Prime Minister 'Maggie', for the same reasons.

3   This is virtually answered in the previous question.

4   A matter of opinion, leading into the discussion that follows. The political attitudes of the readers of the

Guardian and the *Daily Telegraph* are clearly reflected in the editorials and their approach to the Prime Minister, a Conservative.

The *Sun* is less easy to classify, but its popularity seems to suggest that working-class people in Britain are egalitarian in the old-fashioned sense of wanting to make the rich poorer and the poor richer, and very nationalistic, still believing that Britain is the number one power in the world in politics and sport. Of course, the readers may not buy the paper for the editorial or the sports pages but only for the picture of Joan Collins that accompanied the front-page lead story. Our personal view is that this is not true and really a greater insult to working-class people than the assumption that they are unthinkingly nationalistic.

The main purpose of this, in any case, is to allow students to begin a discussion on the newspapers in their own country, where parallels are likely either on political or on design lines, and in some cases in both.

Page 36 Composition

This could be attempted in class, using groups of three who would confer before writing a paragraph each, but is really intended as an individual task. We do not see any value in asking students to imitate the *Sun*, so we expect them to use the paragraph organisation of the 'quality' newspaper as a guide.

7

Narrative: Disasters and accidents

Components	Aims	Grammatical revision
37 Quiz	Introduction	
38 Disaster at sea	Analysis – style and content	
39 Rail and road accidents	Analysis – style and content	
	Information retrieval	
41 Fire!	Paragraph analysis	
	Linking paragraphs	
	Directed writing	Book 3, Exs. 21, 86, 87
	Role play	

Presentation and grammatical revision

The same combinations of tenses are required as in Unit 2, but we also suggest a revision of forms in reported speech prior to the directed writing exercise on page 42.

Page 37 Quiz

The answers here are given at the back of the students' book (p. 184). Use this as an introduction to the topic in general terms. Question A is largely to raise astonishment at the numbers involved, the answer usually being c), but questions B and C offer useful practice of modals that may well be needed in students' compositions (cf. Ex. 14E (which may already have been done in connection with Unit 4), Ex. 17 (linked to Unit 5) and Ex. 20 (linked to Unit 6)).

Exploit to the maximum the students' suggestions such as: *Two planes may have collided, It may have been foggy, An engine might have caught fire* before asking them to look at the options offered in question B, and once they have had time to study them, see if they can imagine the scene, using phrases with **must have . . .** and **can't have . . .** *The pilot can't have seen the other plane on the runway,* etc.

The same kind of treatment can be given to question C, where the possibilities are passive, before allowing students to look at the choices offered, and repeat the practice of **may have . . . might have . . .** and **could have . . .** with the second half of the question. In the

case of the fire, it is also possible to ask how these deaths could have been avoided – '*What should the people have done?*'

Page 38 Disaster at sea

This should be read, if possible, on the same day as the account on the facing page, since some questions refer to both. As usual, if students can be persuaded to read the texts beforehand, much time will be saved. Form groups of three to consider the questions, and in large classes, ask students to deal with only one set of questions (those on this passage or those on the next).

Activity 1

Suggested answers:

1 'There was a perfectly still atmosphere'; 'There was little light that was of any use'; 'No ice was visible'; 'There was no hole . . . except at walking pace'.

2 They realised that there was no engine vibration.

3 'A Rothschild, asked . . . walked leisurely away'; 'Stewards rode bicycles . . . gym'.

4 He would have realised that the bow was lower in the water than the rest of the ship and that this pointed to disaster.

5 He mentions the collision with the iceberg at the beginning, so that we know the ship was certain to sink, but then explains the lack of reaction among the passengers and crew. He begins the second paragraph with a sentence that tells the reader how quickly the ship

was sinking, but once again contrasts this with the lack of concern of the passengers. In the middle of the third paragraph, the extent of the disaster is clear to us, but he still contrasts this with what was apparent to the passengers, something that only an experienced sailor would have understood.

Contrasts: 'her starboard plates which were glanced open' and a series of sentences with the word 'no' prominent in them; the first two sentences of the second paragraph and those that follow; the passengers who saw the iceberg and their reaction; the first five sentences of the third paragraph, especially the second, and the sentence: 'She was in fact . . .'; the detail of the stairs, which seems unimportant, and what it really represented.

Page 39 Rail and road accidents

Activity 2

Suggested answers:

1 In the first sentence. He justifies this amusement by adding: 'No one was badly hurt', and comparing it to a performance in the theatre.
2 Because they were not seriously hurt. Examples: 'writing contradictory reports with trembling hands'; 'was delighted with the whole affair'; 'I am afraid she will grow up to expect too much from trains'.
3 By referring to the train as 'she', and in phrases such as 'had been on top of her form', 'she was giving of her best', 'alas, . . . the signals were against her', 'still at a very creditable speed', 'Our train, however, was in no mood for stopping'. By saying that the driver noticed the signals 'in the course of time'; the trains are not very fast, the brakes did not work, the siding was old and its sleepers were rotten.
4 The first builds up a picture of ominous disaster approaching because he knows that hundreds of people were drowned; the second paints an amusing picture of the scene immediately after the accident, in which no one was hurt, and then explains how it happened in a light-hearted manner, because he survived it and looks back on it as an interesting experience.

The narrative styles are appropriately different because the first writer is a modern journalist still attempting to convey an atmosphere of tension in a situation where most readers know what happened in the end; the second was present himself and recounts the story exactly as it occurred from his point of view, since he experienced it first and discovered the reasons afterwards.

Activity 3, p. 40

This page offers a variation in terms of comprehension since students must understand the texts in order to produce

diagrams illustrating them. Ask students to read all the texts, but depending on the size of the class and time available, either allot one diagram to a pair, or more than one. Indicate the number of drawings needed on the following lines:

1 (a) the situation in the first three sentences; (b) 'my wife accelerated . . .'; (c) the crash.
2 (a) the situation on the pavement; (b) the second half of the first sentence; (c) the change of lane; (d) the crash.
3 (a) the first sentence; (b) and (c) two drawings to show the situation just before the crash, and the crash; (d) the last sentence.
4 (a) the first sentence; (b) the second sentence; (c) the crash; (d) the last sentence.

The answers to the questions are given at the back of the student's book (p. 184).

Page 41 Fire!

Activity 4

The value of this exercise depends primarily on the students' ability to grasp the effect of connectors and modifiers in linking a narrative together in a logical manner and giving it substance. It also tests their understanding of the relationship between paragraphs in a narrative.

Form groups of three or four to deal with this. They should discuss the possibilities and ask for help, or at least clues, if necessary. What is important is that you should be able, in comparing the results, to explain why any solutions other than the one given here are incorrect. The answer will always lie in the connectors producing a *non sequitur*.
Solution:

3	c), b), a).	a) cannot follow c) – 'Instead of that, . . .'.
1	b), d), a), c).	a) must follow d) and c) must follow a).
5	c), a), b).	Sequence of time and place.
2	b), a).	
4	c), b), a).	a) must follow b) and b) must follow c).

Activity 5, p. 42

Before dealing with this, it may be necessary to remind students of the basic rules of reported speech (see Ex. 21) and if necessary, practise them in questions (Ex. 86) and commands (Ex. 87).

Ideally, this should be done in groups of six, so that one member of the group in each case can be allotted a part. Groups should work together to agree on the events in the story, either writing a brief account with one acting as 'secretary', or preferably making notes from which each can develop his part. Make it clear to all those concerned that they should report in detail only the part of the story illustrated to show their role (the roles are given in the same order as the six pictures), using direct or reported speech to highlight this section, and summarise what happened before and/or afterwards in one or two sentences.

8

Rewriting: Timetables and programmes

Components	Aims
43 Deciphering timetables	Information retrieval
44 Social programmes	Directed writing
45 Press release	Directed writing
	Grammatical revision

Grammatical revision

Presentation and grammatical revision

Forms used in connection with future time form an important part of this unit, but no formal presentation of them is necessary in our view, other than to point out in connection with each text why different forms are chosen. The final page of the unit contains a conversion exercise from the **going to** and Present Continuous forms used in conversation about personal intentions to the **will** form used in formal press releases.

Page 43 Deciphering timetables

Students should work in pairs on this introductory exercise. The solution given below can provide useful classroom practice of time clauses in the future and conditional sentences providing students are asked to justify the routes recommended: *When he gets to Chicago, he will have to wait for three hours before catching the plane to Denver* or *If he goes to Houston, he will (may) not have time to catch the connecting flight to Denver.*
Solution:
Outward journey: IB 655 Malaga–Chicago, via New York (La Guardia), connecting with UA 518. AA 604 Chicago–Denver. He arrives in Denver at 10.25 p.m. on Tuesday night, and has time to get over his jet-lag before the conference starts.
He could risk flying 1B 908 via Miami to Houston, connecting with UA 613, but would have only 20 minutes to make the connection with AA 477 to Denver, in order to arrive at 10.05 p.m., only twenty minutes earlier than by the other route.
Return journey: TP 900 Denver–Lisbon will get him to Lisbon by 6.50 p.m. on Monday evening, the earliest possible, since the other flight does not leave till

Wednesday. He must spend the night in Lisbon, having missed the last plane to Madrid. TP 700 Lisbon–Madrid and IB 365, Madrid–Malaga. There is hardly time to make the connection with IB 363 (25 minutes). He arrives in Malaga on Tuesday at 2.05 p.m.

Page 44 Social programmes

Activity 1, p. 45

This is a straightforward task, to be done in pairs, but students normally have difficulty with things of this kind unless given an example, as here, because they have no idea of what tone to adopt. Before asking them to do the activity, make sure that they spend ten minutes comparing the programme with the text, noting in particular the use of the **will** form when announcing future events, the use of phrases like 'should apply', 'are available from', and the modest attempt to encourage readers by suggesting that events will be interesting, entertaining, etc.

Page 45 Press release

Activity 2, p. 46

Again, students should work in pairs, once they have studied the model, but here they must invent the timetable. They should note the **will** form used throughout in the example, the emphasis on travel arrangements, etc. and the naming of people responsible for different things as preparation for the eventual written version they may produce in composition topic 1. The reference to the press, normal in a press release, is not needed here, but it will be in some form or other in Activity 3.

Activity 3, p. 47

This is essentially a transformation exercise in terms of future forms but also in terms of style. It is probably best done in pairs but can also be done individually. Students must understand that they are expected to fill in the details not given in the conversation, mentioning the names of people Buck is going to meet in Rome and Madrid, for example, as well as to omit anything that would not be included in a press release. The press release should include advice to journalists requesting further information on the lines of the *Note* included in the press release on the previous page.

Composition

The first topic is a write-up of the timetable students have produced for Activity 2. The second is a recapitulation of what they have done for Activity 1, transferred to their own circumstances.

Description: Cities

Components	Aims	Grammatical revision
48 Around the world	Introduction	
	Comparison	
50 Cambridge	Analysis – style and content	
52 Lyons	Analysis – writing techniques	
	Paragraph analysis	
54 Getting away	Analysis – style and content	
	Rewriting	

Related texts: *Book 2*, Unit 8, passages 2A–C, provides a follow-up to the final text here, *Getting away*, and could be done immediately after concluding this unit.

Presentation and grammatical revision

While a few structures (e.g. *as if, as though* (*Book 3*, Ex. 24) appear here for the first time in the book, no specific revision is needed for students' classroom or composition tasks.

Page 48 Around the world

Pairs must use the city maps and information provided to decide which cities are being described. This should be followed up by questions about their own or neighbouring cities to see whether they can provide similar information and make a rough diagram of the city's position on the board.
Answers and additional information:

1 (Map D) New York. The river is the Hudson. The city was originally called New Amsterdam. It was taken by the British from the Dutch in the second half of the seventeenth century and renamed. Its brief period as capital occurred before it was replaced by Washington.
2 (Map B) Lagos, capital of Nigeria, developed under British rule in the nineteenth century.
3 (Map A) Leningrad, founded as St Petersburg by Peter the Great. The capital now is Moscow. The river is the Neva. It was given its present name on the death of Lenin.
4 (Map E) Lisbon, capital of Portugal, on the north shore of the Tagus.

5 (Map G) Tokyo, capital of Japan.
6 (Map F) Rome, capital of Italy and also the Vatican City. Founded according to legend by Romulus and Remus. The politician/musician is Nero.

Page 50 Cambridge

Activity 1

The importance of this series of texts is to draw students' attention to the effect of purpose on style and content. Too often, when asked to write compositions like those listed at the end of this unit, students produce either a series of personal impressions in emotional terms that tell the reader nothing about the city, or reel off a whole series of disparate guide-book items, with no attempt to link them together in a logical manner. The texts on Cambridge indicate different approaches, while that on Lyons on the following page provides a model for a well-organised description.

Students should work in groups of three or four. They should read all the texts and first answer questions 1 and 2, which are related, comparing notes in order to arrive at a decision. Ask them to point out stylistic features that influence their choice. In effect, the points listed for q. 1 are intended as an aid, so that they will know what to look for.
Answers:
Text A is from a city history for general readers (2); its chronological presentation (e) reinforces this impression. Students who eventually want to answer composition

topic 2 on page 54 should take it into account as a model.
Text B is taken from an autobiography (1) and consists of first-person narrative (c), as might be expected.

Text C is from a tourist guide conveying general information (4), and this is evident from the information given in tabulated form (a).

Text D is from a specialist guide for readers with specific interests (5); its content is unlikely to mean much to the average reader (d) – e.g. 'alternative bookshops' means bookshops stocking the kind of book unlikely to appeal to the majority; 'the wholefood shop' will interest vegetarians, 'the self-development direction' has to do with an interest in yoga, etc., and, it mentions a good meeting place and where to find out what is happening, but we do not know what sort of thing is referred to.

Text E is from a publicity leaflet aimed at American visitors (3). Students should decide which of the adjectives are superfluous (b). Actually most of them are just meaningless terms of praise – 'famed', 'unparalleled', 'magnificent', 'immortal', etc.

The students' final task in this activity is to make similar notes for their own city, and from these notes they could answer composition topic 1 on page 54, following the techniques indicated in the passage on Lyons.

Page 52 Lyons

Activity 2, p. 53

The same groups should work on this passage, which will be of value to all the students in their composition work.

As a model, students should realise that the first paragraph deals with the history of Lyons and the reasons why it became a great city; the second gives an impression of its climate and people; the third describes its industries and mentions things that would interest a visitor to the city.
Answers:

1   (a) It is a 'great industrial city'; (b) it stands at the junction of the Rhône and the Saône, and also marks the meeting in terms of communication systems and culture of the north and south of France; (c) it is misty and damp; (d) it is famous for printing and silk; (e) its food is wonderful; (f) the people are at first sight grey like the climate, but are 'industrious and inventive'; (g) its attraction for visitors lies in its bookshops, cultural activities and food and drink.
2   The sentences that follow all deal with Lyons as the axis

between the cultures of northern and southern France, so that the junction between the rivers leads naturally to a consideration of a junction between cultures and also explains why Lyons became the 'natural axis of the European road system'.
3   His principal interest seems to be food and drink; the transitional phrase is 'the axis of good eating'.
4   'Comes of age'; at the end of adolescence, people are likely to experience their first love affair.
5   Geographically, culturally and as a centre for good food. Because it suggests the 'middle' and central point of the body, just as Lyons is in the middle, between the cultures of northern and southern France, and because it is the part of the body likely to be filled by good food.
6   Yes, – 'I . . . found it not inapt' – though the double negative does not quite make the positive ('I found it apt'). Daudet suggested the people were like the climate, which is 'grey', sticky and unpleasant.
7   The topic sentence suggests Lyons has attractions. The next refers to fine craftsmanship and suggests a visitor might find examples of it. This is a natural transition to another example of historical and artistic interest. The conclusion is that Lyons 'has its charms', confirming the topic sentence and contradicting the unpleasant, grey picture of the second paragraph.

Page 54 Getting away

Activity 3

The text is publicity material, like text E on page 51. The students' main task is to separate the information from the emotional language in order to rewrite the account in a form much closer to what we would expect to them in a composition. The activity is best handled in pairs.

The answers to the questions are obvious; the phrases listed in q. 3 provide the clue to the kind of emotion suggested by the adjectives that will be found in answer to q. 2.

Composition

Aids for the first two topics have already been referred to. Make clear to students that the third topic must not be answered as if it were a tourist-guide extract, but must contain their personal impressions (and will therefore be a descriptive narrative, mainly written in past tenses, rather than a straightforward description).

Narrative: Journeys

Components
55 Where to go?
56 Abandoned . . . stranded . . . lost

Aims
Information retrieval
Analysis – style and content
Analysis – writing techniques
Paragraph analysis
Linking paragraphs

Grammatical revision
Book 3, Ex. 25

Ex. 26

Related texts: *Book 2*, Unit 8, passage 1, parallel to this unit.
Further grammatical practice: *Book 3*, Exs. 92A–C.

Presentation and grammatical revision

The first task demands a knowledge of conditional
sentences (Present–Future and Past–Conditional) and
for their compositions students would also need to
remember the Past Perfect–Conditional Perfect forms.
Ex. 25 in *Book 3* revises all of these, and also introduces
some less common variants that may be new. It is
advisable to look at this before beginning the unit.
While the various forms of sentences beginning **I wish/
If only . . .** are not directly needed here, we have
always found it useful to teach them in conjunction
with the conditional. Exs. 92A–C could well be
introduced as a follow-up before reading the texts on
pages 56 and 57.

For this kind of narrative composition, it is essential
that students should be aware of the rules governing
the normal order of adverbs of manner, place and time
when they occur within the same sentence. Ex. 26
could usefully be done before students attempt the final
activity on page 58 and should certainly be looked at
before they write their compositions.

Page 55 Where to go?

This is an introductory task, to be done in groups of
three or four, in which students must work out a
sensible route for two people on holiday. The first two
conditional combinations can be practised effectively if
some groups are asked (1) to work out a brief dialogue
between Tim and Barbara discussing the possibilities:
'If we go north-east, along the A64, we can reach

Flamingo Land. I want to see the countryside round
there.' 'I'd like to see some of the interesting houses
around there, too.' 'Yes, well on the way back, there
are several on the route. If we come back on the minor
roads past Byland Abbey, we'll be able to stop at
Newburgh Priory, and we'll also see Sutton Park.'

Other groups can be posed the questions: 'What
would they see if they took the road to Thirsk?' 'Why
would Barbara want to go there?' 'What would interest
Tim near the Moors?' Answers could be linked to
produce an account beginning: 'On the first day, we
think they would go to . . ., because if they went that
way, Barbara could . . . and Tim would be able to . . .'

Page 56 Abandoned . . . stranded . . . lost

The two passages on pages 56 and 57 are
complementary, but need not be read for comparison.
The first demands an analysis of the use of techniques
already referred to in previous units on narrative. The
second demands a similar analysis, but also includes a
greater awareness of the use of atmosphere.

Activity 1

Answers:

1 In the first part of the first sentence: 'It was 10.00 p.m.
   . . train'. This kind of detail is often omitted from
   students' compositions.
2 There are three examples. All of them occur at crucial
   points in the narrative (cf. techniques in Unit 2, p. 11).

3 In the paragraph beginning 'And she was still in summer clothes . . .' and the paragraph beginning 'Now reunited with her husband . . .'. In the first case, to explain this statement and give the background to Karin Edholm's journey; in the second to explain what her husband had been doing while we have been following Karin's misadventures. Point out the use of the Past Perfect tense in both cases.

4 'There was no platform, no station, etc.', and later on, 'nobody answered', 'nobody saw her'. This is done to build up the impression of Karin's isolation and add dramatic effect to her eventual survival.

Activity 2, p. 57

Answers:

1 In the first two sentences. Note that whereas in the first passage, the time (at night) is important, here it is the delay. We do not realise it is night until the fourth paragraph, but this does not affect the point of the story.

2 The dialogue adds life to the narrative, and makes it sound more realistic, because of the comments of the people on India, the suggestion of political influence, lack of bars, etc.

3 In the last sentence, referring back to the offer to translate for the writer.

4 'The station has two rooms, and there are cows on the verandah', and the following sentences: 'Delay of two hours' and 'I decided to look for a beer'.

5 It is a country where modern technology has not advanced very far – 'The engine has packed up', 'there are cows on the verandah'; there is a combination of dirt and things not being well-looked after – 'Grass tufts grow out of the ledge of the booking-office window. It smelled of . . . cow dung'; 'drinking milky tea out of cracked glasses'; there is an atmosphere of quiet resignation and acceptance of the inevitable – no beer, no car, but 'Have some tea' – and only a few quiet grumbles – 'if there was a cabinet minister on the train . . .', 'This is the real India', which is said 'under [the man's] breath'.

Activity 3, p. 58

The passage here should be handled in the same way as in Unit 7, page 41.

In all cases, groups should again discuss the possibilities. Here, the logical order of sentences and paragraphs is determined by the time and place references, and it is important that students should use the same kind of references to order their own compositions. Solution:

3 c), a), e), d), b). The initial sentence is a topic sentence for the whole composition. c) gives the time reference. a) introduces the 'German girl', who is referred to as 'her' in e). In d) 'there' refers to 'Switzerland' in e), and b) is the natural conclusion for the beginning of the journey.

1 c), b), a). This paragraph clearly comes before 5, because of the place reference. c) precedes b) in place reference, and 'it' in a) refers to the 'gleaming modern train' in b).

5 b), a).

2 c), e), a), d), b). 'All I knew . . .' in c) refers to the opening sentence. The remaining sentences are governed by place reference.

4 b), e), a), d), c). 'the hotel' in b) clearly refers back to the end of the previous paragraph. 'He' in a) is the taxi driver, referring back to e). The time reference and the mention of 'the other hotel' in d) shows that it is after a), which ends with the mention of 'another hotel', and c) is obviously a final comment, relating to the taxi-driver's behaviour in d).

Composition

Students are free to use any of the three texts as a model for this. What is important is that they should use the place and time references illustrated, and also give the narrative 'life' by the use of (a) direct speech at crucial moments; (b) descriptive detail to make the atmosphere surrounding the journey clear. While a chronological narrative is the best plan to follow, students should note the use of Past Perfect tenses where they are required.

Discussion: Women in society

Components

59 Questionnaire

60 The historical background
62 Two modern views
63 For or against

Aims

Introduction
Clarifying ideas
Comparison of style and content
Comparison – writing techniques
Directed writing

Grammatical revision

Presentation

No grammatical revision is required here that has a direct relationship with the content. Students may nevertheless be well advised to look again at **It's + adjective + for/that** (Ex. 8), purpose clauses (Ex. 16) and emphatic constructions: **it, what, the thing that** (Ex. 23), introduced in connection with previous units.

The unit is the first in which techniques for presenting a convincing argument are the main topic for students' attention. It is as well to point out from the beginning that there are various approaches that can be made to any general discussion topic but that basically our response to a statement made in general terms is (1) to argue strongly for or against it; (2) to present a balanced case, considering both sides in an impartial way; or (3) to react by wanting to redefine the terms of the statement to make it more accurate or more relevant, whether or not we sympathise with it in general. These three approaches are illustrated in this unit, in Unit 15, and in Unit 19 respectively.

Page 59 Questionnaire

The questionnaire is designed to produce instinctive, rather than considered, reactions to the statements made, all of which reflect to a greater or lesser extent the feminist point of view. Students should decide within a few seconds whether they are strongly in favour of the statement, agree with it in general terms, disagree or are outraged by it. The middle column (0) must be explained as meaning not only that students have no opinion but as including the attitude that the statement is too vague to justify a clear expression of opinion one way or the other.

Depending on the constitution of the class in terms of sex ratios and also on the vehemence you may or may not expect on the subject because of the students' social or religious background, either ask for a show of hands on each question or collect the questionnaires. Make a note of those statements that call forth the most disagreement, and expecially any where there are a number of votes at the two extremes. These will either be the subjects on which a discussion should be based or the subjects to avoid, depending on the freedom of speech students are accustomed to.

Students may need guidance in answering q. 4 (i.e. to explain the modern preference for 'Ms' over Mrs and Miss) and q. 5, where the point is that the father's surname does not form part of the child's name in Britain, as it does in some other countries, any more than a wife on marriage officially retains the use of her own name, as she would do in some other countries.

A discussion on any of these subjects can be introduced at any time in the unit on the basis of the questionnaire, but is probably most likely to be fruitful later on, e.g. after completing page 61 or after completing page 63, by which time students will have had the opportunity of hearing some different points of view to relate to or react against.

Page 60 The historical background

Some students may think that the struggle for sexual equality is of relatively recent origin; these four texts, given with the date of publication, disprove that idea. The object here is primarily for students to comprehend the ideas being put forward and understand the topic in a rational way, without giving way to instinctive prejudices. All the texts on pages 60 and 61, of course, were written by women. If possible, students should read all four before coming to class and then be split into groups working either on Activity 1 or on Activity 2 on page 61, though if time permits, they can attempt both.

Activity 1, p. 61

Suggested answers:

1 Because she thinks that it is social custom that has made man woman's protector, not that it is in fact natural.

2 The second passage shows Rosamond getting her own way by means of using her charm and weakness as a weapon against her husband. (In fact, she is not pretending, but genuinely believes in her own suffering because she is so self-centred.)

3 Lydgate assumes that he should protect Rosamond because it is his responsibility, having married her. He cannot help thinking of her 'as if she were an animal of another and feebler species', which directly relates to Mary Wollstonecraft's argument that a 'fragile' woman, appealing to her protector for help, is bound to be despised.

4 Not at all. She is precisely the opposite, obtaining power by 'charms and weakness', and also clinging to her husband with 'parasitical tenacity'.

5 The general impression given by Mary Wollstonecraft is that women, traditionally brought up, are rather pathetic, even though she also finds them exasperating. George Eliot's last sentence suggests that this apparent weakness and use of tears is a very powerful weapon and Rosamond, from this time on, will be the dominant partner in the marriage. George Eliot definitely sympathises with Lydgate, a 'loving-hearted man', and is too good a novelist to say openly how much she hates Rosamond.

Activity 2

Suggested answers:

1 They are similar, in that both are thinking of women as independent, reasoning begins, not relying on men for support. Mary Wollstonecraft, however, is primarily concerned with women being educated so that they can play a part in society as individuals, while Virginia Woolf is concerned with women who have been educated in this way but must consider how far their careers and independence must be balanced against other considerations.

2 She means an independent professional position, rather than the right to live alone, though that is also implied.

3 Because for Rosamond, whose whole aim in life was to get married, a woman is bound to share her life with her husband and children.

4 She thought they were 'frightening people . . . of their heads'. The picture was confusing because such women,

cut off from the mainstream of society, dressed alike and became a recognisable minority, 'the very antithesis of freedom'.

5 The 'natural protector' of the first passage and Lydgate in the second are bound to despise women's intelligence, and regard them as beautiful living dolls, capable of feelings and attractive, but not rational beings.

Page 62 Two modern views

These passages are intended for detailed analysis of the way in which the argument is presented. Students should work in pairs, having read the passages, in the first place to establish their understanding of them.

Activity 3, Part 1

Suggested answers:

1 Not really. The first passage is about a woman's struggle to remain a complete individual in a married relationship, the second about being a 'successful', self-satisfied wife. But in general terms, they both deal with the problems of married women.

2 An open-ended question, but we imagine that the first is writing for women in need of advice on how to develop their own personalities, the second for women who want to get on well with their husbands. (It may be rather more difficult for students to realise from the style, although the content may indicate it, that the first passage is obviously aimed at a higher intellectual level than the second, and that the second is clearly American).

3 'A complete person' for Greer is a woman who is still herself as an individual but also capable of loving unselfishly; 'a total woman' for Morgan is a housewife who lives her own life on good terms with her husband.

4 Again, an open question, but they would not be likely to have much in common because Morgan assumes that the 'total woman' is married, and her main object is to organise her marriage on the right lines, whereas Greer distrusts marriage and is concerned that women should be fully developed individuals without the need to depend on others.

In detail, Greer blames women who sacrifice 'their personal responsibility for themselves' and encourages them to be 'self-reliant'. Such women must be 'hard' and not 'surrender', in order to retain their completeness as individuals. They must allow lovers freedom and expect it for themselves. Morgan thinks women must always 'adapt' to their husbands, and it is the king who makes the final decision'; right or wrong, the wife must agree with it out of loyalty. She must have her own opinions, but allow her husband to overrule her if they disagree. (However, the second and third sentences suggest that the husband is likely to be strongly influenced by his wife once he has made a fool of himself!)

5   Greer – the main risks are loneliness, broken love affairs and not having children, because men will not allow women to be self-reliant.

Morgan – the main risks are that the husband makes a lot of wrong decisions and the wife is unable to go on graciously adapting to him, in the long run a situation leading to divorce.

Greer assumes that most women have been brought up to think of marriage as the main end in life, but is convinced that this is wrong and that their aim should be self-realisation, at all costs.

Morgan seems content with the idea that most women are brought up with marriage as their main aim, and is concerned that they should get the best bargain possible.

Activity 3, Part 2

1   Greer (first paragraph). The paragraph is built up (1) by example – the second sentence is an example of the statement made in the topic sentence; (2) by further exposition – the fourth and fifth sentences illustrate and develop the third; (3) by example, the last two sentences acting as an example of the previous three.

Greer (possible counter-arguments). (1) Isn't it likely that a woman will appear hard if she tries to show her independence? (2) How do you know that self-reliant women are always loved? What guarantees can you give? (3) Isn't it likely that this sort of behaviour will lead to divorce?

2   Morgan (second paragraph). The paragraph begins with a metaphor and each sentence indicates points that justify the relationship in terms of a king and a queen. The success of the argument depends on whether the metaphor is really applicable to a husband and wife.

Morgan (possible counter-arguments). 'Now, hold on, I know just what you're thinking.' 'I would like to say right here that in the beginning I was as dubious as anyone about adapting.'

3   Both passages are convincing in terms of technique, though it is evident that the first is a much more convincing argument because it is established by example and definition (first paragraph), by anticipating possible disagreement (the instances stated above) and by a logical argument that relates the paragraphs. Of course, it depends in part on unsupported statements (e.g. the first sentence of the second paragraph) but not to the extent of the second.

The second passage depends almost entirely on an extended metaphor. If we accept the metaphor, we accept the argument, which is consistent within those terms. The fifth paragraph, with its conclusion, is already summarised in the topic sentence at the beginning of the first. Such techniques, however, are dangerous for students to follow, since they can easily lead to endless repetition of the same point, which may not be valid in the first place. Ms Morgan's argument seems to depend on the husband being a fairly well-off businessman capable of 'spoiling his wife with goodies', on his wife being able to behave in a gracious, queenly manner, presumably because she is dressed for the part and not weary from the household chores, and on their decisions being matters like choosing a new house, not fighting for survival.

Page 63 For or against

Activity 4

This is a directed writing exercise aimed at showing students how to argue a case by taking a stand one way or the other. We have chosen the topic from the original ten in the questionnaire where the statement made obtained least support from students in pretesting, irrespective of their sex.

Students should use the plan and the opinions presented in order to build up a case against the proposition, whatever their own views may be. Draw attention to the way in which paragraphs 2 and 3 should be organised. It is always convincing in a paragraph that depends on a list of points (2) to build up from 'In the first place' to 'Above all'. Remind students of connectors used for this purpose by telling them to consult the Appendix, p. 164.

Few students ever take into account that there can be any view other than their own in writing compositions of this type; the instruction for the third paragraph forces them to recognise it, but also indicates that the opposing arguments must be introduced in order to be destroyed (cf. the final paragraph of the *Daily Telegraph* editorial on page 32 'The newest profession', already referred to in the notes in this connection). Draw students' attention to such connectors as 'At first sight', 'However'.

We suggest that students should work together on the first and last paragraphs to establish continuity, but should each handle one of the middle paragraphs demanding greater technical skill.

Composition, p. 64

While there is no reason why students should not give their own opinions on any of these topics, make it clear that from the point of view of developing their technique, it would be preferable if they wrote on one where they have a strong argument for or against, rather than one on which they feel indifferent. The opportunity for practising 'balanced' compositions will come later.

Rewriting: Dialogue and speeches

Components	Aims	Grammatical revision
65 To extend or not to extend	Introduction	
66 Summarising dialogue	Summary techniques, rewriting	*Book 3*, Exs. 96A–C
68 An informal speech	Rewriting	
69 Formal speeches	Rewriting	
	Grammatical revision	

Further grammatical practice: revision of *Book 3*, Exs. 21, 86, 87.

Presentation and grammatical revision

A unit containing exercises in which dialogue must be summarised and transformed into continuous prose necessarily requires that students not only handle reported speech confidently in terms of form (already practised in Exercises 21, 86 and 87 in association with Unit 7) but are also aware of the variety of introducing verbs commonly used. The exercises on these verbs, 96A–C, will almost certainly need to be done before students attempt the summary of dialogue.

Page 65 To extend or not to extend

A good idea of students' control of reported speech and reporting verbs can be gained from this task. Play the cassette, having first asked students to read through the points listed as arguments for and against. Pause briefly after each of the phone-in speakers to allow students to tick the arguments he or she has put forward. Then play the whole broadcast through without stopping so that students can confirm that their understanding is correct. In asking students to explain which arguments the speakers put forward, elicit answers in reported speech by referring to the cassette in the past: 'Was Mrs Brewster in favour of the airport expansion? Why was she against it?' Students can either transform the arguments given in the list into a reported form or try to paraphrase or repeat in the same form what they have actually heard: 'She was against it for two reasons: she said people in areas disturbed by noise would have to be rehoused' or 'She complained about the noise'.

Page 66 Summarising Dialogue

Students who have been using *Book 3* of the course in conjunction with this one will have no difficulty in understanding the techniques required here, which are the same as for summarising a piece of prose (see *Book 3*, Section 2, Unit 3).

Activity 1

One side of the argument (Susan's) has been summarised here, and students must summarise the other side, Henry's. This is largely a matter of finding the sentences that express the main points, as already illustrated for Susan, and then reordering the information in a logical way. Warn students not to attempt to answer this simply by copying down the relevant sentences without reordering.
Suggested answer:

Henry agrees that examinations are not always satisfactory but thinks they are necessary because they are the only fair way of judging people's abilities. Individual teachers could not be relied on to apply the same standards. He also considers examinations are a good test of people's response in a real-life situation where they would have to show their knowledge under stress. He is aware that examinations can have a bad effect on teaching methods but considers that this does not justify doing away with them; the answer lies in improving them, and improving teaching methods.

Activity 2, p. 67

As in the case of the previous dialogue, play the cassette twice to add authenticity to the situation before allowing students to look at the text. The exercise is an extension of the previous one, where students must summarise both sides of the argument. It can be handled in one of two ways. Either the class is divided into pairs, and one member of each pair summarises one side of the argument, or alternatively, with an eye to the examination, students make notes in class and discuss the main points, but must complete the activity as an individual task at home, summarising both sides of the argument.

Page 68 An informal speech

We are sceptical of the value of expecting students to imitate the conventions of speechmaking in English, considering how few native speakers are capable of saying anything worth listening to, but Cambridge appear to be insistent on including this kind of task. We have therefore concentrated on speeches a student could reasonably be asked to make. The main difficulty is to convince students that by comparison with speeches they have heard in their own language, the English are so inarticulate, and anything resembling a speech in Spanish, for example, would be regarded as pompous because of its literary organisation.

The first example indicates that an informal speech in English is like an impromptu monologue. Play the cassette twice so that students can get used to the tone and style, and then ask them to study the notes, together with the speech, to see how one is transformed into the other.

Activity 3

In effect, students are being asked here to come as close as they can to the models in a similar situation. The value of the exercise can only be obtained if they make the speeches from notes with books closed, not if they read out a copy of the original.

Page 69 Formal speeches

The speech here is rather more like what a student might one day have to make in English in real life. The essence of it is good organisation, based on notes.

Activity 4

Students should first order the speaker's notes before listening to and reading the finished speech.

Ask students to work in pairs to decide on a logical order for the notes. The order in the speech itself is in fact 4, 2, 1, 3, but play the cassette without telling students this so that they can confirm it for themselves. Then ask them to comment on this order or presentation and see whether they think it is appropriate, and if so, why.

The pairs can be retained, or preferably larger groups of three or four formed, to deal with Activity 5.

Activity 5

The final versions of these speeches form one of the composition tasks at the end of the unit. What is needed from the group work is the provision of notes in a logical order from which the compositions can be written. This is a necessary stage for many students, who find it difficult to put themselves into a situation they have not previously encountered in real life. Go through the notes with the groups, supplying ideas when necessary, and in listening to the final versions, draw students' attention to omissions and also to possible inclusions that might not be appropriate to the situation.

Activity 6, p. 70

Students can hardly be expected to make political speeches in a foreign language. This task is intended for grammatical revision of reported and direct speech, and should be done for that purpose. Once versions in reported speech exist for all the contributions, however, either in the book or in students' versions, students could then be asked to summarise the debate in a few sentences (one or two for each paragraph in the text).

Composition

Students must either write an informal speech for a situation where they might be likely to make one or else write up the notes they have made in connection with Activity 5.

13

Description: The past

Components
71 My husband and I . . .
72 Two famous men
74 Britain between the wars
76 Memories of India

Aims
Introduction
Grammatical revision
Comparison – style and content
Grammatical revision

Grammatical revision

Book 3, Ex. 14E (revision) 16 (revision)

Ex. 32

Related texts: *Book 2*, Unit 10 (parallel with this one), passages 1, 2A and 2B.
Further grammatical practice: *Book 3*, Ex. 33.

Presentation and grammatical revision

Previous units devoted to description have largely concentrated on decriptions in present time. Descriptions in past time, the subject of this unit, necessarily resemble narrative, with the distinction that they do not tell a story. The composition topics at the end of this unit include potted biography, life at some time in the past in the students' country, and changes that have recurred in a place students know well. Students need to have a thorough grasp of the following in order to deal with all of them:

1 the use of modals in the past, particularly those regulating speculation and deduction (**may have . . ., might have . . ., must have . . .**); these could well be revised prior to handling the first two passages (pp. 72 and 73);
2 the use of **used to** and **would** to describe what was customarily true in the past, but is no longer true. The exercise in *Book 3* listed above (Ex. 32) could well precede the exercise given here on the use of these forms in continuous prose.

The three texts in the parallel unit of *Book 2* afford parallels to the subject of the two passages compared here on Britain between the wars and also prepare students for the topic of changes in a familiar place; this unit could well be done before students write their final compositions.

Page 71 My husband and I . . .

Play the cassette as an introduction to the topic twice to

see if students can identify the three well-known figures seen through the eyes of their wives. Then allow students to study the text for comprehension and attention to the style, and ask them to work in groups of three on the activity that follows. Needless to say, this is intended primarily as light relief, and can be omitted if time is pressing.

Additional points of information that may arise in questions are as follows:

1 Julius Caesar, assassinated on March 15, 44 BC, in the Forum. In Shakespeare's version, based on Petrarch, there was a storm the night before, and Calpurnia, his wife, the 'speaker' here, tried to prevent Caesar from going (though not for the reasons given here!). Caesar campaigned in Britain in 55 and 54 BC, and complained about the climate.
2 Henry VIII married six times and executed two of his wives. He *did* pride himself on his knowledge of Latin and the Bible. Catherine Parr (his last wife and the 'speaker') was very learned. She afterwards married the Lord High Admiral, Thomas Seymour (said to have been the first lover of the later Queen Elizabeth I).
3 William Shakespeare had three children when he apparently left home around 1585, probably to join a group of actors. He returned a rich man and built a new house in 1597 before eventually settling down with his wife and two surviving children about 1609 in Stratford-on-Avon. His plays were very popular with Queen Elizabeth I (died 1603). Shakespeare's father, once Mayor of Stratford, *did* go bankrupt, and his mother, born Mary Arden, was of a higher

social class. The views on the theatre expressed here by the 'speaker', Anne Hathaway, were typical of middle-class attitudes at the time.

Page 72 Two famous men

The texts here serve as models for composition topic 1, but are also aimed at revising the structural points mentioned above.

Activity 1

The passage lends itself to straightforward comprehension questions before students attempt the activity, involving practice of the third conditional and in particular of its use with modals (**may** and **might have . . .**).

Activity 2, p. 73

Here students must work in pairs to produce their own speculations and deductions, using the modals. Prompt with questions of your own, using the suggestions given in the instructions in the students' book, to aid them.

Page 74 Britain between the wars

The two passages on pages 74 and 75 are contrasted, and should be read on the same day; if possible, students should read them before coming to class. Their main interest for students is the content, and they can work in pairs on the activities, prior to a general discussion on the implications of the contrast shown here which can of course be extended to consideration of changes in their own country over the past fifty years or so.

Activity 3, p. 75

Suggested answers:

1 'Hold a candle to' – approach in quality, brilliance, etc.; rival. 'Stunt party' – a party at which the guests were expected to act or perform a music-hall turn on a stage (a stunt). 'Do a turn' – act, sing, dance, etc. as in a music-hall. 'Dragoon' – force the guests to take part (in a military manner, like a dragoon).
2 By realising that 'even the most unlikely people were open to bribes', and gaining the favour of rich people by allowing them to win prizes and giving them presents.
3 Both adjectives mean 'shining', and the favourable accounts of the parties may have been influenced by the beautiful presents guests received.
4 Because they were not invited to dinner.
5 The point was to ensure that the most distinguished guest won, not really by luck but by arrangement. 'The most exalted guest' was the one with the highest social position and the one whose favour the hostess was

most eager to obtain. It is called 'a very noble ticket' because it had been given to an aristocrat.

Activity 4

Suggested answers:

1 Because in that case they would save fifteen shillings a week and part of his compensation would be paid by the social security services.
2 As a sign of respect.
3 Social position, as seen by other people; we demand what we have a right to legally or morally, and he was entitled to the money, but had to ask for it, as if it were a gift.
4 He is different because he is a bourgeois and is treated more respectfully in a bank because of his dress and accent and social class.
5 It means 'even a bourgeois who is so poor (and not very well dressed)' because people whose shoes are 'down at heel' need new ones or cannot afford to have them repaired.
6 Because the bank clerks are polite, treating him as a gentleman.
7 Many observations could be made, but what is obvious is the enormous difference in terms of wealth and the treatment of people on class lines. The greatest contrast is between the aristocrat being given an immensely expensive prize to obtain his favour while the miner has to beg for what is owed him. The first passage, as indicated, relates social events of 1927; Orwell's journey to the depressed areas of the north of England took place in the early 1930s.

Page 76 Memories of India

As indicated, this should be preceded by revision of **used to** and **would** (Ex. 32 in *Book 3*). It is difficult to indicate their use except in continuous prose, but equally difficult to test understanding of it because the Past Simple tense can always be substituted for either. Ask students to read the text carefully, noting the changes from present to past tenses and vice versa, and also the introduction of **used to** and **would**, prior to attempting Activity 5, for which the passage serves as a model in structural terms, as it does for composition topic 4.

The principal points students should note are:

1 The passage begins and ends in the Present Simple because it describes weather conditions in India (which have not changed) but gives way to the Past Simple as the speaker begins to reminisce about his own experiences. Note the time reference: 'When I first went out . . .', which introduces this sequence.
2 **Used to** is substituted for the Past Simple tense, indicating the speaker's awareness that these are no

longer his customs. **Would** is only used in connection with repeated actions that occurred at the same time every day.

NOTE: In common with most native speakers, the speaker uses **one** and **you** indiscriminately in speech, shifting from one to the other to describe general impressions affecting everyone. The tendency to shift towards **you** is probably a means of identifying the listener with the situation. In written English, however, students should be reminded that they should themselves be consistent on the point (see *Book 3*,

Ex. 91, introduced in association with Unit 9).

Activity 5

As far as possible, students should endeavour to use this themselves as a means of employing all the points mentioned above.

Composition

The topics and the relevant models have already been referred to.

Narrative: The future

Components	Aims	Grammatical revision
77 Film posters	Introduction	
78 Views of the future	Comparison – style and content	
80 The distant future	Analysis – writing techniques	*Book 3*, Ex. 34
	Grammatical revision	

Further grammatical practice: revision of *Book 3*, Ex. 25.

Presentation and grammatical revision

Narratives and general compositions relating to future time can be written in a variety of tenses, depending on whether the student is asked to speculate with regard to the future from the point of view of now or imagine that he/she has been transported into future time. From a grammatical point of view, it is essential to concentrate on the former, where complex tenses such as the Future Perfect, together with the employment of time clauses and conditionals of types (1) and (2), will be required. Exercise 34 from *Book 3* is best introduced before activities where students will be obliged to use these forms in the classroom (p. 80).

Page 77 Film posters

This is an introductory exercise primarily aimed at presenting the theme of imaginary visions of the future. Students should have seen some or all of the films illustrated here and are likely to participate in a lively discussion.

Page 78 Views of the future

The passages on pages 78 and 79 can be contrasted but need not be read on the same day. Students should realise immediately that the first is a forecast made in present conditions and therefore written primarily in present and future tenses, the second a narrative supposedly written in the future but narrated in past tenses.

Activity I

Suggested answers:

1 Examples are plastics; DDT; hovercraft; Concorde.
2 The short answer is widespread birth control.

Obviously, this passage lends itself to discussion of all the points it raises, and can best be used for that purpose.

Activity 2, p. 79

Suggested answers:

1 It is a totalitarian state where the individual is controlled by the Thought Police.
2 The television can transmit and receive simultaneously; it can see and hear people in the room. The city is dirty and dilapidated. Most of the houses are old and there are bombed sites everywhere which have not been cleared up.
3 Great Britain is now an outlying province of Oceania. It has been bombed in a war.
4 The language has been streamlined, but above all the meanings of words have been so distorted that they now mean the opposite of what they meant before; the Ministry of Truth is really the Ministry of Lies. This has been accomplished by perverting language; the slogans are made up of opposites being suggested as synonyms.
5 An open question for students' discussion. The key question is whether the collapse of the present system would be followed by war and the kind of state Orwell envisaged.

Page 80 The distant future

The passage leads to three activities, one of which is a matter of analysing it, while the others are mainly intended for grammatical revision. Students should study the passage in pairs and decide on the answers to Activity 3.

Activity 3

Suggested answers:

1. a) the trains leave every two and a half minutes; b) the helicopters and monorails; c) the trains are segregated according to the caste of the passengers.
2. He is disgusted. The sentences describing the landscape are deliberately poetic ('the bright shore of the western sky', the colours of the sunset) but the factory 'glared' and its brilliance was 'fierce' and 'electric' – in other words, aggressive and unnatural. The houses of the lower castes were 'barracks'; they are treated without much consideration, like serving soldiers.
3. The dead are used for the benefit of the whole of society, in producing phosphorus, etc., but it is strange to Lenina that the lower castes, so rigidly separated in life, are just as useful when they are dead, proving that the society is unjust.
4. Henry speaks (or rather, thinks, because he speaks 'telegraphically' by thought transference) like someone who has learnt a lesson by heart. When Lenina raises a doubt, he replies 'sententiously' with a quotation.
5. The apparently well-organised society is based on predetermined inequality and the need to brainwash everyone.

6. It demonstrates that such a society can only function on this basis, where such questions cannot be answered without disrupting the system.

Activities 4 and 5, p. 81

These provide open-ended grammatical practice, first of the Future Perfect tense and secondly of the conditional in the combinations of Present-Future, and Past-Conditional.

Activity 6

This is again an exercise on the control of tenses in future time, which should confirm students' grasp of *Book 3*, Ex. 34. Students should note that they are expected to use appropriate modals, whenever this would add to the sense of the passage.

Suggested answers:

(1) continues; (2) will have used up; (3) will make; (4) is; (5) came up with, produced, suggested, etc.; (6) exhaust, use up; (7) ought, could try, should try, will have; (8) should be bred, reared, etc.; (9) can live; (10) has been done; (11) will fly, go, etc.; (12) will have changed, transformed, turned; (13) have done; (14) will be, will have become; (15) lands, sets foot, etc.; (16) falls; (17) will have to; (18) should/will live; (19) will suffer, undergo, should suffer, undergo; (2) will be living.

Composition

The first topic is the only one which obliges students to use the range of the future tenses. Topic 3 demands use of the conditional forms.

Discussion: Education

Components	Aims	Grammatical revision
82 Examination results	Information retrieval	
83 Grading students	Analysis of style and content	
	Discussion	
86 Discipline	Comparison – style and content	
88 State and private education	Analysis – writing techniques	
90 Arguing for *and* against	Using writing techniques	

Related texts: the parallel unit in *Book 2*, Unit 12, also takes education as its theme but the texts are not directly relevant to students' compositions.

Presentation

No specific grammatical revision is required for this unit, but students would be well advised to study the connectors and modifiers in the Appendix, especially those used to modify or contrast with previous statements.

Page 82 Examination results

This introductory exercise will not recommend itself to teachers averse to the interpretation of statistics, but provides interesting points for discussion and directly relates to composition topic 1. It is also a useful corrective in classes where men have been brought up to feel instinctively superior to women in intellectual or academic achievement, and this is important in a unit aimed at showing students how to write 'balanced' compositions showing both sides of an argument.

Before asking students to study the tables and answer the questions, point out the differences between 'A' and 'O' level and draw attention to the fact that in Britain each subject is dealt with individually and students' chances of further educational progress depend on the number of subjects they pass and the levels they obtain, not on a global scoring system or one where failure in one subject means failure overall.

Help students unfamiliar with this kind of task in the following ways, having first divided them into groups of four so that they can pool their efforts.

The first question depends on listing preferences of

boys and girls in descending order, in the same way as the overall entries. Comparisons should be made by comparing the proportion of boys to that of girls, so that e.g. physics is much more popular with boys at 'O' level (73–27).

In q. 2, students should see whether subjects rise or fall in order of the number of entries, in general and for boys and girls separately; the total number of entries is not relevant, since far fewer students take 'A' level.

In q. 3, students must compare the pass rates, first at 'O' level, then at 'A' level, and see whether there are noticeable differences (i.e. more than 5% difference between the two). They must also look out for subjects where the ratio of boys and girls passing changes noticeably from 'O' to 'A' level.

Solutions:

1 'O' level	Boys	Girls
	English Language	English Language
	Mathematics	Mathematics
	Physics	Biology
	Geography	English Lit.
	English Lit.	French
	Chemistry	Geography
	Biology	Art
	History	History
	French	Chemistry
	Art	Physics

'A' level

Boys	Girls
Mathematics	English
Physics	Biology
Chemistry	History
Economics	Mathematics
Gen. Studies	Gen. Studies
Geography	French
English	Chemistry
Biology	Economics
History	Art
Art	Geography
French	Physics

At 'O' level, physics is much more popular with boys than with girls, and chemistry is considerably more popular; considerably more girls take biology and French than boys.

At 'A' level, far more boys take physics and mathematics, and considerably more take chemistry and economics; far more girls take French and English, and considerably more take art. The pattern of preference seems to be that boys favour scientific subjects, excluding biology, and girls favour languages, literature (since at 'A' level English is basically literature) and art.

2 In general terms, physics and chemistry rise most up the scale, together with the new subjects, economics and general studies; geography and French fall most down the scale.

Chemistry and the two new subjects attract more attention from boys at 'A' level than at 'O' level, while the proportion for English is similar to that for English Literature.

English Literature and history become more important for girls, while geography shows the greatest decline.

3 Boys appear to do noticeably better in mathematics and biology at 'O' level than girls; girls do better than boys at English Language and Literature and art.

At 'A' level, boys do better at economics and general studies, girls at English.

In some cases (e.g. English) the results are similar, and girls appear to be better than boys; in the new subjects, economics and general studies, boys do better, perhaps because of aptitude or interest, perhaps because the subjects are taken more seriously by teachers.

The changes – e.g. the improvement of the girls in mathematics and physics (better than the boys at 'A' level) and of the boys in art (almost equal with the girls) – are to be accounted for in our view by the fact that the proportion of girls taking the former and boys taking the latter is small, and those who have continued are no doubt very dedicated people and score well.

Page 83 Grading students

The passage on page 84 is once again the basis for a possible discussion topic and relates to composition topic 2.

Activity 1, p. 84

Note that although this becomes pair work, individuals should form their own opinions in answer to the questions and discuss them with their partners afterwards. Some of the questions are open-ended, but suggested answers for the rest are as follows:

2 They did not think the teacher was taking the class seriously and were annoyed that they were no longer receiving good marks.
3 The rest took things easy because they assumed it did not matter.
4 Perhaps they thought he would suddenly change, or the procedure was a trap.
5 E.g. 'Haven't you forgotten to mark the papers?'
7 They suspected a trap, with everything depending on a sudden examination, for example.
8 Because the students were in a competitive situation, and were rivals.

Activity 2, p. 85

1 54% were against, 37% in favour, and 9% neutral.
2 A students were 2 to 1 in favour, Bs and Cs were evenly divided, Ds–Fs were unanimously opposed.

(These answers are given at the back of the students' book.)

Page 86 Discipline

As previously stated, the main object of this unit is to aid students in writing compositions where they put forward a balanced argument. Part of the preparation for this is to compare two systems of education, totally opposed to each other, but both apparently successful. Before looking at the passages students should get into the habit of seeing the other side of the question by deliberately looking for arguments that probably differ from their own (Activity 3).

Activity 3

Ask students to work together to find arguments to oppose the 'progressive' point of view, and then consult pairs to see how many sensible ones they have come up with. Find out how many of these views are genuine and take this into account in organising the subsequent discussion.

The best way to handle the two texts that follow is to insist that they should be read before students come to class so that you can deal with problems of comprehension from the start and pairs can begin working on Activities 4 and 5.

Activities 4 and 5

Essentially, these questions are open-ended, and aimed as a stimulus to prepare students for the general discussion on education that follows. In effect, the discussion topics listed should develop out of the discussion of the points in the two activities, begun in pairs but to be opened out once students have had time to consider the questions.

Page 88 State and private education

For the benefit of students and non-native-speaking teachers we have preceded the text on page 89 with some information on the background to the article. Ideally, students should read this before coming to class so that they can then spend most of their time in class on the article itself.

Activity 6, p. 89

The article is intended as a model for a balanced composition. Students should work in groups of three, analysing the techniques employed.
Suggested answers:

1   Arguments for: 1) they provide better education, proved by statistics; 2) grammar schools, separating children by intelligence, are socially and morally wrong; 3) they break down class barriers.
     Arguments against: 1) they provide worse education, proved by statistics; 2) children within comprehensive schools are also separated according to ability so this is presumably admitted to be educationally preferable; 3) children from comprehensive schools do not do so well in examinations and entrance tests to universities. The writer devotes the second paragraph to the views of those who support comprehensive schools, the third to their opponents, but in the second paragraph includes the other point of view and in the third implies it.
2   The topic sentence refers to the continuing debate; the conclusion indicates why it is likely to continue further. 'The argument about comprehensive schools is basically political'. The paragraph is developed by constant comparison and contrast. The effect is to make the reader aware at all times that there are two sides to the question.
3   In paragraph 2 by saying that the local authorites 'were determined that their experiment should be seen to succeed' and by suggesting they were prejudiced against grammar schools. In paragraph 3 by saying 'It is difficult

to believe . . . that this defence is inspired purely by a desire for academic exellence' and so questioning the motives of those opposed to comprehensive schools. By using the connecting phrases 'on the one hand' and 'on the other hand'.

4   The topic paragraph referred to the debate continuing. The concluding paragraph explains why the two sides are unlikely to agree, and why the debate will not be settled by compromise. The important question is whether comprehensive schools are preferable to grammar schools and whether grammar schools should be retained or revived. One is that 'the different circumstances in which' the schools 'operate make accurate comparison difficult'. The other is that the two opposing groups' criteria 'have little to do with education', and are fundamentally political.
5   1) The choice between comprehensive and grammar schools; 2) The attitude of those who support comprehensive schools; 3) The view of those who defend grammar schools; 4) The effects of the meritocracy; 5) The unresolved debate.

Page 90 Arguing for *and* against

Activity 7

Pairs must now attempt to put into practice the techniques indicated for paragraph organisation and development in this kind of composition. The topic is one on which students should in general not have very strong views, effectively comparing the system of global evaluation used in some countries with the greater specialisation normally required in Great Britain.

As this is an exercise in technique, students should be advised to follow the instructions and not allow their own views to intrude on the composition. It does not matter much which of the arguments students choose to balance against each other. All that matters is that they should present them in a balanced manner, providing a coherent transition from one paragraph to another in line with the plan given and ensuring that each paragraph performs the function laid down for it.

Composition

The topics listed relate to the four main areas of discussion presented in the unit and follow the sequence of presentation.

Rewriting: Advertisements

Components	Aims	Grammatical revision
91 Choosing a flat	Information retrieval	
	Introduction	
92 Properties	Rewriting	
94 Jobs	Analysis – style and content	
	Rewriting	
95 Classified ads	Analysis – style and content	
	Rewriting	

Related texts: Unit 13 in *Book 2*, planned to appear in parallel with the next unit of this book, is also devoted to the topic of advertising, but in its social and linguistic aspects. In this unit, we are concerned with different ways of rewriting or responding to classified advertisements.

Presentation

No specific grammatical revision is required for this unit. What is important in the presentation is that students should observe the style in which the different kinds of advertisement appear.

Page 91 Choosing a flat

Before working in small groups to find an appropriate flat for the different people listed, students should check the abbreviations against the full forms and match them. The flat-choosing is partly open-ended; its value lies in the students being able to justify their choice of a particular flat for a particular person.

Activity 1, p. 92

This is a light-hearted excursion into the personal columns. The task for groups is to show you that they understand what is being advertised.
Suggested answers:

1   The Countess of Beckenham is looking for a servant. Anyone interested should consult the 'Domestic Situations' section of the classified advertisements in the paper. Draw students' attention to the difference between 'see' and 'look at'.
2   An enormous bath is being advertised at a reduced price. If you needed one, and considered the price fair,

you would telephone the number. Of course it is an anomaly that emperors should be thought of as needing larger baths than other people.
3   A Jack Russell is a breed of terrier, not a child, and this one would be happier in the country. If you lived in the country and wanted it, you would telephone the number.
4   Someone claims to have discovered an exciting cure for those who stutter. Such people might ring the number.
5   A professional writer would like to contact someone who wrote a diary or has a collection of letters from the Second World War. He hopes to edit them and publish them. If you had what he is looking for, you would write to the paper, using the box number. The author would tell you who he was if he felt that what you had to offer would be of interest to him.
6   'Beaver' (probably a young man) is trying to contact his girl-friend, 'Squirrel', who had a row with him last night. If you were Squirrel, had forgiven him, and believed his professions of adoration, you would meet him next Friday as suggested.

Page 92 Properties

Students should first of all study the letter on page 93, comparing it with the advertisement for Burleigh House to see how the information given there is used. They should use this as a model for Activity 2.

Activity 2, p. 93

Groups of three or four should work on this, with one student acting as 'secretary'. It is important that they should not only consider what might be wrong with the houses, but also that they should compose the letter in a convincing way, with an introductory and concluding paragraph, using the information given as the basis for the middle two paragraphs. In order to speed up the task, groups of three can be used, in which one student undertakes to begin and end the letter, while the others work out the defects and the form of criticising them.

Page 94 Jobs

The two advertisements are deliberately contrasted in style, and students should take these into account in Activity 4.

Activity 3

First of all, however, they should work in pairs to make sure they understand what is involved in each case.
Suggested answers:

1. The job for a salesman/woman places restrictions on all five categories, which is forbidden by law, although by 'qualifications' it means suitable previous experience, rather than anything on paper. The educational advertisement insists only on academic qualifications.
2. In the first case, you would write to the Sales Manager. In the second, you would write to the Registrar for an application form and further information, and if you were still interested, consult three people to see if they were willing to support your application.
3. Five. Previous experience, with a good selling record, preferably selling the same sort of thing, and an extrovert personality. All those listed, together with others not specified.
4. In the second case the amount of money the applicant is likely to receive has already been determined ten years in advance, whereas the first group of applicants have the opportunity to increase what they earn through commission, according to their sales. The word

'currently' indicates that the scale will not necessarily remain the same for ten years.

Activity 4

This is a test of students' awareness of style. Obviously, an advertiser who asks questions in capital letters, reaching a crescendo of enthusiasm, would only be impressed by someone who used a similarly aggressive approach to selling himself as to selling a product. The same kind of approach, used in the second advertisement, would be hilariously funny, but disastrous.

Monitor groups while they are working on this task, and draw their attention to such points and also to the importance of a convincing and logical beginning to the letter, following normal commercial or academic practice.

Page 95 Classified ads

Activity 5

Students are again asked to compare style here, though their answers would not need to imitate the style used. Their task is to make notes in preparation for composition topic 3, where they are asked to answer both advertisements or letters appropriately. This activity is a useful 'filler' to end a class, and you should use it to draw students' attention to the formality of the first advertisement and letter: e.g. the use of the conditional – 'We should be most grateful if you could . . . that would . . .' – which they should follow themselves in letters requesting a favour.

In the second case, there is little difference in style between the advertisement and the brochure, but it is worth asking students what techniques the advertiser is using in order to interest readers. Point out, if students do not see this for themselves, the insistence on 'royal or noble blood', and also the emphasis on economy ('as little as £150'), as well as the more straightforward claims made.

Composition

The topics are based on the different activities in the unit.

Description: Customs

Components	Aims	Grammatical revision
96 Superstitions	Introduction	
97 Marriage customs	Analysis – style and content	
	Grammatical revision	
99 Origins of soccer	Paragraph analysis	
	Linking paragraphs	

Presentation and grammatical revision

Reference is made in the activities on the last two pages of the unit to the change of tenses from Present to Past forms and *vice versa* in this kind of composition, where customs that are still valid are referred to in the course of the writer's description of his experience of these customs, or where general statements in anthropological terms are contrasted with their origins. No additional exercise is needed for this, which is a matter of logic as well as observation. The unit as a whole is aimed at the description of events which take place within a context of tradition, but the fluent change from one tense to another referred to above is also required for discussion topics where general statements are supported by examples from personal experience.

Page 96 Superstitions

This is an introductory exercise aimed at producing an interesting discussion, comparing superstitions and folklore traditions in Britain with those of the students' own country. Students must look for equivalents, and can then raise others of their own, which may also have equivalents in Britain not listed here.

Page 97 Marriage customs

Activities I and 2

The two texts on pages 97 and 98 should be read in conjunction, preferably before the class begins. Pairs should work individually and then compare impressions before supplying the answers in the form of general discussion. In all cases, while the questions demand an understanding of the texts, and you should ask general comprehension questions to make sure these have been understood, they are really intended to stimulate students into a consideration of the parallel customs and attitudes of their own culture. The answers, particularly to Activity 2, are in this sense almost always open-ended. The discussion that evolves is directed at composition topics 2 and 3.

Page 99 Origins of soccer

Activity 3

This is an exercise in paragraph organisation and linking, similar to those in Units 7 and 10. Students should decide on the basis of the linking words and phrases how the sentences should be re-ordered, and on the basis of the topic sentences what the correct order of the paragraphs is. The grammatical point emphasised in this unit, the relationship between Present and Past forms in this kind of account, is of importance in deciding on the ordering of paragraphs and sentences.
Solution:

4 d), b), a), c). 'that hunting period' in d) refers to the topic sentence, and is also 'It' at the beginning of b); a) must follow b), and c) provides the transition to the next paragraph.

2 c), a), b). The sentences develop the topic sentence from the beginning to the end of the hunt.

1 b), d), c), a). b) is an example of the topic sentence, and 'It' in d) refers to 'The switch' in b); a) is further exposition of the ideas in c).

3 c), b), a). The change of tense, reverting from the hunters to a modern soccer team, occurs in b) and for

this reason alone 'this is no accident' in a) must refer to b).

The tense changes from present to past and past to present occur in paragraph 1 (here, 4) in the second sentence, (d). Here the writer shifts our attention from modern soccer to 'that hunting period', in order to explain its origins, and the shift naturally takes us into the Past tense; in the final paragraph (here, 3), having completed his description of the hunting pack in sentence c), the writer reminds the reader of the parallels between this description and a soccer team and prepares for the next sentence in the Present tense.

Suggested answers:

1 The origins of soccer; How men became hunters; Co-operation in hunting; Parallels between hunting as a team and soccer.

2 Both sentences are written in the Present tense. The last sentence of the final paragraph justifies the statement made in the topic sentence of the first. What has come in between is an evolutionary description to establish the parallel.

3 Soccer has its roots in the development of Man from a vegetarian into a hunting species. This development required physical changes for men to catch their prey, but it also demanded a change of attitude, emphasising team-work. The same aggressive ends and team-work are evident in a soccer team.

Composition

The techniques required for these compositions and the information necessary should have been obtained from the models and following discussion within the unit.

Narrative: Possibilities

Components		Aims	Grammatical revision
100	If I were . . .	Grammatical revision	*Book 3*, Ex. 25 (revision)
		Analysis – writing techniques	
		Discussion	
102	Critical situations	Grammatical revision	Ex. 14E (revision)
		Information retrieval	
104	Embarrassing situations	Grammatical revision	Ex. 20 (revision)

Further grammatical practice: *Book 3*, Exs. 92A–B (revision).

Presentation and grammatical revision

This unit concentrates on composition topics that depend on the use of conditional forms and of modals, particularly in past forms. While the first two pages require sure use of the second (Past-Conditional) form, the last three demand fluent use of the third (Past Perfect – Conditional Perfect), **might have . . .**, **could have . . .** and **should have . . .** It may well be advisable to revise the relevant exercises mentioned above before reaching each stage. While **I wish/If only . . .** (Exs. 92A–B) is not an essential structure for the compositions, it would be an appropriate place to revise it.

Page 100 If I were . . .

Activity 1

A role-playing exercise, practising the second conditional form in a wider context.

Activity 2, p. 101

Students should study the model not only to find out how their own interests differ from the writer's, but also for its organisation. They should use it as a basis for answering composition topic 1. The principal difficulty with this kind of composition is that it can easily become a wearying series of sentences beginning 'I would . . .' Students should note that the beginning, setting the scene, avoids this, and then should realise that it is important to group ideas together in paragraphs instead of putting one wish after another in a haphazard fashion.

These activities do not demand much supervision, other than the inevitable monitoring and preparation required for role-playing and the organisation of possible discussion arising out of the preferences expressed in Activity 2.

Page 102 Critical situations

Once again, the text is a model, this time of a composition where students are required to consider 'What would have happened if . . .?' or 'What might have happened?' Students should note that what is of most importance to them technically in preparing for composition topic 2 is contained in the last paragraph. The previous paragraphs merely set the scene, as students should do, though not necessarily at such length.

Remind students of the modals in Exercise 14E before they read the passage; you may also need to give metrical equivalents to the sizes mentioned, so that they will fully understand the problems discussed. The average soldier is about 1.7m tall, weighs about 70kg and takes continental size 41 or 42 boots. The narrator is 1.97m tall, weighs over 95kg and takes size 46 or 47 boots. The wires were about 8m off the ground.

Activity 3

Suggested answers:

1 He was of average height, weight, etc. It suited the army

because they could then manufacture uniforms, equipment, etc. to a standard size.

2 Because common sense must have told them that most soldiers were not average, but it was inconvenient to accept this.

3 Because he no longer wears boots.

4 Because it had to be specially made. It was an advantage because he did not have to take part in parades.

5 Soldiers were supposed to lift the rifle by the muzzle while standing to attention. Because his legs were so long, he could only balance it between his fingertips, so in order to lift it, he had to bend over to grip the muzzle firmly.

6 (If the text is not sufficiently clear for students to understand, you will have to draw it on the board. The point is that when half-way across, the tension forced the wire close to the writer's neck, and in avoiding this, he put his head under it and lost contact with the lower wire.)

7 Because the fear of losing his grip again was so strong that his memory has deliberately erased it from his mind. This is the true explanation, though others are possible.

Activity 4, p. 103

While the previous activity dealt with a close escape, this one deals with turning points, offering further practice of the third conditional and modals. Students should work on the situations in groups of three; each group need do only one of the situations. The answers are for the most part open-ended.

Activity 5

This is in fact an opportunity for students to relate the previous activities to themselves and their own lives. After having given everyone a few minutes to think about it and make notes, it is best to ask for volunteers in the first instance. Other students should be encouraged to ask questions when they have heard the story.

Page 104 Embarrassing situations

The same kind of practice is extended to the use of **should have . . .** You may need to prepare for it by referring once again to Ex. 20 in *Book 3*. Students should use it as practice in pairs, which you can monitor by inviting them to tell the rest of the class their conclusions. The answers are to some extent open-ended, but should be given in the form: 'He should have found out who the man was before calling him an old bore', etc.

Composition

The three topics are based on Activities 2 and 5, using the models associated with Activities 2, 3 and 4.

Discussion: Sociology

Components	**Aims**	**Grammatical revision**
105 Questionnaire	Introduction	*Book 3*, Ex. 40
	Clarifying ideas	
106 Surveys and opinion polls	Analysis – writing techniques	
108 Generalisations	Analysis, writing techniques	
110 Using the definite article	Grammatical revision	

Related texts: the three passages in the parallel unit, Unit 15, in *Book 2*, and in particular passages 1 and 3, are closely related to the aims of this unit, and could well be used as follow-up material before students attempt their compositions.

Presentation and grammatical revision

This unit deals with discussion topics presented in abstract terms and teaches techniques for dealing with them. In our experience, the most common error in compositions written by advanced students, found most often in compositions on abstract topics, is uncertainty over the use and omission of the definite article. While this is practised in the exercise on the last page of the unit, it would be advisable to go through the rules listed in *Book 3*, Exercise 40, as a preliminary to the unit as a whole, and also to attempt the accompanying exercise. Our view is that students cannot be reminded too often of the normal rules of English usage in this connection.

The main aim of the unit, however, is to approach the most difficult kind of composition for the majority of students by demonstrating how good writers deal with questions that are generally too vague in their expression to be handled either with a strong argument for or against (Unit 11) or by presenting a balanced argument (Unit 15). The difficulty that must first be overcome is the inability of most students in examination conditions to think clearly enough to realise that the proposition in such compositions is too vague to be answered satisfactorily except by the presentation of facts, rarely at the students' disposal, or by redefinition.

Page 105 Questionnaire

For this reason, the unit begins with eight quotations from former Cambridge examination papers, scarcely any of which can be answered convincingly in a straightforward manner. As in the previous use of a questionnaire (Unit 11) students should answer within a few seconds, and you should either ask for a show of hands on each question, or collect papers and assess the results. In our view, it is virtually impossible for anyone who has considered the issues involved to respond to any of the statements by taking an extreme stand. The notes for students that follow take into account the possibility of such views, but emphasise that the statements presented are either too vague or extreme to be accepted as they stand, or else cannot be accepted without further definition. Students should work together in pairs, having responded individually, to decide which of the three possible categories each statement belongs to, and if they have responded in an extreme way themselves, why they have done so.

Once separated into the three categories, the statements should be modified to such an extent that students could accept them. An example is given for q. 1, where most people would object to the use of the word 'never' and would want to qualify the circumstances in which they would prevent children from being aggressive. Pairs should then be asked to say how far they have redefined the original statement, and why. Obviously responses to this series of questions are a matter of opinion, but from a logical point of view, we would suggest the following guidelines, to be put to students to clarify their point of view:

1 'Never' is too extreme. In what circumstances should aggression be suppressed?

2 Which idea in which parts of the world are we talking about? Punishment for different crimes in different parts of the world varies, and some countries consider criminal acts that are accepted in others.

3 How often is 'often', and what are 'vice' and 'virtue'?

4 Are students always qualified to judge the most useful subjects for study and the effectiveness of different kinds of teaching methodology?

5 Is this statement limited to human beings, or do we include animals, and if so, in all circumstances or only in certain circumstances?

6 Is 'essential' justified here, or do we mean 'useful', assuming we agree in general terms?

7 'Always', for everyone, or only for the speaker?

8 What is meant by 'patriotism'?

The end-product of this, we hope, will be to make students think more carefully before expressing their views on topics of this kind.

Page 106 Surveys and opinion polls

These two texts should be read together, preferably before the class begins and again on arrival. They should be studied carefully for the effectiveness of the techniques used in argument.

Activity 1, p. 107

Suggested answers:

1 a) Surveys are aimed at interpreting human behaviour, and people frequently complain that they are unnecessary because they only tell us what we already know. If we consider a number of statements with a logical explanation we can see how this attitude arises. The fact that all the statements mentioned are false justifies the need for research. Since almost all general statements can be made to appear logical it is necessary to do research to prove whether or not they are really true.

b) The paragraphs are logically related. The first asks a question, suggesting that surveys are unnecessary. The second appears to give an example of why they are unnecessary. The third turns this argument upside down by proving the assumptions to be false. The fourth demonstrates why the suppositions of the first are false, based on this evidence. Their relationship is to lead the reader along one line of argument in the first two paragraphs in order to prove the opposite in the last two by showing that what he or she has accepted is in fact not true.

2 a) The first sentence indicates the complexity of social surveys; the last suggests that this complexity is unnecessary if social surveys only prove the obvious.

b) It is convincing because we are normally convinced by anything listed in this manner, which seems to have been thoroughly planned and well thought out.

c) The sentence in italic type. You ought to be surprised, if not shocked.

d) It resolves it by forcing us to accept that we would have believed whatever conclusions the survey quoted had reached and so it cannot be assumed that conclusions reached are a matter of common sense and there is no need to investigate them scientifically.

3 He uses an extended example to prove his point but differs in that he expresses his doubts from the beginning instead of leading us into a situation where we accept what is false as true.

4 The subsequent paragraphs are an illustration of the statement that concludes the topic paragraph.

5 In the first case, the examples are presented as genuine and then said to be false; in the second, they are presented in contrast to demonstrate the effect of a change in wording.

6 An open question, but it could be argued that the second writer would accept the first writer's case for surveys if they were scientifically conducted and people asked to respond had really been given time to consider the questions involved in depth.

Page 108 Generalisations

The first passage here is meant to illustrate the rare case where the student has sufficient knowledge at his or her disposal to dispute a general statement on the basis of fact. Students should concentrate their analysis on the way in which the account of Eysenck's method is presented as a series of logical steps.

Activity 2

Suggested answers:

1 The argument is (1) that identical twins are much closer in intelligence than fraternal twins, so heredity must be more important than environment; (2) that children brought up in the same conditions show as great a range of intelligence as those brought up in different houses, so the difference cannot be due to environment; (3) that intelligence tends to average out from generation to generation so that the provision of an ideal environment for intellectual development does not seem to change what must be due to hereditary factors. The implication is that education will not make much difference, so they are wasting their money.

2 a) very little; b) much more noticeably. Eysenck argues that environment only has a great effect on hereditary intelligence if people are starved and this affects the

development of the brain. Therefore greater equality in society, preventing this, will lead to environment having less effect on intelligence.

3   A matter of opinion, but Eysenck has taken into account the fact that children may be considerably better fed, according to their social status, in some societies than in others. What he has not mentioned is (a) that intelligence tests may not be perfect and may favour those brought up in a certain kind of environment; (b) that 'success' in a given society does not necessarily depend on intelligence. These factors do not necessarily affect the validity of his argument, but they certainly affect its practical applications.

Activity 3, p. 109

Given that students are not usually in the position to argue intelligently on the basis of information at their disposal, because they lack the statistics, etc. to make a satisfactory case, they are nevertheless able to deal with statements that are vague or extreme on the basis of requiring a more adequate definition. The model, taken from George Orwell, illustrates the way in which a master in this art goes about the task.

Suggested answers:

1   He is attacking the proposition that everyone should be scientifically educated. The concluding sentence indicates that he attacks it because the proposer does not define clearly what this means, and it is capable of more than one interpretation. 'As usual' indicates that other people before Mr Cook have made the same error in failing to define what they mean (which discredits their argument) and 'merely' suggests they have not thought deeply enough about the subject. He fixes readers' minds on the last sentence by saying: 'This is of great importance'.

2   The second paragraph explains the alternative definitions of science which affect our idea of a 'scientific education'. The title of the article relates to the problem of definition.

3   The third paragraph assumes that the second has established a 'confusion of meaning', and goes on to describe the reasons for it and possibly dangerous effects.
    He takes the confusion to its logical (and extreme) conclusion by suggesting that if scientific education means what it is popularly supposed to mean, scientists are necessarily wiser than other people.

The phrase 'even on the arts' emphasises the absurdity of this by implying that an expert in one field, science, necessarily knows more about another field than someone who is an expert in it.

4   He would accept the definition of 'implanting a rational, sceptical, experimental habit of mind'.
    He says it is due to 'professional jealousy' because scientists would in that case lose some of their prestige. The phrase is 'which is partly deliberate'.

5   The formula students should reach is 1) What does this phrase 'mean'? 2) It could be taken to mean (a) but it could also be taken to mean (b). 3) If it means (a) it is unacceptable because . . ., while if it means (b) it is unacceptable because . . . 4) In fact, it would be possible to accept the statement if it were modified as follows –

Page 110 Using the definite article

If students have fully understood the rules laid down in *Book 3*, Exercise 40, and completed the exercise satisfactorily, they should be able to complete this. It would be unwise to assume, however, that further revision of this kind is not necessary before they attempt compositions on abstract subjects.

Activity 4

Solution:

(1) —; (2) the; (3) —; (4) the; (5) —); (6) the; (7) —; (8) —; (9) —; (10) the; (11) —; (12) the; (13) the; (14) the; (15) the; (16) —; (17) the; (18) the; (19) the; (20) —; (21) —; (22) the; (23) —; (24) the; (25) the; (26) the; (27) —; (28) —; (29) the; (30) —; (31) —; (32) —; (33) —; (34) —; (35) —; (36) —; (37) —; (38) —; (39) —; (40) the; (41) the; (42) —.

It could be argued that the definite article could be omitted from 4 and 6 because these phrases are in apposition to that containing the definite article, 2, and this is a needless repetition. It is essential for 12 and 19, where the passage refers to species of human beings, for which the only alternative would be a plural form ('efficiency experts'). This also applies to 22, a species of technique.

Composition

Students can write on any of the subjects listed in the questionnaire, but should endeavour to imitate the techniques presented in connection with Activities 2 and 3.

20

Rewriting: Letters to the editor

Components	Aims	Grammatical revision
111 Protest	Introduction Rewriting	
112 Opinion and reply	Rewriting, Analysis – writing techniques	
114 Comments on the news	Information retrieval Discussion	

Presentation and grammatical revision

No specific grammatical revision is required for this unit, although as in all cases where students must rewrite in order to present an argument, they should look at the use of appropriate connectors and modifiers in the Appendix, page 164.

Page 111 Protest

The task here resembles one set in a past Cambridge Proficiency paper. Essentially, students should use it rather like the examples of headlines given in Unit 6. In class, the main thing is for them to reword the slogans in such a way that they can demonstrate their understanding of meaning and implications. Subsequently, the points that emerge should be noted down so that students can use them again in connection with composition topic 1.

Page 112 Opinion and reply

The two letters presented on pages 112 and 113 are models of the kind of letter that often appears in 'quality' newspapers. They are also intended as models for study of technique in argument and of style, though the second should be adopted by students as the one to imitate. First, ask pairs to read the first letter and answer the questions. Before students study the reply invite ideas on how a Welsh person might respond to this, and what form his or her argument might take. Allow time for the questions to be answered and points

of technique discussed before moving on to Activity 3, which is primarily intended as active follow-up both in the classroom and as the basis for subsequent composition.

Activity 1

Suggested answers:

1 Those in authority; the way things are normally done in society; there is an inversion of the natural order; I have no grudge or prejudice.
2 'While I am no racist . . . receive their due'; 'I hasten to add that I have no axe to grind as far as Welsh people are concerned'.
3 By picturing himself as a hard-working man, relaxing in his armchair after a long day and being disappointed by the TV programme; because they have experienced similar situations.
4 Why didn't you realise that the programme was likely to be changed?
5 He uses it by pointing out the unnecessary expense of making special Welsh sub-titles for a Hungarian film which would have been understood by the audience with the English sub-titles that were presumably already available.
6 Because the way the authorities have organised things in the past might not seem natural to them (it assumes that programmes in English are more natural than those in Welsh) and because they would not consider Welsh a foreign language in Wales.
7 'an audience who all understand English'.

Activity 2, p. 113

Suggested answers:

1   By referring to the date of publication of the previous letter and quoting from it.
2   1) on the ground that he ignores the fight that Welsh people have had to get their language recognised; 2) on the ground that he puts his own convenience before other people's rights.
3   'long, hard struggle', 'hard-won rights'; 'rigidly chauvinistic', 'little Englanders'.
4   Because Ms Hopkins is being ironic, and does not think him generous at all.
5   He should have written to the television service. No one would have seen the letter in print.
6   She uses the phrase 'foreign language' to apply to English, instead of Welsh, as well as referring to compulsion and understanding; the technique is effective because she can speak and write the 'foreign language' as well as her own, while her opponent can't.

Activity 3

The group work here should be organised so that students deal with one of the five topics in each group. This is often necessary to help those students who are short of ideas and imagination. Depending on the time available, and the numbers in the class, the group can write up their answers in letter form, and other groups, given the outline of their arguments, can write replies.

The main point is to ensure that students eventually write both sides of the same argument as convincingly as possible in the composition topic, since in an examination they might have either side's argument thrust upon them. It is for you to decide whether they follow the plan suggested in their book, writing up their notes on the topic they have done as group work, and then providing a convincing answer, or you ask them to do this for a topic handled by another group because both sides of the argument have been satisfactorily dealt with in class.

Page 114 Comments on the news

Activities 4 and 5

These are primarily aimed at information retrieval and the comprehension of ideas presented in the form of comparison, and as such are allied to work done on comprehension in *Book 2*, particularly in Unit 16, passage 3, which follows this unit if the books are used in conjunction. Both topics concerned here can be used as the basis for discussion in connection with comparable situations in the students' own country.

Suggested answers (Activity 4):

1   STOPP feels that the depiction of beatings in comics could affect children and 'encourage sado-masochism'. The readers think the comics are good fun and have no effect of this kind. They accuse STOPP of not having a sense of humour.
2   They say children enjoy the comics, and that although they have read them themselves and their parents did, too, they have neither been beaten nor become aggressive as a result.
3   Because they are both children of the age the comics are intended for — one is nine and the other eleven.

Suggested answers (Activity 5):

The Government is planning to replace £1 notes with coins (a) because the pound has declined in value; (b) because notes have a short life of only 10 months, while coins last longer; (c) (possibly) because notes are dirty and tattered after a short time.

Miss Baldwin is in favour because the coins are attractive and she thinks no one carries notes in wallets these day; Ms Raphael thinks notes easily become dirty and carry germs. Mr Fraser thinks carrying a lot of coins is inconvenient, and there are too many already. Mr Lancashire thinks coins are too big and heavy, and other countries continue to produce notes even though they have a short life.

Most men carry coins in their trousers pockets, which wears them out quickly, while they carry notes in wallets. Women, even if they wear trousers, usually carry all their money in purses.

Composition, p. 115

These are based on the introductory exercise and Activity 3.

21

Descriptive compositions

Components	Aims	Grammatical revision
116 Planning your composition	Planning Analysis – writing techniques	
117 Describing houses	Directed writing	
118 Describing holidays	Directed writing Analysis – writing techniques	

Further grammatical practice: *Book 3*, Exs. 1, 2, 10, 11, 25, 32.

Presentation and grammatical revision

This unit, together with the two that follow, revises the techniques students should have learnt in the course of the book for dealing with different kinds of composition. The revision exercises indicated above are those that would be of most importance in completing the composition tasks here, but it is to be hoped that at this stage students would not normally need to do them again. What they should do is glance at them before writing their final compositions at the end of the unit.

To a considerable extent, these final units expect students to analyse things for themselves, given the aid that appears in their book. From a teacher's point of view, it is therefore not so much a matter of formal presentation as of effective monitoring of the pair work and group work tasks provided. Give further advice where required, but above all make plain to students that in preparing for an examination, what is important is to ensure that one's technique is adequate for the task. As we customarily tell our own students: 'No examiner cares where you went on your last holiday, or what you think about any subject under the sun; all that matters to him or her is whether you can express your ideas or experiences clearly in English. If you also succeed in arousing the examiner's interest, that is a bonus, and even then good technique is more likely to do it than the ideas or experiences in themselves.'

These remarks are in our view even more appropriate when one considers the (understandably) boring topics given to students to write about in the examination. All the models we have chosen closely resemble Cambridge Proficiency topics in past papers.

Page 116 Planning your composition

Descriptive compositions are primarily a problem of lexis (knowing the right words to make the description interesting and accurate) and in some cases of structure – e.g. word order of adjectives and adverbs, use of tenses in some cases. Go through the plan, drawing students' attention, in particular, to the following:

1. The three topics lend themselves to different main tenses; the third in particular can easily become a whole series of sentences in the conditional tense (Cf. Unit 18, Activity 2, Notes).

2. Before they start, students should be able to answer all the questions listed on each paragraph. Truth is not necessary – i.e. if they think of a particular house, but cannot describe all its features in detail for lack of vocabulary, they should adapt the features, not invent the vocabulary, as many of them do!

3. The third paragraph is the one where life can be given to the description. It may require changes of tense, which is all to the good.

Activity 1

This should be done individually, for obvious reasons. Students should speak from notes, and not attempt a full written version. Ask questions in an attempt to provide ways of expanding the information given in the third paragraph.

Page 117 Describing houses

Activity 2

The group task is intended to provide further practice of the same kind; this time, however, each group must provide a description fitting the three categories indicated on the previous page. Groups of three should be asked to discuss all the houses, decide on one appropriate for a description in each category, and then split the work between them, each person writing the notes for one house.

Your task here is mainly to monitor with helpful vocabulary, and at the end, in the course of comparing different choices for and different versions of each category, teach any additional words that could be used, as well as checking on the grammatical points mentioned above in each case. The notes students make can form the basis of final compositions.

Page 118 Describing holidays

Here students are asked to work in pairs, primarily on the organisation of a descriptive composition into paragraphs. The three topics chosen are the seaside parallels to those on houses in terms of the use of tenses, etc., and all that varies from the original plan is the lexis required.

Activity 3

Given the first paragraph, which is all-purpose for a large number of seaside resorts on different coasts, students split up the work on subsequent paragraphs between them, as instructed. Essentially, they must respond to the prompts of the questions given in order to fit the place they are thinking of into the model provided. It is of course true that students may protest that they would rather write about somewhere that does not fit the description, but they will have the opportunity to do that later; for the moment, technique is all-important.

Activity 4, p. 119

This is the same kind of thing, applied to the past. Depending on the time available, and the number of students, the same pairs may attempt this, or you may prefer to offer pairs from the outset the choice of Activities 3, 4 or 5 or assign them to different pairs yourself.

Activity 5

The notes here are intended to show the students the way round the traps that many fall into. They emphasise the importance of technique for success, rather than strict adherence to the truth. There are various suggestions for avoiding the monotony (and for most students, the strain) of writing in the conditional tense throughout.

Composition

Students are free to develop any or all of the composition topics they have previously made notes for or to attempt one that they have not themselves done in pair work or group work.

22

Narrative compositions

Components	Aims	Grammatical revision
120 A party	Paragraphing	
	Analysis – writing techniques	
	Directed writing	
122 First meeting	Directed writing	
123 A quarrel	Directed writing	

Further grammatical practice: *Book 3*, Exs. 6, 7, 14E, 17, 20, 21, 26.

Presentation and grammatical revision

As in the previous unit, the main aim is the revision of writing techniques for a specific purpose. The exercises listed are those that will be useful in completing the composition tasks. It is to be hoped that a reminder to look at them once again will be sufficient at this stage.

The advice given in general terms in the previous unit on the handling of this sort of technical revision also applies here.

Page 120 A party

Students first read the narrative in order to decide on the order of paragraphs. Unlike other exercises of this kind, this one does not also require the reordering of sentences, since what we are concerned with here is simply the sense of narrative flow as a model for students to follow.

Activity 1, p. 121

1 Solution: 2, 5, 3, 1, 4.
2 and 3 This analysis is satisfactory if it reminds the students of the use of the Past Continuous for actions taking place simultaneously; the use of the Past Perfect for actions preceding the moment in the narrative – e.g. 'who invited us along to the party, which had been organised. . .'; the use of modals, 'must have been', 'might have been'.
4 Because it is the crucial point in the narrative (see earlier examples in the book from *Unit 2* onwards).

5 Suggested: 1 Establishment of time and place; 2 description of atmosphere; 3 background to the main incident at the party; 4 the main incident; 5 conclusion, relating the main incident to time, place and atmosphere.
A Bastille Day party in North Africa; the scene on the beach; a journey at midnight; an unexpected meeting; how it happened.

Activity 2

Here students must use their imagination to complete a narrative in two paragraphs, given the situation. Pairs should discuss the probable developments together before attempting one paragraph each.

As in the previous unit, you should aid them by monitoring, supplying ideas as well as lexis where required, and take advantage of the comparison of different versions to check the grammatical points already mentioned and the effectiveness of the narrative techniques employed.

Page 122 First meeting

Activity 3

This is a similar task with a different topic to be handled in the same way. Draw students' attention to the necessary changes of tense – i.e. the use of the Present Perfect – that will be required in the last paragraph. Students are given questions to answer with relation to these last two paragraphs which, if answered correctly, effectively guide them to the conclusion.

Page 123 A quarrel

Activity 4

Here, a different topic is dealt with the other way round, in that students have to provide the first two paragraphs to a story which is ended for them. The story may be considered a little old-fashioned in its social background in some cultures, but by no means in all. Students need more imagination here and greater powers of logic to deal with the first two paragraphs than in the previous activity, but once again the correct answers to the questions provide guidance. What needs emphasis here, perhaps, is the need to fit the beginning to the narrator and his attitudes later on.

Composition

Here students should write about the same topics, but their narratives should only resemble what they have done before in terms of organisation and the use of techniques, the correct tenses, etc.

23

Discussion essays

Components		Aims	Grammatical revision
124	Approaches	Analysis – writing techniques	
125	For *or* against	Analysis – writing techniques	
		Directed writing	
127	The balanced approach	Comparison – writing techniques	
128	The analytical approach	Comparison – writing techniques	

Further grammatical practice: *Book 3*, Exs. 3D, 4, 8, 13, 16, 31, 40.

Presentation and grammatical revision

As in the previous units, the main aim is the revision of writing techniques for a specific purpose. The exercises listed are those that will be useful in completing the composition tasks. It is to be hoped that a reminder to look at them once again will be sufficient at this stage.

The advice given in general terms in Unit 21 on the handling of this sort of technical revision also applies here.

Page 124 Approaches

This page, together with the notes preceding the texts on pages 127 and 128, is intended for study at home. Students should relate what they have already learnt about the use of connectors and modifiers to plans suited to different approaches, and these approaches are once more outlined. Essentially, there are four: 1, arguing for the proposition (see Unit 11); 2, arguing against the proposition (see Unit 11); 3, the balanced approach, page 127 (see Unit 15); 4, the analytical approach, page 128, working on the basis of redefinition of the statement, normally because it is too general or misses the real point at issue (see Unit 19).

Page 125 For *or* against

The text here and accompanying activities relate to the Approaches 1 and 2.

Activity I

While this could be dealt with as a pair work task or in groups of three, it is essentially an individual test because of the opinions involved.

Suggested answers:

1 By suggesting that he is not prejudiced, and therefore that his opinions are valid; on this basis, he is free to launch an attack on rock music. His argument is based on his son's apparent deafness, and his own experience of a rock concert. The experiences are connected because he went with his son to the concert and discovered the reason for the 'deafness'. 'with enough common sense to see its potential dangers', 'an unnaturally loud voice', 'something wrong with his hearing', 'these affairs'.

2 1) the noise produces mass hysteria; 2) it also eliminates people's individuality through this effect; 3) it reduces human beings to the level of animals: 'collective madness', 'mass hysteria', 'faceless crowd', 'demented monkeys', 'degrading human spectacle'. Which of these phrases is an exaggeration is a matter of opinion. The writer adds to his argument the effect produced by noise, and what he considers to be the animal behaviour that results.

3 He mentions that some people argue that the music has quality, that the young have a right to enjoy themselves in their own way, and that the rock world provides them with freedom. In all cases, whether or not we consider he is unfair or exaggerating is a matter of

opinion, but in fact the technique is to contradict or undercut the points made (a) by questioning the validity of the witnesses – 'so-called serious music critics', 'glibly and hypocritically', 'know full well that. . .'; (b) by suggesting that such people pretend ignorance about the damage rock music does to hearing; (c) by suggesting that they are biassed in their definition of freedom. He is never 'fair' because he is arguing a case to win. The adjectives and adverbs mentioned above are all intended for emotional effect.

4 Basically, the argument that the music destroys individuality (paragraph 2) and the opposing argument with regard to freedom (paragraph 3): 'sheep-like', 'striking absurd provocative poses', 'stupid, unintelligible words', 'jerking marionettes', 'mindless zombies'.

5 Paragraph 1: the first, effectively the main clause.
Paragraph 2: the second.
Paragraph 3: the first.
Paragraph 4: the first.

Activity 2, p. 126

This is a self-explanatory task preceding Activity 3.

Activity 3

This could again be done individually, though in some cases, where pairs had similar views, they would be able to work together. The paragraph given suggests one approach, though not necessarily the only one. Students using it should be aware that it conditions the line of argument in the following paragraphs to a considerable extent. If possible

they should follow it, but could consult you on alternative lines of their own.

Page 127 The balanced approach

Page 128 The analytical approach

These passages are intended as models of Approaches 3 and 4. Students should trace the way in which the argument follows the plan laid down for the approach given above it, and consider the part played by connectors and modifiers.

The passages can be used in one of two ways. Either students can work in groups to deal with one of the topics listed below, making notes as the basis for an essay employing one or other of the approaches, or you can move straight into a discussion of the topic itself, and the passages, once understood in technical terms, will serve as models when students attempt compositions of their own. This question depends largely on the intellectual sophistication of the class, and the extent to which they could be reasonably asked in groups to attempt one or other approach without choosing for themselves.

Composition

Students should make a plan and indicate which approach they propose to adopt before writing their compositions, and in part these should be judged on the student's ability to put the plan into practice.

24

Rewriting: Official language

Components	Aims	Grammatical revision
129 Formal/informal letters	Comparison – style and content	
	Directed writing	
132 Formal protest	Rewriting	

Related texts: *Book 2*, Unit 15, introduction and Passage 1. Further grammatical practice: *Book 3*, Exs. 3, 4, 18, 33, 36.

Presentation and grammatical revision

The constructions listed relate to composition tasks but it is to be hoped that by this time students would normally need only to glance at the exercises to remind themselves of the problems involved. What is almost certainly necessary here is for you to aid students in their appreciation of what constitutes official English.

If they have read the examples given in the Orwell passage in Unit 15 of *Book 2*, they may be surprised that Cambridge have at times in the past expected candidates to reproduce the formal style affected by Government departments. We have chosen the course of representing it, but do not expect students to imitate it, only to recognise that it should not be answered in the same way as an informal letter to a friend.

Page 129 Formal/informal letters

Activity 1 (Part 1)

The activity has three parts, which must be dealt with in sequence. Students first read an informal letter which explains the problem in question in straightforward language.

Students should note in this letter (1) the use of short forms, not to be imitated in formal compositions; (2) the friendly introductory paragraph; (3) the way in which it is written as if the mother were talking, not writing; (4) the informal modes of address.

Activity 1 (Part 2), p. 130

Students must now compare this with a formal letter, which is really their model for style. It is written as an effective

argument, but does not make use of jargon. Students should note (1) the statement of the reason for the letter; (2) the organisation of the points in the argument; (3) the polite use of the double conditional in the last paragraph ('I should be most grateful if the committee could. . .').

Activity 1 (Part 3), p. 131

Before reading the Council's reply, students should note any reasonable objections they can think of to Mr Sutcliffe's application. The official reply is by no means as full of clichés as it might be, and of course is grammatically free from error.

Suggested answers:

2   Examples of bureaucratic language: 'has been given due attention' = has been read; 'after consultation with' = and by; 'it is with much regret that I have to' = I regret; 'which was originally constructed. . .one building' = built as one house, but later split into two, counts as one for planning purposes; 'with the consequent implication that' = which means that; 'albeit for the sole benefit of your neighbour' = although only your neighbour has the right to use it; 'was not of sufficient gravity to merit. . .Sub-Section 2A' = was not serious enough for the Committee to change its interpretation; 'May I express my regret' = I am sorry.

As far as possible, students should attempt to rephrase the examples quoted above, the rephrasing counting as a reason for the avoidance of bureaucratic language.

3   a) Leading out of the above, students should be able to deal with this.

b) Suggested answers:

1. I am sorry that the Committee cannot grant your application; 2. Your kind of house, although it has been split into two, is only entitled to one garage under the law; 3. The Committee did not think the case of hardship you mentioned was serious enough to change their interpretation of the law; 4. I am sorry that the Committee cannot grant your application.

4   The final question should be attempted either by individuals or in pairs. The model here is the first informal letter, and the exercise therefore demands a written version of what has been done as q. 3 a).

Page 132 Formal protest

Activity 2

Students should listen to the dialogue, with books closed, before reading it as the basis for their final composition question. The exercise requires a combination of the skills in summarising dialogue already learnt in Unit 12 with the ability to imitate a letter like the second model here, Mr Sutcliffe's letter to the Council. Students should first list the points to be made, and then consider the organisation of paragraphs, ensuring that the first introduces the subject and circumstances of the complaint clearly, the second lists the complaints, the third justifies the letter and requests action on behalf of the company.

Prescribed books

In all cases the aims of the following units are as indicated in the General Introduction to this book:

1 to introduce students to the necessary lexis for writing critical essays on prescribed books;
2 to provide examples of model compositions of different types which at the same time help to define the problems involved and the best ways of dealing with them;
3 to ask a series of key questions, enabling students to transfer what they have learnt about technique in connection with the books used as examples to the book they are reading.

   Assuming that teachers will normally be concerned with teaching only one book, either a novel or a play, the majority of pages and key questions are specifically devoted to one form or the other, so that almost half of them would normally be omitted.

Presentation and grammatical revision

The only grammatical revision necessary is outlined on the first page of Unit 25. Subsequently, the techniques to be applied will in different cases resemble those of description (e.g. essays on characters), narrative (e.g. those on plot) or argument (e.g. those on dramatic or narrative technique).

   The teacher glancing at the units in the student's book must inevitably see his role as largely passive, but they have not been written entirely for home study, even though most of the reading involved is designed to be done at home. In effect, they will only be of use to students if you are able (a) to relate the key questions asked to the book students are studying, which involves considering it in the light of the comments made on *Emma* and *Othello*; (b) to help students to analyse the way in which the model essays, as distinct from paragraphs explaining literary techniques, have been organised, so that they will be able to organise their own essays in a similar way.

   What we are really asking you to do, therefore, having provided the basic concepts and models, is to adapt them imaginatively to the book you are teaching. Short of providing new material for every change the examiners make in the list of prescribed books at annual intervals, we felt this was the most satisfactory way of proceeding. The notes that follow are simply aimed at clarifying a few points in the units that may not be immediately clear.

Page 133 Unit 25 Plot and theme

Talk the students through the grammatical point noted and the terms and definitions to be employed, and then deal either with the treatment of plot and theme in drama or in the novel. In both cases the student's need to make a synopsis is emphasised and ways of doing this are suggested. Lead all study towards the key questions on the relevant pages, and relate them to the book students are studying.

Activities

1 The answers are a) *Macbeth*; b) *Othello*; c) *Hamlet*; d) *King Lear*.
2 Depends on an understanding of the text. The main point is for students to separate plot from theme.
3 The authoress's comments are 1, 2 and 9. In 3, 4 and 5, Mr Woodhouse and Mr Knightley illustrate their own personalities. In 6, 7 and 8 the relationships between characters are illustrated. We learn that Mr Woodhouse is timid, a hypochondriac and thinks Emma can do wrong; Mr Knightley is sensible and knows Emma is spoilt, but tells her about her faults in a kindly spirit because he is fond of her; Emma is young, playful and lively, as well as spoilt, but fond of her father, and respects Mr Knightley.
4 A matter of information retrieval. Everything, or almost everything, that is said, is based on the notes opposite. Students should at the same time be aware of what would be drawn from a synopsis, and which comments are a matter of interpretation, and see how the interpretation depends on the constant use of examples.

Page 140 Unit 26 Character

The only activity here concerns a similar analysis of the final model essay on *Othello*. Character is looked at from a variety of angles in this unit, and it may sometimes be necessary to overlap a little from the basic categories of play and novel, illustrated by the same two books as in the previous unit.

In one sense, this kind of essay is a parallel to the description of people in Unit 1, with similar problems concerning the choice of appropriate adjectives and the need to place them in the right order. In another, however, it is important for students to realise that characters are not real and that they fulfil the role the writer has designed for them. Students unused to literary criticism sometimes adopt the naive approach that characters are to be approved of or not because they behave as the reader would behave in a hypothetical situation, rather than in line with the background, personality and experience given to them. The examples given here are very relevant, though even some well-known critics have blamed Othello for being deceived by Iago, and don't like *Emma*, the novel, because they disapprove of Emma, the girl. The first key question should therefore be dealt with in depth for as many characters as are relevant. Where identification with characters is considered (Key Question to p. 142) it is in a different context. NOTE: in connection with the final essay here on *Othello*, it is relevant to note that in Shakespeare's time, 'jealous' could mean 'suspicious', and Othello's self-justification depends to some extent on this double meaning. Emilia, quoted above, uses the word with both meanings, too.

Page 147 Unit 27 Narrative technique

This unit is aimed primarily at students reading a novel or continuous prose narrative for the examination.

Questions on technique are by far the most difficult to answer unless students have had previous training in literary criticism. However, in some ways the study of technique is the most helpful among the three possibilities presented in these units in so far as a real understanding of the book is concerned. We would consider that the unit is well worth doing even though only the more sophisticated students could be expected to deal satisfactorily with a question of this kind. As always, the key questions are the focus of the content, but there are also a few activities that can be done in class.

The first section, on the structure of the novel, may appear unusual in its attempt to present novels in terms of diagrams, but this is a method that works very well in our experience with students unfamiliar with literary criticism, and it will considerably enhance students'

understanding of the book they are reading if they can produce similar diagrams for it, though this task cannot be attempted, obviously, until they have read through it once.

Activity 1, p. 148

The answer to the equation is that Catherine Earnshaw was the daughter of Mr and Mrs Earnshaw, was in love with Heathcliff but married Edgar and became Mrs Linton. Her daughter, born Catherine Linton, was forced to marry her cousin, Linton Heathcliff, becoming Catherine Heathcliff, but after his death married Hareton Earnshaw, and so became Catherine Earnshaw.

Activity 2, p. 150

To some extent a matter of opinion, but suggested answers are as follows:
Dickens addresses us like an audience at a public meeting. Note the rhetoric of the repetition, and the direct appeal to us as 'men and women, born with heavenly compassion in (our) hearts'. Thackeray is coy. He imagines the reader as a beautiful young lady and takes advantage of the situation to give her some advice, like an old uncle. Trollope regards us as people reading for entertainment, at all times conscious that this is 'only a novel', and stops to explain his problems as a writer. Jane Austen makes ironic comments on the world which take for granted that we are as intelligent as she is, so they will not need further explanation.

Most modern readers do not like to be addressed by the author in this way, especially if the novelist gives them a character and personality which is not theirs (Thackeray) or breaks up the story and spoils the illusion (Trollope).

Activity 3, p. 151

The answers here are given in the students' book, but are repeated here.
1 *Felix Holt*   The theme is political in the context of the General Election of 1832, but the novel is also a study of families in society. The heir to the estate returns home in the first chapter and decides to stand as a candidate for Parliament. Clearly, we read on to find out who was expected, and we are also made aware of the 'memorable year', the first in which relatively democratic elections were held in Britain.
2 *Daisy Miller*   The story is about a young American girl in Europe in the 1870s, and compares European and American society and values. We realise from the beginning that we are likely to read about travellers in Europe.
3 *Northanger Abbey*   The novel is a parody of all the romantic novels current at the time (about 1800). The ironic opening sentence tells us Catherine is the heroine, but also says she is not typical (of novels). We read to find out what was different about her.

4   *Bleak House*   A sombre portrait of different levels of Victorian society, set mainly in London, which also involves satire of the law and its obscurities. The powerful opening gives us an impression of the atmosphere, moral as well as physical, in which the novel takes place, and we read on to discover what sort of people will be introduced, and what will happen.

5   *The Day of the Triffids*   A science-fiction novel about most of humanity being blinded and at the mercy of killer-plants. The splendid opening arouses our curiosity. What was wrong?

Activity 4, p. 152

Suggested answer:

The first quotation shows that Emma was not seriously upset by what she had done, and woke up the next morning feeling much happier, simply because it was the morning (previous sentence). On the second occasion she is fully aware of what she has done, and 'Time did not compose her'. The more she thought about it, the worse she felt. Her greater maturity is shown by the fact that she judges herself

now by the action and its consequences, and is not influenced by such things as daylight.

Answering a question on narrative technique

As in previous units, the most important work students have to do, having considered different key questions, is to study the technique employed in writing the model essay, so that they can plan and write similar essays themselves.

Page 156 Dramatic technique

This unit is aimed primarily at students reading a play for the examination.

As before, the texts are used as a means of explaining dramatic technique by means of examples so that students can refer the key questions that result to the play they are reading. The activities, for the most part, consist in this case of comparing the play they are reading to the examples given. As in previous units, the final model essay should be used for study of the techniques of planning and the use of notes made beforehand and quotations.

NEW PROFICIENCY ENGLISH
Book 2
Reading Comprehension

Introduction

Relationship with the course as a whole

The chart at the back of this *Teacher's Guide* indicates the way in which the 18 units of *New Proficiency English Book 2* are interrelated with the 24 language units of *Book 1*. The three units in each of the six sections of the book have been written in parallel to the first three of every four units in the corresponding sections of *Book 1*; in most cases, but not all, there is an overlap in thematic terms, developing further the range of lexical items associated with a context. Teachers using the books in conjunction would normally deal with the material in *Book 2* once a unit in *Book 1* had been completed, though there is no reason why passages in *Book 2* should not be interpolated in the teaching of *Book 1* for the sake of variation.

Lexis and comprehension

The Cambridge examination in Reading Comprehension consists of two sections which require related, but to some extent, different areas of knowledge and technical skills. I have discussed them separately below but it is not my intention to suggest that they should be divided off. In effect, the units of the book serve two purposes throughout; they exemplify lexis in context, the only way in which they can be satisfactorily learned and subsequently used, and they also serve as passages for comprehension. I have used a wide variety of exercises in this connection, explained below. These exercises, preceding and following the passages, are presented in the order in which I habitually use them in the classroom.

Lexical problems at advanced level

The meaning of words can only be learnt in context and students must overcome, if they have not done so already, the habit of asking what words mean and expecting an instant translation, which is likely to be imprecise, particularly at advanced level, where what governs the choice of a word is as often a matter of common usage as of definition in dictionary terms. It is essential that students should be trained, with the aid of techniques suggested in the course of this book, to work out meanings for themselves wherever possible.

At the same time, anyone with experience of teaching for the Proficiency examination will be aware that while it is of most value in the classroom for students to learn new items of vocabulary in a thematic way, associating them with a context, the items that appear in lexical tests are only to a very limited extent dependent on the choice of the correct word for an object (e.g. fishing *rod*, as distinct from 'stick' or 'pole'); it is also far less often the case than in the First Certificate examination for them to be based on words that are commonly confused either because they are similar in form and meaning in English (e.g. *lie* and *lay*) or because they are deceptively close to words with a rather different range of usage in the students' own language (i.e. *advertise, advise, announce*, etc. for speakers of Latin languages). In the majority of cases, the student must recognise terms customarily used in articles appearing in 'quality' newspapers and be aware of the prepositions that follow them or other structural variations implied automatically by their use. Here is a typical example:

His irresponsible behaviour put the whole operation in

_____ .

A risk   B doubt   C jeopardy   D condemnation

It is virtually impossible for a teacher to prepare for such an item in advance, and virtually impossible to explain why 'jeopardy' is correct, and 'risk' and 'doubt' are not, except by saying that that is what people say, whereas they would say 'put the whole operation at risk', or 'put the success of the whole operation in doubt'. The approach I have adopted in this book has therefore been to take such eventual examination difficulties into account without departing from a thematic approach, which I consider to be indispensable for classroom work, and one that will eventually be of more benefit to students outside the classroom.

It must be added that the lexical range of the Proficiency examination is infinitely greater than that of First Certificate (limited to the classification of the *Cambridge English Lexicon*) and consequently that no selection of texts, however varied, could possibly deal with the potential coverage of the examination. To a considerable extent, the remedy is in the students' own hands; those who read a great deal in English will inevitably have a much wider vocabulary than those who do not, irrespective of their comparative linguistic abilities elsewhere. I am nevertheless convinced that the variety of approaches I have adopted and the care with which test items have been constructed and pretested, always based on vocabulary that has previously occurred in the book, will help all students towards the achievement of a pass level.

Types of lexical exercise

Introductory exercises

Each unit begins with an introductory exercise, introducing the theme; in many cases these are a means of checking the range of vocabulary students already possess, and expanding it. This kind of exercise is of particular importance for subjects like Finance (Unit 16) and Crime and the Law (Unit 18), where a large number of technical terms must be used with precision.

Unfamiliar words

Wherever words appear in the passages that are likely to be unfamiliar to students, I have either explained them in marginal notes (either because they are items of cultural knowledge, or because I do not think their meaning can be worked out from the context) or, in the majority of cases, drawn students' attention to them and asked them to explain their meaning. The first unit contains a long section showing students the techniques that they can apply in order to aid their guesses; subsequent exercises of this kind provide clues in cases where the context in itself would only supply the answer to students with a wide vocabulary range. In almost all cases, I have placed these exercises immediately after the passage and before the comprehension questions on it, since in my experience students' most urgent requirement after reading a passage is to clear up their difficulties with words that are new to them; the exceptions are some passages where students are asked about the gist of the passage, and the unfamiliar words do not affect their answers.

Synonyms

In some of the early units of the book, I have included exercises as a variation on those on 'Unfamiliar words' where students are asked to find the words in the passage similar in meaning to those given; the words given are usually more familiar than those in the passage, so that this is a means of confirming their understanding of any that may be new. True synonyms are, however, rare, so that in the more complex passages that begin to appear in the second half of the book, I have discontinued this approach as being likely to lead to an inadequate understanding of the items involved.

Words often confused

Every unit contains exercises comparing words used in the passages that are commonly confused by students with others that are a source of the confusion. Here, my object has been to provide contexts in which the differences in meaning can be clearly recognised. As already explained, this is increasingly a matter of usage, rather than definition. Such exercises must not only indicate, for example, that we talk of an *exhibition* of pictures but the *exposure* of a fraud; students must also grow accustomed to recognising the association of words in idiomatic expressions, and seeing that we habitually speak of a *chronic* illness, but *durable*, hard-wearing shoes.

Vocabulary expansion

Just as it is justifiable to introduce new lexical items in association with a common theme, for example by asking students to indicate through pictures with arrows and empty labels the parts of a car, it is also useful to expand vocabulary by considering differences in association, i.e. a dog lives in a *kennel* and *barks*, but where does a lion live and what noise does it usually make? There are a number of exercises of this kind in the second half of the book, together with others based on common prefixes, comparing words like *overlook*, *overtake, overcome*, etc. While students are likely to find them very interesting, I have placed them last because I consider them to be the group that can most readily be omitted if time is short.

Lexical tests

There are six Lexical Progress Tests, appearing at the end of each section of three units; in all cases, the items are based on the vocabulary presented in the previous passages and exercises. The Tests have been thoroughly pretested with the help of over 500 students in Barcelona, all of whom were attending courses between First Certificate and Proficiency at schools where classes are homogeneous and a high pass rate is obtained in Cambridge examinations. The statistics given in this *Teacher's Guide* in relation to the Tests should form a yardstick for comparison; a detailed explanation of how to interpret them is given with the notes on Lexical Progress Test 1 (see page 88). In each case I have provided (1) the scores obtained by students attempting the Test at this stage of their progress from First Certificate to Proficiency level; (2) an estimate, based on comparative statistics, of the difficulty of the Test, compared to Cambridge Proficiency level; (3) a discrimination analysis indicating the relative reliability of the Test in individual cases; (4) a target pass mark for students to aim at, bearing in mind that unlike the students who originally attempted the items, they will be doing so with the aid of the previous exercises on the lexis.

The three Test Papers at the end of the book include three further lexical tests of much higher accuracy in terms of discrimination analysis, to be attempted not long before the Cambridge Proficiency examination. Results on the three Tests taken together provide a very accurate indication of students' chances of passing.

Comprehension

I argued in the Introduction to *Proficiency English Book 2* (1977) that multiple-choice questions, whatever their merits as testing instruments elsewhere, are unsuitable for testing comprehension because they give rise to ambiguity and very often test students' logical powers rather than their understanding of language. For this reason, as I believe that students' real understanding of texts can only be tested by direct questions and such an approach is indispensable in the classroom, I have continued to use them in this book. But because Cambridge continue to use multiple-choice questions, presumably because they are a convenient form for marking, I have followed the practice of including them as a check on the direct questions that precede them, and in tests have imitated the examination format.

Types of comprehension exercise

The Cambridge sample examination paper, published in 1983, and subsequent modifications, indicate that students might be expected to answer questions on three out of four of the following kinds of passage: (a) those where they are expected to understand the gist of the content; (b) those where a close attention to detail is required; (c) those in which they must interpret nuances of style and register and the writer's use of language; (d) those consisting of comparison between two or more passages of a similar kind.

Each of the units in the book contains at least two, and generally more than two, of the above types. I have indicated, however, that some variations in technique are advisable. Passages to be read for the gist are best approached by general questions that require an understanding, for example, of the content of each paragraph; in multiple-choice form, the student must learn to recognise a paraphrase of what he or she takes to be the overall meaning of part of the text. Questions of detail demand the capacity to eliminate wrong answers by process of elimination, studying the text carefully to see which details indicate that only one answer is acceptable, and it is important to train students here to explain why the wrong answers are wrong, and to justify their choices by reference to the text. Perhaps the most difficult passages for students without experience of living in Britain are those that depend on stylistic nuances. I have in general used direct questions on humorous passages as a means of drawing students' attention to the devices used by writers to produce a given effect. The first such passage,

on page 19, is accompanied by notes that help students to see what they should look for. Comparisons are of different types, ranging from straightforward information retrieval (e.g. eliminating the exceptions to the statement made in four or five letters or advertisements) to genuine comparisons of passages written in a different style or from a different point of view. In all cases, passages that can best be handled in conjunction with others throughout the book are indicated (i.e. Unit 6, passages A and B).

Presentation of passages and exercises

The instructions for dealing with passages and exercises vary little during the book. Below, I give general advice on how they can best be handled, and these guidelines apply throughout. I have given a checklist of answers throughout the book, although I am aware that it should not really be necessary. I have done so primarily to clear up doubts over usage for non-native-speaking teachers and also, with particular reference to multiple-choice comprehension questions, to justify the correct answers and explain why I would reject distractors; this is necessary in a form of test where even native-speaking teachers frequently become involved in arguments about the correct choices! In all cases where cultural knowledge is involved and in such introductory exercises as the cinema quiz beginning Unit 6, I have provided the necessary information.

Introductory exercises

These should normally occupy the first ten minutes prior to dealing with the first passage in a unit. Their object is to introduce the theme of the unit, in many cases checking on students' knowledge of the relevant vocabulary and introducing useful terms. If students can be persuaded to read passages beforehand, this will be a tremendous advantage and save a great deal of time, and make it possible for the introductory exercises to be done in the right atmosphere. Small groups (i.e. of three people) or pairs should be formed for these exercises, which are not in any sense tests, in order to obtain prompt replies to the questions.

Lexical exercises and tests

I recommend the use of pairs for all lexical exercises. Given that the gaps in lexical knowledge in otherwise homogeneous classes tend to be much greater between individual students because of the varying quantity of reading they are likely to do outside the classroom, it is time-consuming to depend on individuals for answers, but also probable, if groups are formed, that one individual in each group may do almost all the work. The main teaching requirement for such exercises is that students should thoroughly understand the need to make sensible guesses of their own whenever they are faced with an unfamiliar word, and that at this level it should be made clear that word-for-word translation and even supplying synonyms is seldom reliable. As far as possible, I have indicated the association between meaning and context, and the aim is to ensure that students can make a similar association. I have suggested situations in which students could best confirm their understanding of usage by making sentences of their own, but my suggestions are in no sense meant to be prescriptive, and if time permits, this is always a valid exercise.

The lexical tests, as explained above, are of value in measuring students' progress against a reliable criterion that has been thoroughly pretested. If set as tests, 20 minutes should be allowed for students to answer the 25 questions. If not, the most useful revision procedure is to form five groups or pairs, each of whom must answer five questions, but to insist that minority votes or disagreements within the groups should be recorded, since the value of the test consists not only in affording useful information on comparative progress but also in offering a further opportunity to clarify the differences in meaning and usage between the correct and wrong choices.

Passages and comprehension questions

It is obviously preferable for students to read passages before coming to class, and, if necessary, to re-read them on arrival. I have recommended differing approaches to questions, depending on whether the passage is to be read for gist or detail, etc., and these also apply to presentation. Essentially, in handling a passage where the gist is what matters, the approach should be to find out from general questions whether the content as a whole has been understood; such questions are generally posed in the student's book, and in many cases a series of correct answers adds up to a summary of the passage. The questions can either be addressed to the class in general, or pairs can be formed that will subsequently handle the multiple-choice variants of the direct questions.

Passages demanding an understanding of detail are always preceded by questions on unfamiliar words to clear up any doubts presented by the lexical content as such. Here, pairs are useful to consider why the wrong answers are wrong, and find evidence in the text to demonstrate it. This kind of passage, above all, requires the application of logic, where two heads are almost always preferable to one. Passages requiring an appreciation of the use of language and those that involve different kinds of comparison are also best dealt

with in pairs, or in small groups of three or four. The first demand a feeling for language, the second an eye for detail and the ability to set two or more texts side by side and see the differences. Such abilities can be developed by example in all students, but in the first instance are likely to be found only in individual cases because of wide reading and logical capacity, respectively.

The comments already made indicate that I would not normally expect students to answer any questions of this type at home, alone. The value of the passages and what can be derived from them should be shared, and they are not intended as tests of ability. Individual work should be concentrated on the responsibility to read the passage before coming to class to save valuable time for the exploitation of it for the benefit of the group as a whole.

For the reasons I have already given, I have used direct questions either alone or in combination with multiple-choice until the closing stages of the book. As a general rule, I have begun with direct questions for passages demanding an understanding of gist, in most cases in such a way that the correct answers will provide a summary of the whole. Once students have mastered the basic techniques of summary explained in *Book 3, Use of English*, Unit 3, such passages can also be used as useful training for that purpose. There are multiple-choice questions in almost all cases as a confirmation of students' understanding and in order to accustom students to the examination format. Passages requiring knowledge of detail are always accompanied by multiple-choice questions, but those where questions of style are involved are best dealt with in class through direct questions, and I have only introduced multiple-choice variants in the final stages. The use of direct questions for comprehension assumes that if teachers wish to test students at any time with these exercises, the degree of understanding shown in the answer is the main criterion for correction, rather than the accuracy of the students' English. I have provided answers in all cases; particularly in the case of questions of interpretation, these are to be taken as an approximation students should aim at, rather than as a definitive yardstick against which their answers should be measured.

Comprehension tests

While any of the passages can be used for testing purposes, the only ones that have been pretested as a reliable guide to standards are those that appear in the three Test Papers. An indication of standards to be reached is given in the introduction to the Test Papers on pages 125–6.

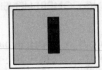

People

(Corresponding unit in *Book 1* – Description: People)

This unit should be dealt with as slowly as time permits since it draws students' attention to the techniques to be developed in dealing with the different kinds of exercise. To ensure that students grasp the advice given, you should emphasise its importance by going through it in detail in class.

Introductory exercise

This serves simply to introduce the subject, and should not occupy more than 10 minutes. If students have already done a similar introductory exercise in *Book 1*, this offers an opportunity to invite them to check what they have learnt by supplying appropriate adjectives to the features they point out.

From East to West

As indicated in the general introduction to *Book 2*, students should have read the passage before coming to class. Ask a few general questions, e.g. whether anyone has seen *Heat and Dust* or films made in India or about India, and what the class know about India and Indian customs, particularly the relationships between men and women, before proceeding to the analytical questions in Exercise A.

A   Reading for gist

Encourage students from the beginning, before they attempt the exercise, to look for the contrasts contained in the paragraphs, and then, in their own words as far as possible, to say what they are. Students should work in pairs, and should produce something like the following, using the instructions in Exercise 1 as a guide:

1 Madhur Jaffrey teaches cookery, but is also a film star; 2 she looks young and beautiful but plays a character much older than herself in the film, and did not need special make-up to do it; 3 her family was

traditionally Indian, and some members of it were like the character in the film, but she herself is open in manner, elegant, charming, etc.; 4 she appears Western, but remains deeply Indian; her daughters have grown up differently in the West, but she has some regrets about this; 5 she led a sheltered life as a child, which had some attractions, but rebelled against it; 7 in spite of having been conquered, Indians have no inferiority complex and are very self-assured, compared to Westerners, in her opinion.

Having done that, students should recognise similar paraphrases to their own in the statements made in Exercise 2. The relationship is: a) paragraph 4; b) paragraph 7; c) paragraph 5; d) paragraph 2; e) paragraph 6; f) paragraph 3. Paragraph 1 is not summarised.

B   Unfamiliar words

Make sure that students fully understand the techniques described here before attempting the exercise. If necessary, ask what part of speech the following are, and what the likely meaning of the word is in the passage: *mistress, wicked, menace, worn, resourceful, swore, escorted, face, vastness, submission, backwardness, question.* Allot one word to each student in advance to save time. Then ask the class in general to indicate the meanings of the words in Exercise B, along the following lines:

sari: a noun, something an Indian woman wears – in fact, the typical dress of the country;

reluctantly: adverb, against her will, although she doesn't really want to;

resentment: (see also *resented* (line 67)), which helps to make the meaning clearer; noun, bitter or angry feeling because of ill-treatment;

land: verb, get or obtain.

elegant: dressed stylishly; *eloquent:* fluent in expressing herself. Note the similarity in sound which helped to dictate the writer's choice of words.

drab: dull and colourless;

lustrous: rich in colour and texture.

C Words often confused

1a plenty of; full of; full of; plenty of.
1b grew up; brought up; grew up; brought up; grown up.
2 Everyone in the class should attempt this, and a number of sentences should be asked for.
3 When they understand other people's problems or feel sorry for them; when they feel they have been badly treated, and are bitter.
4 This should be attempted by everyone in the class, and more than one sentence should be asked for in each case.

First meeting with Sven

This passage should be attempted on a different day, and read beforehand. It is lexically advanced for students at this point in the course, but has been placed here to give maximum opportunity for them to develop their techniques in intelligent guessing.

D Unfamiliar words

The form of the exercise here is one that is followed in many later units. The clues should make the correct answers clear, but it will probably be necessary to define some words more precisely:
1 b; 2 a; 3 b; 4 b; 5 a; 6 b; 7 b; 8 b

E Reading for detail

In contrast to the previous comprehension exercise, Reading for gist, students must here develop the ability to read carefully enough to justify right answers and indicate wrong ones by reference to specific sentences or phrases. Deal with the first set of direct questions on a classroom basis and then ask students to work on the multiple-choice variants of the same questions in pairs, in each case justifying the correct answers and saying why the wrong answers are wrong, as in the examples given. In this way, the first set of questions should be used as a genuine test of how closely the students have followed the text, the multiple-choice questions as practice in the correct technique to follow.
Suggested answers:

1 No, because he kept changing his mind and sending 'contradictory telegrams'.
2 He thought he looked like a cave-man, looked very strange, etc.
3 Because it had two holes on either side that looked as if they had been made for a horse's ears to go through.

4 Because his voice went up and down.
5 Because she did not know what to say to such a strange man, and he was eating and drinking, and perhaps shy.
6 A Answer already given.
   B False. He had sent 'contradictory telegrams'.
   C True. 'at last turned up', 'kept having to make and unmake his bed'.
   D False. They 'had had some warning'.
7 A Answer already given.
   B False. Artists may sometimes dress in an unusual way, but normally have better taste.
   C False. The opposite is suggested.
   D True. 'enormous', 'Neanderthal'.
8 A False. No evidence.
   B His head was large, but this is not the reason given. False.
   C False. It was a straw hat, not a crown.
   D True. The 'two holes'.
9 A False. 'with scarcely a trace of an accent'.
   B False. 'His English was impeccable'.
   C True. It 'wavered . . .'.
   D False. He was a middle-aged man. Draw attention to 'as though', which implies hypothesis or imagination, not fact.
10 A False. He 'stared', 'smiled', etc.
   B False. No evidence.
   C True. She 'desperately searched her mind . . .'.
   D False. She invited him to tea, smiled, etc.

F Synonyms

1 consternation; 2 hordes; 3 resemblance; 4 clad; 5 voluminous (enormous); 6 ponderously; 7 enchanted (point out that this indicates Sven's English was not quite perfect, since nowadays we would always say 'delighted'); 8 impeccable; 9 scarcely; 10 extended

G Use of language

1 driven; 2 made, wound, came; 3 bore; 4 searched; 5 filled. Point out that 'make one's way' also exists. *Wind* is preferred here because the drive was presumably winding, with many bends.

H Words often confused

1 forecast; 2 threat; 3 promise; 4 warning; 5 (piece of) advice. Stress that *advice* is uncountable, and indicate the use of 'piece'. Sven might have *knelt* to pray, to beg forgiveness, to do a job of work that required it, etc.; *nodded* to show agreement, to greet someone in the street formally; *stooped* to pick something up

2

Work

(Corresponding unit in *Book 1* – Narrative: Work)

The theme of this unit may not appeal to younger students, but the lexical content is vital. I have endeavoured to make it more interesting by including an amusing passage on page 19.

Introductory exercise

1 Company organisation

Younger students may know very little of how companies are run, and some help may be needed. Up to 15 minutes could be allowed, depending on the level of interest. In practice, the Managing Director is the 'boss' of a firm, but he must report in most cases to a Board. The Chairman's job may be honorary, or he may be the owner of a large block of shares, a former Managing Director, etc. The titles of President and Vice-President are seldom used in Britain, but common in the USA, where it is also customary to distinguish between honorary and executive (i.e. working) presidents. A director is any member of the Board, and it is important to point out that no one would talk of 'the Director', but would say 'the Managing Director' or 'the boss'.

1 A foreman is in charge of men on the shop floor. He would report to the Works Manager.
2 Almost certainly, her future boss, the Research Director, and the Personnel Manager.
3 The Marketing Manager, the Works Manager and the Sales Manager.

2 The balance sheet

a) what is paid to the workers and executives; b) the things needed to make the product; c) the fall in value in machines, etc. as they get older; d) new machines and equipment, installations that must be bought; e) expenses such as telephones, paper, facilities for the workers.

   Cash flow refers to the money coming into and going out of the company. The company's customers may owe it money and may not have paid their bills at the same time as the company had to pay its workers, buy raw materials, etc.

Why do We Work?

A Reading for gist

The correct answers to the questions here build up into a summary of its content. This is, in my view, the best way to teach students what is required of them in understanding the gist of a passage. The first lesson on summary writing in *Book 3*, Use of English, occurs after this in Unit 3 of that book.
Answers: 1 (A); 2 (A); 3 (B); 4 (B); 5 (B); 6 (A)

B Synonyms

1 necessity; 2 fortunate; 3 continue; 4 unduly;
5 actually (point out that it always means 'really' or 'in fact' and not 'currently'); 6 indicate; 7 tenet;
8 creature; 9 deduced; 10 pace (note 'pace' as verb and noun in connection with walking); 11 output; 12 tedious

C Use of language

1 climate; 2 destroying; 3 vast; 4 mixed; 5 isolation

D Words often confused

1 private; particular; private; special; particular; special; private
2 job; craft; work; (employment); job; work; employment; craft
3 award; reward; profit; award; benefit
4 1 economic; 2 economical; 3 economics; 4 economy; 5 economy; economical; economics

Starting your own Business

E Unfamiliar words

This exercise is a new variation in the book, relying as it does on the comparison between the meaning of words in this context and in the context where students may previously have encountered them. Students should be asked, once the exercise has been completed, to use the words in sentences of their own with the alternative meaning.

Answers: 1 (a); 2 (a); 3 (b); 4 (b); 5 (b)

F Reading for detail

This exercise combines techniques previously used in association with Reading for gist in the direct questions with the suggested approach to multiple-choice questions illustrated in the passage on page 11. Ask the whole class the direct questions, but use pairs for multiple-choice.

Suggested answers:

1 A strong demand for what you have to offer. (Note that this information is provided at the end, a necessary corrective for those students who expect all questions to appear in the same order as statements in the passage. The rubric warns them about this.)
2 Independence and job satisfaction.
3 It guarantees loans made by banks.
4 They fail within a few years, the majority within 2 to 5 years.
5 There are more skilled workers available, looking for jobs.
6 The key word is 'essential'. C is the only choice that meets this test.
7 D is clearly stated at the beginning of paragraph 2.
8 A Tax relief does not mean 'tax-free'.
    B This is what it says. The right answer.
    C The Government does not lend money. It encourages the bank to do so by guaranteeing it against loss.
    D The Government recommends 'going it alone', but not specifically for redundant workers.
9 The statistics given at the end of paragraph 3 clearly indicate B, not A. There is no mention of C, and D is clearly false, in view of B.
10 A is clearly stated in the last paragraph.
    B and C are obviously wrong for common-sense reasons.
    D is contradicted in the last paragraph.

G Synonyms

1 businesses; 2 set up; 3 retailing; 4 fledgling entrepreneurs; 5 materialises; 6 stressing; 7 judged; 8 getting your hands on; 9 labour; 10 in the short term

H Words often confused

be dismissed (sacked); were dismissed (sacked); retire; be made redundant; resign

It's a Hard Life for Commuters

This is the first passage in the book in which students are asked to recognise differences in usage between the common word they may expect and a word or phrase used for effect, in this case with humorous intent. Such passages are often the despair of native-speaking teachers, in particular, who find them funny themselves but are confronted with blank faces. For this reason, I have laboured the jokes on this occasion in the hope that students may see how such passages depend on techniques like those explained here. This passage should be attempted on a different day from the others in the unit, and students should be asked to read it previously, and say whether they find it amusing, and if so, why, without having read the exercises that follow and accompanying explanations. On this occasion, it will probably save time if students are invited to supply answers without being divided up into pairs at first. The few who have read widely are likely to stand out from the rest by showing that they understand.

I Use of language

1 a) those who are going to work (*bound for toil*); b) as the east wind blows (like a scythe cutting not grass, but their faces); c) uncomfortably close (but not exactly in his eye); d) travelling smoothly and silently – the implication is of a very comfortable car, used by politicians; e) worrying (but they are not *in agony*); f) splashed; g) steamed. In the last two cases it is the extent of the splashing and the time of the steaming that forms the exaggeration.
2 a) cowboys preparing to round up cattle; b) a train going through a tunnel; c) distant places in the desert or jungle; d) cf. the use of 'turnover' in its business sense in the Introductory exercise to this unit; e) a log cabin in, for example, Alaska; f) a frightening series of stories, for example, about air crashes; g) 'lunch' is seen as being necessary to 'restore' the writer to health; h) 'fodder' is food for animals, who cannot be expected to distinguish between truth and fiction. In all cases, the joke is essentially the same. We have to imagine the 'typical' British commuter as a cowboy, etc. and create an absurd visual image.
3 a) Deflating the importance of the Chancellor of the Exchequer by making him seem like a corner-shop grocer, with the national till downstairs; b) if the rain 'cascades' like a waterfall, it is hardly 'soft' and 'refreshing'.

J General understanding

I have deliberately withheld multiple-choice questions at this stage for this kind of passage because they would be likely to cause confusion. What is important here is understanding.

1 The fact that the journey to and from work is so exhausting.

2 London Bridge. There is no shelter for people waiting for buses.

3 Because the weekend is nearer, and he can begin to look forward to it.

4 Because they are responsible for a great deal of work in the country. Because they are too exhausted to work properly after their journey from home. Because they have good bus shelters.

5 More work would be done. He would not get wet waiting for the bus.

K Interpretation of text

Here the answers are not directly stated. Pair work is recommended.

1 Because grocers do not have to face a long journey to work.

2 He assumes people will say he really does not like the idea of working, is lazy, etc.

3 Because he always travels to the same station. Of course, the joke is that the others are so close, and he pretends not to know what happens there.

4 Because they do not come very often.

5 At London Bridge station. He has heard them all before.

6 The lack of bus shelters at London Bridge. Almost certainly, he got wet while waiting for a number 13 bus at London Bridge on his way to work.

3

Country Houses

(Corresponding unit in *Book 1* – Discussion: Britain)

There is no direct relationship with the unit in *Book 1* in lexical terms, but there is a close connection with the summary in the corresponding unit of *Book 3*, which deals with Country Parks.

Introductory exercise

A brief warm-up exercise as in previous units, which should precede teaching the first passage, preferably read beforehand. The main idea is as usual to give students an idea of contexts in which a given word would be the most appropriate, rather than attempt dictionary definitions. The class should be divided into three groups, handling one question each, to save time.

1 Fields

(a) a *common* may in London resemble a park, but in the country is normally open land adjoining a town or village. The main point is that this land is for recreation and is the survival of land that was not enclosed (see '*enclosures*' in the passage that follows);
(b) a *heath* is generally wilder and never cultivated. In general this term is used in the South and Midlands, while in the more mountainous country of the North and Scotland, it would be called a *moor* (d);
(c) a *meadow* is for animals to graze in, as distinct from a *wheat field*, *potato field*, etc.; (e) a *park* may be found on a private estate, as in the following passage, or may be a recreation ground. The essential details are that it is man-made; English parks, unlike many on the Continent, tend to be less carefully designed and to have sports facilities, opportunities to walk and lie on the grass, etc., as well as flower beds, seats, etc.

2 Boundaries

(a) *walls* – stone or brick;
(b) *hedges* – vegetation, usually bushes;
(c) *fences* – wood or metal. Many students associate them with purpose, rather than the material used. A *ditch* is most commonly found at the side of the road or

for drainage between fields; a *moat* around a castle, to form a barrier against attacking troops.

3 Farm buildings

(a) *barn* – for storing crops, farm implements, etc.;
(b) *dairy* – for making butter, cheese, milk products;
(c) *shed* – for cows, but also for gardening tools, etc., in a private house;
(d) *stable* for horses and
(e) *sty* for pigs.

Georgian Houses

The normal pattern is followed here of clearing up lexical difficulties with unfamiliar words before attempting the comprehension questions.

A Unfamiliar words

1 (b); 2 (b); 3 (a); 4 (b); 5 (b); 6 (a)

B Reading for gist

This should be done in pairs. It provides good pre-teaching experience for the summary techniques taught in the corresponding unit of *Book 3*.
1 B is correct. A is a misreading, referring to Denmark, and C refers to Denmark.
2 A. B is the effect later on. C did not cause the change.
3 B. A is incorrect ('ruins') and C substitutes 'fields' for '*parks*'.
4 C. The first sentence of paragraph 3 says so. Other styles fit in with the countryside, too (A) and B refers to earlier and later buildings.
5 A. By deduction (last sentences of paragraphs 3 and 4). B is relevant, but they could have reacted against that. C is imagination.

C Synonyms

1 submerged; 2 squalor; 3 embellished; 4 shire;
5 mode; 6 by and large; 7 thrall; 8 quips; 9 plump;
10 decked out

D Use of language

Note that students ought to make sentences of their own to get the most out of this exercise.

1 *based on* – formed by, on the basis of. Note: 'His argument is *based on* fact but 'the house is *built, constructed* on sound foundations'.

2 *wore on* – drew towards a close. 'The day *wore on*, and still there was no sign of the missing children.'

3 *round off* – make them rounded, and so, neat, complete. 'He *rounded off* a good afternoon by scoring the decisive goal.' (brought it to a successful close)

4 *gave way to* – were replaced by. Note: *make way for; give way to* an argument, a person's wishes (allow to pass, prevail).

5 *were decked out in* – were dressed elaborately (or comically). There is always a sarcastic or ironic intention behind the use of this. 'The bride's mother *was decked out in* all her finery, and looked pompous and ridiculous.'

The National Trust

This represents a new departure in the book, and should be dealt with on a different day. Students may at first be put off by the rubric, but with careful reading, this form of comprehension should be the easiest of those that may be set in the examination. Insist that students read all three for gist, making notes if necessary, before considering the questions.

The titles actually used for the three leaflets from which these extracts were taken were: (A) 'Join and enjoy the National Trust'; the purpose is to encourage people to join and contribute money – see the first five paragraphs and the last; (B) 'The National Trust: An Introduction'; the purpose is general, to explain what the Trust does, how it is organised, and when and why it was founded; (C) 'The National Trust: Advice to Teachers'; this purpose is clear from the phrase 'you can bring your pupils', and the suggestions on what children can usefully do when visiting a house.

E Comparison of texts

Groups of three, or pairs, should be used for this exercise. Students' answers should include the following information:

1 Because he/she is interested in preserving historic buildings, the countryside, etc. Free entry to National Trust properties, information on properties and activities, a magazine, the satisfaction of helping a good cause.

2 'National' because it is organised throughout Britain, but not in the sense that it is a public institution, run by the Government.

3 By concentrating on particular aspects, and through activities such as drawing, drama and music.

4 (a) by gift and purchase; (b) by donations from individual members, by charging admittance to non-members, and by grants from individuals and organisations.

5 The preservation of buildings, whereas the other co-founders were more concerned with the preservation of the countryside.

F Synonyms

1 diverse; 2 care for; 3 rely (Note: '*It depends what you mean*' and example of usage in first sentence of 2C); 4 suitable; 5 aspect (Note possible confusion with a person's features, expression); 6 comprehend; 7 growing; 8 jealously (Note more common usage of this); 9 on behalf of; 10 threat

G Use of language

This sort of question is the most difficult for students to answer, and in an examination would be framed in multiple-choice form, but it is good training for them to have their attention drawn to the way in which passages are written and the writer's intention, and to work out their own explanations in English. Pairs, or groups of three, should be used.

1 Because the suggestion is 'unfortunately, very quickly', and this indicates his concern for the disappearance of the countryside.

2 Bridges, factories, etc. They are 'monuments' because they are physical structures and commemorate past history.

3 The owners and their servants.

4 Music of a particular period in history; because they could sense the atmosphere of life at that time better.

5 Organisations operating according to 'statute', or legal requirements, such as professional associations; because the conditions must fulfil the law, and also not affect the Trust's independence of action.

6 Her foresight. She was looking towards the future.

7 To emphasise how cheap it was at that time. Cf., only £10.

H Words often confused

1 A **historic** event is one that 'makes' or changes history later on; a **historical** event is any event that occurred in history, important for the future or not.

2 We **depend/rely** on people, services, etc. when we trust them; but actions **depend** on circumstances/previous actions (they are influenced by them) and

the use of the two verbs **depends** on the meaning and context (is determined by it); cf. 'It **depends** what you mean' (my interpretation or action will be influenced by which meaning you intend).

3   A **discussion** is a friendly or formal exchange of views; unlike an **argument**, it does not automatically imply disagreement and the possibility of verbal attack on others.

4   Our national **heritage** is something we have all inherited from the actions of our countrymen in the past; an **inheritance** is something left to us personally in someone's will.

5   Because we only **look forward to** things that we want to happen, as well as expect to happen, so we do not look forward to a threat; a) foresee; b) predict; c) forecast.

Lexical Progress Test 1

In common with the other Tests in this book, this Lexical Test was submitted to rigorous pretesting, using the same criteria as the Cambridge sample test, published in 1983 with the new regulations. The Tests are derived from a larger number of items, and those where students provided more than 85% or less than 20% correct answers were eliminated.

All items were subjected to discrimination analysis, comparing the results in each case of the top 20% and bottom 20% of students in samples of over 100 students. The discrimination analysis is given, taking into account that the hallmark of a successful test is 0·30, indicating that the number of 'good' students with correct answers was 30% greater than the number of 'weak' students; the Cambridge sample test had a rating of 0·34. It is therefore possible in the case of a particular item to have negative correlation, where the weaker students scored better than the top group; all such items were eliminated.

In view of the long periods of time involved in most Proficiency courses, tests were administered to groups of students ranging from those who had had 50 hours' tuition since passing the First Certificate examination to those preparing for the Proficiency examination, with up to 250 hours' additional tuition. The results are calculated, nevertheless, according to the standard that could be expected of students attempting the Test at a given stage in the course, in this case one-sixth (or some 50 hours' tuition) of the way towards Proficiency standard.

The object of the Progress Tests is rather different from that of the Tests at the end of the book, and the statistics must be interpreted accordingly. The Progress Tests deliberately incorporate most of the items contained in previous exercises in this book (Words often confused); in all cases, the vocabulary occurs either in the previous three units of this book or in the corresponding units of *New Proficiency English Book 1*. The Tests at the end of the book are also based on the lexical items that have been presented, but have been selected to provide maximum effectiveness in terms of discrimination. As a result, the analysis figures are correspondingly higher.

It must also be taken into account in interpreting the statistics that they were obtained from students who had not previously studied these units in sequence, and therefore had no aid from practice or memory. Consequently, it is to be hoped that students with this advantage should score higher than the averages given here. The students who did the Tests nevertheless provide an excellent guide to the real difficulty of items, since they were drawn from a total of over 500 studying at two schools where they had been placed in homogenous classes at three levels between First Certificate and Proficiency. In each case, I have provided statistics indicating the average score of the students tested at a corresponding level to that of the students at the relevant stage in the book; an estimated Cambridge pass level showing the real difficulty of the Test in relation to Cambridge Proficiency; the discrimination analysis, indicating the reliability of the Test in individual cases; a target figure, indicating what I consider to be a reasonable score in view of the help given by preceding exercises.

Note that there is no obligation to do this Test as a test, even though it should provide teachers with considerable information, especially with regard to persistent sources of error. If you prefer to do it as a classroom exercise, the most effective, time-saving method is to divide the class into five pairs or groups and give each five questions to do in five minutes. Indicate that all disagreements should be noted, since in many cases the wrong answers provide as much information as the right ones.

The time for this and subsequent lexical progress tests should be 20 minutes, though in the first instance an extra minute or two could be allowed.

Statistics for Test 1

Average score: 13·6/25 = 54·5%
Estimated Cambridge pass level = 21
Discrimination analysis = 0·33
Target score = 19
On the basis of pretesting, the most difficult questions and awkward distractors are: 4 (decay); 7 (economic); 10 (road); 13 (place); 19 (disregard); 21 (excitement, nervousness); 22 (referendum); 23 (overrun).

Answers:

1 A; 2 C; 3 B; 4 D; 5 D; 6 B; 7 C; 8 B; 9 B; 10 D; 11 A; 12 C; 13 D; 14 C; 15 C; 16 C; 17 A; 18 B; 19 D; 20 C; 21 D; 22 B; 23 C; 24 B; 25 B

4

Health

The unit corresponds in part in lexical terms to the first topic in Unit 5 of *Book 1* Description: Processes, which has to do with dieting, and to the summary in Unit 4, relating to the provision of vehicles for handicapped people, both of which should have preceded it if the three books are taught in conjunction.

Introductory exercise

This short preliminary topic for discussion is open-ended, but most of the causes of worry are explained in the first passage, which should have been read beforehand.

Worrying

A Reading for gist

The technique, by now established, of asking direct questions, the answers to which summarise the passage, and then following up with multiple-choice questions as a check on the previous answers, is adopted here.

1 The main causes are conflict and stress; examples of the first are given in paragraph 1 and of the second in paragraph 2.
2 The difference is that conflict has to do with our uncertainty about what may happen in the future and our difficulties in making decisions about future actions, while stress has to do with our concern about what may happen to us and those we care for, or is the result of what has already happened.
3 Worrying is normal. It requires medical help if people are no longer able to lead normal lives because of it.
4 Either the sufferer becomes tense and frightened for no obvious reason, or reacts to specific conditions, e.g. enclosed situations. The causes can only be determined by reference to some incident in the patient's past. (The latter is not explained in the text.)

5 Worry is not always negative; it can be positive if it causes us to face up to our problems by seeking to understand them, or in causing us to concentrate, on our work for example, and become more determined to succeed.

Note the instruction given to students when answering multiple-choice questions relating to the gist of the meaning. They should look for paraphrases of the original text without worrying too much about the significance of all distractors. The answers are:

6 A; 7 C; 8 A; 9 C; 10 A
Before accepting these answers as correct, ask students to justify them by reference to the text, as follows:

6 'we can rarely predict...' (line 3)
7 'fear of death is as strong...' (lines 22–3)
8 'We can manage perfectly well...' (lines 34–5)
9 'In practice, anxiety is judged...' (line 37)
10 'But at less intense levels,...' (line 59)

B Unfamiliar words

In this exercise, students are asked to develop their techniques for guessing meaning further by relating unfamiliar words to those that occur in the surrounding context. There are five variations on this theme:

1 synonyms: **go awry** relates to 'get seriously ill', 'crash'; **taut** to 'tense', 'dry', 'feeling of agitation'; **galvanises** to 'energises'
2 opposites: **cursed** relates to 'blessed'; **pathological** to 'normal'; **counterproductive** to 'recovery' and 'helping us to come to terms with reality'
3 logical context: **accrue** means 'grow out of', and can be deduced from 'advantages and disadvantages', 'action we may be contemplating; **stave off** means 'hold back' or 'prevent for a time', related to 'understand better' and 'breakdown'
4 previous content: 'triple-checking the front door' is an example of a **quirk**
5 subsequent content: **curtails** means 'limits', and can be deduced from what follows

C   Synonyms

1 anxiety; 2 rarely; 3 precise; 4 contemplating;
5 dreadful; 6 care for; 7 basis; 8 curiously;
9 widespread; 10 cope with

D   Use of language

1   To indicate that the ability to think about the future is at the same time an advantage and a disadvantage.
2   Advantages and disadvantages.
3   It is used to explain more clearly what has just been said, in this case, using psychological jargon; the fact that we may not understand such jargon and he feels he must clarify it.
4   In theory; any sign of abnormality may in theory be pathological, but is not taken seriously except in the conditions indicated.
5   Because they are in rising degrees of importance or seriousness.

E   Words often confused

1   1 slang; 2 cliché; 3 slogan; 4 jargon; 5 slogan;
6 jargon; 7 slang; 8 cliché
2   1 reasonable; 2 rational; 3 irrational;
4 unreasonable
3   1 elderly; senior; antique. 2 senile
4   chores; errand; task; assignment

The Cold War

Introductory exercise

This is open-ended, for general warm-up discussion.

F   Unfamiliar words

For the first time, no clues are given. Students should deduce that 1 **draught** means a current of cold air;
2 **layman**, someone not technically qualified;
3 **congestion**, a medical condition in which too much liquid collects, blocking the passage of air, etc.;
4 **sedation**, being put to sleep; 5 **soothing**, comforting, relieving symptoms

G   Reading for detail

As in previous exercises of this type, students should explain by reference to the text why the distractors are wrong.

1   A Getting wet is discounted as a reason. False.
B False. Viruses cause colds, but the person could have a different one.
C False. Draughts are not the cause.
D True.
2   A True. That is why it is preferred to aspirin.

B and C. False. Aspirin has the same effect.
D Decongestants are contained in various remedies. False.
3   C is correct. Decongestants are specifically mentioned.
4   D. The old wives' remedy contained alcohol. Antihistamines are used for purpose A, and will put you to sleep, which is satisfactory for B and C.
5   A 'grossly inflated the price'. True.
B False. They do not do so.
C That is not the reason for the writer's criticism. False.
D False. There are warnings on the packets.

H   Words often confused

1   1 expelled; 2 relegated; 3 discharged; 4 evicted;
5 extradited; 6 dismissed
2   1 adhered to; 2 acknowledge; observe; comply with;
3 acknowledge; comply with; 4 conform to;
acknowledge; adhere to
3   a) viewer; b) observer; c) spectator; d) onlooker;
e) watchman; f) sightseer
4   1 discount; 2 omitted; 3 overlooked; 4 ignored;
5 neglect
5   1 avoid; prevented; 2 escaped; evaded; prevent;
3 hindering; avoid

Giving Blood

This passage resembles the third passage in Unit 2 in that students are asked to demonstrate their understanding of the use of language for humorous effect.

I   Unfamiliar words

1 **pack in**: give up, resign from; 2 **gory**: bloody, bloodstained, but 'horrible', 'revolting' would do in context; 3 **squeamish**: made to feel sick, upset;
4 **woozy**: dizzy, with one's head not clear; 5 **soothing**: comforting

J   General understanding

Small groups of three or pairs should be used to pool their ideas on the best answers available here and in the following exercise.

1   She felt 'good', charitable because it was a fine, bright morning.
2   The young woman treated her in a business-like way, while the doctor was kind and comforting, aware of her fears.
3   The fact that he had left because another donor had just fainted, and the nurse was not at all comforting.
4   He had received 500 dollars for promising the hospital, that in the event of his death, they could

make use of any part of his body.

5   Because he was hoping to rub out the mark indicating that he had made a bargain with the hospital, either because it embarrassed him or because he wanted to make a similar bargain elsewhere.

K Use of language

1   Because it is bright red, and reminds us of blood.

2   Because it reminded her of blood, and she must have imagined that he used them to wipe bloodstains from the floor, etc.

3   Because they had given blood, and she imagined that this had had such a serious effect that they had lost their natural colour.

4   Because, after telling us not to worry, she immediately gives all the details she believes will worry people.

5   Children are told bed-time stories to help them sleep; generous contributions are usually made to good causes in cash. In this case, the kindly doctor was talking to her as if she were a little girl, and she had generously given her blood, not money.

6   A 'vampire' sucks blood (Dracula). The nurse collecting the writer's blood is spoken of as if she were drinking the blood herself. 'Maracas' are shaken with a violent rhythmical action hardly appropriate in a hospital. 'Drowning men' are supposed to see their whole lives just before they

die, so it implies the writer was about to die from giving blood.

7   'Spare parts' are used to replace defective components in cars, machines, etc. Here, it means parts of the human body, and makes a surgeon sound like a garage mechanic.

8   The fact that he had in a sense 'sold' his body to the hospital, so it physically belonged to them while he was alive as well as after death.

L Words often confused

1 dripping; 2 dripping; 3 leaking; 4 spill; 5 drained; 6 drain; 7 leaking; 8 dripping; 9 draining; 10 spilt
The next section depends on the explanations given; students must provide their own sentences; small groups could be asked to deal with three or four words each.

M Vocabulary expansion

1   The first group are best demonstrated. People **chant** in church or at football matches, demonstrations. The difference is that they do not always sing, and the words are either sung on one note or repeated over and over again.

2   1 a queue; 2 a row; 3 file; 4 a row; 5 a row

3   1 whisper; 2 mutter; 3 murmur

4   1 rinse; 2 brushing; 3 swept; scrub; 4 wiping; 5 Brush; 6 rinsed; wipe

5

The Press

(Corresponding unit in *Book 1* – Discussion: The press)

Introductory exercise

This should be done in small groups, either asked to answer all the questions, or given four questions each out of the total of 16.

A *cartoonist* draws (amusing) drawings that comment on political events and figures, etc.
The *City Editor* is responsible for pages dealing with the financial affairs of the City, advice to shareholders, economic trends, etc.
A *compositor* sets the type.
Our own correspondent is a reporter sent by the newspaper, and this indicates that the report was not received from an agency.
The *Editor* is in overall control of the content of the paper.
The *Features Editor* is responsible for special articles given some prominence in the paper (*features*).
A *freelance journalist* works for himself, and submits articles to papers that may be interested.
A *gossip columnist* writes a regular series of notes about people in society – e.g. film stars, royalty – and their private lives.
A *newsagent* sells papers from a shop.
A *news vendor* sells them in the street.
The *proprietor* owns the newspaper, but does not necessarily have anything to do with its content.
A *reporter* is sent to report on events. Note that a *journalist* is a rather more distinguished title, suggesting people who write original articles, although all reporters are journalists.
A *reviewer* comments on books, films, art, etc.
A *sub-editor* cuts the reports sent in, places them on the page and writes headlines.
The *Sports Editor* is responsible for the pages dealing with sport.
A *typist* types copy, letters, etc.

Sub-Editor on *The Times*

A Unfamiliar words

1 Not demanding (hard work); 2 uncontrolled, undisciplined; 3 with a reddish, excited face; 4 using few words; 5 comments made in a sharp, humorous manner, likely to hurt; 6 sharp comments, like arrows; 7 here, sensational; 8 savour, taste; 9 when there was little to do; 10 unpleasantly hard

B Reading for gist

The technique of using direct questions that summarise the passage as a whole, followed by multiple-choice questions to confirm understanding, is used here.

1 Because he works in agreeable company, has time for his own creative work, and learns to write clearly and concisely.
2 The fact that it is varied and does not follow a routine.
3 The ability to 'compress a story to the minimum length possible without ruining its effect'.
4 Because he respected him professionally and came to realise that underneath his harsh exterior, he cared genuinely for the writer's future; because Colonel Maude was not willing to take risks by giving him work that might be too difficult for him.
5 Because he was afraid that he would fail as a writer, and have no security for the future.
6 A is correct.
  B is obviously nonsense; C may be true, but is not the main advantage; D is not true. There were 'rare periods of rush'.
7 A is not the reason for the work not being dull.
  B and D are absurd. All writers use different words all the time.
  C is correct.
8 B is correct. A is not mentioned. C and D are advantages, but not 'the most useful lesson'.
9 A refers to Maude in part, B only refers to a short time and a stage in the writer's career. C is wrong because Anderson's humour was not 'good' for the

writer, or at first appreciated. The correct answer is D.

10 The answer is clearly C, given in the phrase 'He foresaw a time...'. The others are all the product of reading into the passage what is not stated.

C Use of language

These questions are intended as an aid to students in answering the following exercise.

1 We normally **drive** horses, or cars, **hard**, to produce more speed, better performance. Anderson's sarcasm was aimed at producing the same effect on the writer.

2 Stretch one's arms, the rules, etc. (cause them to reach to the maximum extent). Here, cause him to use his abilities to the maximum extent.

3 Because we suppose what he had drunk made his face redder.

4 **Heavily** refers to quantity, **badly** to the quality of the cutting.

5 In digging trenches, etc. for protection against attack. Anderson was trying to defend himself against adverse criticism and disappointment as a writer.

D Reading for detail

1 D is correct. A is contradicted by insistence on good work; B was not part of their training; it is not stated that he 'stood over them' (C).

2 D is correct; 'heavily' could only refer to the quantity of the cutting. C is true, but is not 'the point of the story'.

3 C is true – 'would have acquired a tang of friendliness'. There is no suggestion that he had been drinking 'heavily' (D).

4 C is correct. B is not true; his translation was published. A and D are imagination.

5 The only reasonable supposition is D. The rest are pure guesswork.

E Words often confused

1 1 matched; 2 fits, suits; 3 match; 4 fit; 5 takes after (Note that this can only be used of ancestors, blood-relations); 6 suit

2 1 disappointed; 2 disappointed; 3 discontented; frustrated; deceived; disappointed; disillusioned (a matter of degree); frustrated; discontented

F Vocabulary expansion

Note that in this exercise students must supply alternative meanings and contexts, ideally by forming sentences, wherever these are possible, as well as deciding on the meaning of the word in this context.

1 **career**: b). It does not mean a), as many students assume, or c). Note *university course*, *vocation to be a priest*, etc.

2 **conservative**: a). It does not in itself mean b). Conservative parties are right-wing.

3 **enclosed**. c). *Locked up* in prison. *Restricted* in one's movements, *restricted* to an area, *restricted* information, etc.

4 **expression**: c). *Idiom* is a commonly used phrase, not a language. The creative writer's problem is finding the appropriate words, rather than understanding *meaning*. Note *facial expression*.

5 **fancied**: c). *Desired* to be back at school (*wished that I was*). *Guessed* the answer. Note I *fancied a cup of tea*.

6 **courteous**: c). It implies the other two together; *polished*, with excellent manners.

7 **episode**. b). *Chapter* of a book, of one's life (= stage in). Compare *episode* of a TV, radio serial. *Period* of one's life, in history.

8 **apprehension**: a), relating to the future. Policeman may *apprehend* (= arrest) a criminal. *Dread* is too strong a word here for the same kind of feeling.

9 **resign**: b). *Abdicate* the crown, responsibility. *Retire* from a job because of age, ill health, not voluntarily. Note *resign one's claims*, *resign to the inevitable*, but *resign a post*, *resign from a committee*.

10 **arguing**: c), here. The main confusion is between *discussing* (amicably, without trying to prove a point) and **arguing** (bitterly, to win the argument). *Quarrelling* involves potential violence, etc. Note **arguing** a point of view, and confusion of *argument* with *subject* of an article, paragraph, etc.

Writing letters becomes popular again

This section serves two purposes. It helps to reinforce students' awareness of the differences in style and approach adopted by different newspapers, a main topic in the corresponding unit of *Book 1*, and also gives them practice in distinguishing between similar articles and drawing information from the comparison of passages on the same subject.

While students can be divided into three groups to answer the questions on interpretation, they must read all three articles in the first place in order to deal with the comparison questions.

G Unfamiliar words

1 expressing sympathy in loss, bereavement; 2 strongly active; 3 producing the greatest quantity; 4 the general direction, tendency; 5 love lasting for ever; 6 something they were very fond of; 7 accounted for, explained...by, attributed...to; 8 delighted

(excessively); 9 coming close to equalling; 10 do as well as; 11 registered, recorded; 12 attraction; 13 group temporarily working together for business reasons; 14 scored (see *clocked up*); 15 getting used to, accustoming ourselves to

H Comparison of texts

1 (c). The headlines rule out (a), and there is no criticism of the statistics presented as unreliable, etc.
2 Passage C. The headline sets the trend.
3 Passage A, which is written tongue in cheek. Note 'the pink writing paper trade', and the whole of paragraph 8.
4 Comparing Passages A and B, the 1940s and 1950s, though a bureau release implies the age of 'their grandparents', and Passage B also suggests the Victorian era. The argument advanced is the greater use of the telephone, which was installed in the majority of homes in the 1950s. A reason not given, but almost certainly relevant, is that families were widely separated during and immediately after the Second World War.
5 The point here is that there were more people who were illiterate in the 1930s, and could not write at all, but it is believed that those who are literate now do not write as accurately and well as their parents or grandparents who were literate. A left-wing newspaper is more likely to point to the improvement in standards, a right-wing newspaper to a decline, probably because of differing views on the effectiveness of state education over the past 30 years.

I Use of language

1 Writing a letter; letter writing is increasing. The number of letters written is increasing.
It suggests a teenager writing a letter to his/her father to explain why the phone bill is so high because of conversations with a boyfriend or girlfriend. To suggest the beginning of a letter. 'Odds' refer to 'the explosion of electronic communication, declining standards of literacy, the difficulty of buying a stamp on Sunday'.
2 *A reverse* would mean that letter-writing began to increase, *a pause* that it temporarily ceased to decline.
3 To thank people for presents, etc.; to write to friends abroad they have arranged to correspond with, usually without meeting them; to express their admiration of pop stars, etc., ask for pictures or autographs.
4 One of the people writing long accounts of incidents in their lives, like compositions.
5 They are upset by the size (amount) of the bill. Teenagers may discuss the state of the world or their future happiness (*everything*) or simply gossip (*nothing*).
6 'Love makes the world go round.' The phrase is relevant because such a large proportion of the mail is made up of love letters.
7 In sports competitions. The suggestion here is that different age-groups or people from different areas of the country are competing to write more letters, and those *at the top of the league* have written the most.
8 Letters that are useless to the recipient, such as circulars advertising products.
9 A young lover; because Romeo is the archetype of the romantic young lover; because young men do not appear to write many letters, compared to their girlfriends.

J Words often confused

1 manipulating (possibly regulating); 2 handling; 3 regulate; 4 see to; 5 handles; 6 supervising, handling; 7 cope with; 8 manipulate, regulate

Cinema

(The corresponding unit in *Book 1* is not relevant, but the topic of the summary in *Book 3*, Unit 8, which will follow this if the books are used in conjunction, deals with the decline of the Western.)

Introductory exercise

This quiz is best dealt with in pairs. Pretesting suggests that 'film buffs' in the class can score as high as 18/20, and the average student will know about half the answers.

1 Marlon Brando; 2 Dustin Hoffman; 3 Jacques Tati; 4 Orson Welles; 5 Humphrey Bogart; 6 Warren Beatty and Faye Dunaway; 7 Paul Newman and Robert Redford; 8 Gene Kelly; 9 Liza Minnelli; 10 Anthony Perkins, Janet Leigh; 11 Anthony Quinn; 12 Humphrey Bogart, Ingrid Bergman; 13 Bing Crosby and Bob Hope; 14 Alec Guinness; 15 Gene Hackman; 16 a train, Buster Keaton; 17 a boat, Humphrey Bogart; 18 a sledge, Orson Welles (in *Citizen Kane*); 19 a shark, Roy Scheider (in *Jaws*); 20 King Kong

Some categories may overlap. The following is a rough guide: crime 1, 4, 5, 6, 15; comedies 3, 13, 16; westerns 7; musicals 8, 9; adventure films 12, 17; war films 12, 14, 17; social films 2, 11, 18; fantasies 19, 20; horror films 10

The Birth of a Star

A Reading for gist

1 He had 'no clear idea of what he wanted to do in life'.
2 He was convinced that he could make money there.
3 Because he had considerable experience of riding horses.
4 He advertised his ability, helped by an agent.
5 The actor originally chosen was unable to take part, and Cooper had stood in for him while the company were waiting for him.

6 A; 7 C; 8 B; 9 B; 10 A

B Unfamiliar words

Here I have reverted to offering clues.

1 a); 2 b); 3 a); 4 a); 5 b); 6 c), and not just a); 7 a); 8 a), though b) is implied; 9 b), though a) is close in its basic meaning; he was offering his services for sale, however; 10 c). Note that an *understudy* must be prepared to speak the lines, while a *stand-in* does not. Note also the term *dubbing* for voices.

C Interpretation of text

These questions test students' ability to understand the nuances of the passage.

1 Because he had been brought up on a ranch.
2 Because it involved considerable physical discomfort, through continually falling off horses.
3 Because there were other actors called Frank Cooper in Hollywood.
4 The dog, 'Lightnin''.
5 Because he was 'standing in' for the actor chosen to play the part, and the public were not supposed to recognise any differences between them.

D Words often confused

1 1 sensational; 2 sensual; 3 sensitive; 4 sensible; 5 sensuous
2 1 adequate; 2 suitable, qualified; 3 adaptable
3 1 casually; 2 by chance; 3 occasionally; 4 eventually

Good and Bad Reviews

The comparison here is between a favourable and an unfavourable review. The first is a good model for students to follow in writing reviews of their own. All students should read both passages.

E Unfamiliar words

1 keeping people under close observation; 2 telephone wires; 3 a verb, suggesting the way in which a spool of

film or tape emerges from a machine; 4 having no clearly responsible person for its actions to face the public; 5 falling short of a standard previously established; 6 involving awkward sudden movements or changes of facial expression; 7 neat and careful with details; 8 because he had not expected a present, not having given or deserved one, and because he might suspect that it contained a bomb.

9 sits down clumsily; 10 a bed with four posts; 11 suitcases; 12 on the way to; 13 dress; 14 suggesting that one is sceptical or amused because of superior knowledge; 15 lazy, inactive slowness; 16 in the mountains, above the line where the snow still remains in summer

F General understanding

The first questions demand an interpretation of the text; the multiple-choice questions are used for confirmation.

1 People who admire films that are well-written and organised (*immaculate screenplay*).
2 Through Harry Gaul's professionalism, but primarily through his realisation that what he is doing can affect other people's lives, and is not just a job he can do well.
3 He indicates the character perfectly, without overacting.
4 Clothes, fashion, the life of the very rich and idle.
5 It is long, boring, and there is no real story.
6 A; 7 C; 8 A; 9 D; 10 C

G Interpretation of text

1 Because there is so little action.
2 Because she is obviously so rich, and can afford to die so comfortably.
3 The film is so confused that it is not clear whether the writers worked together on it, and the result is the work of a committee, or each had a little piece to do, without knowing what the others were doing.
4 She gives away her 'pretty things'. We cannot change our minds about dying unless we are contemplating suicide.
5 It is absurd that a person who has been suffering from a serious illness should have been dressed ridiculously to go to the mountains. An 'above-the-knee-line number' means an attractive short dress presumably designed to show off Miss Dunaway's legs, without reference to the situation in the story,

since people going to the mountains usually try to keep warm by wearing wool.

H Use of language

From this time on in the book, I have endeavoured to suggest to students that it is important for them to recognise the differences between similar words rather than to assume words of similar meaning are interchangeable. This marks a step towards fluency in the sense that students must increasingly learn to choose the most appropriate of a number of words they know, rather than recognise that an unfamiliar word is similar in meaning to the only one they already know. At this early stage, any reasonable attempt to indicate an understanding of the differences is to be commended.

1 **ambiguous** implies two meanings at the same time, deliberately planned, where *unclear* would mean vague and confused, without intention.
2 **indictment** means a formal, public accusation, and is much more precise than *criticism*.
3 **immaculate** means without a fault of any kind, while *excellent* means very good, with few faults.
4 **devout** is used primarily in connection with religious conviction, and also suggests observation of religious feasts, attendance at mass, etc.; *convinced* has to do with rational acceptance, not faith.
5 **plagued** is much stronger than *troubled* – cf. *a plague*.
6 **remorse** is also much stronger than *regret*. It implies deep feelings of guilt, not just feeling sorry.

I Words often confused

1 noticed, commenting, added, allege, remarked
2 comment, remark, allegation, notice, addition
3 1 appearance, complexion; 2 outline, aspect
4 1 gesture; 2 characteristic; 3 traits, mannerisms
5 1 restored, recovered; 2 revived, survived, restored; 3 repair, restores
6 1 recovery; 2 revival; 3 restoration; 4 repairs; 5 survival

J Vocabulary expansion

1 stage; 2 hero; 3 rehearsals; 4 lines; 5 first night; 6 dress; 7 speech; 8 producer; 9 performance; 10 costume; 11 cue; 12 scene; 13 footlights; 14 heroine; 15 make-up; 16 audience

Lexical Progress Test 2

For interpretation of the statistics, please see the notes on Lexical Progress Test 1, on page 88.

Statistics for Test 2

Average score: $13.6/25 = 54.3\%$
Estimated Cambridge pass level = 18
Discrimination analysis = 0.20
Target score = 19
On the basis of pretesting, the most difficult questions and awkward distractors are; 3 (works); 5 (outlook, reference); 13 (dismissed); 16 (consent, perform); 17 (outbreak); 23 (elderly)

Answers:

1 A; 2 D; 3 B; 4 B; 5 A; 6 B; 7 A; 8 D; 9 D; 10 C; 11 C; 12 D; 13 A; 14 A; 15 B; 16 B; 17 D; 18 B; 19 A; 20 C; 21 A; 22 A; 23 D; 24 D; 25 A

7

Animals

(There is no direct correspondence here with units in *Book 1*. The topic of the summary in Unit 11 of *Book 3*, however, is the threat to wild life. This corresponds to Unit 9 of *Book 2*.)

Introductory exercise

A brief warm-up to establish some useful terms that may not be familiar, or may be confused. The class could best be divided here into four pairs or groups, taking one group of words each.
Answers:

A bee–hive; bird–nest; fox–lair; lion–den; rabbit–warren
B bird–feathers; cat–fur; cow–hide; pig–skin; sheep–wool
C cat–paw; eagle–talon; horse–hoof
D bird–beak; elephant–trunk; pig–snout

Intelligence in Animals

The usual approach to reading for gist is adopted here.

A Reading for gist

1 'To study the way they behave when set different kinds of puzzles.'
2 Because it does not 'tax enough attributes of the mind'. Rats are better at this sort of test than human beings.
3 By the fact that it can remember the lighted door indicating where food can be obtained without continuing to look at it.
4 Monkeys show their superior intelligence by being able to reason, work out a system for getting food, etc.
5 They are incapable of abstract thought.
6 C; 7 B; 8 A; 9 D; 10 A

B Unfamiliar words

1 a); 2 a); 3 b); 4 c); 5 b); 6 a); 7 b); 8 a); 9 c); 10 c)

C Reading for detail

1 B. 'In the end, . . .'. This proves some thinking capacity (A); C is clearly contradicted ('a lot of mistakes'). D is absurd.
2 'The light is shone as before . . . and is then extinguished.' D is therefore correct. A and B are contradicted. There is no evidence that the test is not repeated (C).
3 A is correct. B applies to dogs and rats. C is contradicted ('25 seconds'). D is false – they do this during the test.
4 C is correct. The example is a system for getting food.
5 A. C may suggest the monkey was 'charming', but not the story.

D Words often confused

1 1 instruments; equipment; 2 tools; 3 gadget; 4 instruments, equipment
2 1 won; 2 beating; 3 earning (winning); 4 won; 5 gained; 6 beaten; 7 gain; 8 won; 9 beaten; 10 earned (won). Note on 3 and 10: we *win* prizes, but in the days of professionalism throughout top-class tennis, it has become customary to talk of *earning* money by *winning* matches.
3 1 try . . . on; 2 experimenting on, test, analysed, proved, try . . . out; 3 trying out; sample; 4 analysed, proved, tax, trying . . . out (on)

Try on, in the last example, could be used with the meaning of 'behave disobediently to see how far it is possible to get away with it'.

E Vocabulary expansion

Note that students should make sentences of their own here to reinforce their understanding of the different movements. An extrovert class should be encouraged to mime them, and see if the other students can guess the word intended.
a) march; b) crawl; c) stroll; d) shuffle; e) stagger;

f) pace (up and down); g) wade; h) stride.
1 pace; 2 stride; 3 crawl; 4 march

Wild Animals: the Raccoon

F   Unfamiliar words

1 laughable, ridiculous; 2 suffering from; 3 walk in the water; 4 using its open paw, and beating downwards; 5 held carefully; 6 bite off its head; 7 throw away with a sideways gesture; 8 self-confidence and balance; 9 attachments to the crab's legs for holding things, attacking; 10 made to feel uncomfortable

G   Reading for detail

1   A 'with a pessimistic air'. B is false (first sentence); C false ('in search of food'); and D false ('shuffled slowly').
2   B. 'The trophy was always...dealt with...on dry land.' A reverses the order of the actions, C is contradicted, D is false because the raccoon bit off its head.
3   D. It bit both creatures to death (A), and killed both on shore (B and C).
4   A. It was 'frustrated' and 'would fold up and squat'. It had regained its balance before the fight began (B).
5   B. 'tapping them on his carapace...'. C is false – 'followed the crab around', and D is imagination.

H   Use of language

The amusement comes in all cases from transferring human characteristics to the animals, and retaining a picture of the human situation out of context.
1 'Chilblains' are painful swellings on the toes, usually caused by getting cold, wet feet; 2 a person looking in a mirror and not being pleased by what he sees; 3 someone about to take an examination, etc.; 4 someone who has just received an unexpected present; 5 someone who has been embarrassed, or has made a social error, but got over it; 6 a child saying it doesn't want to play any more; 7 Pekinese dogs are associated with old ladies as favourite pets; 8 a businessman, once the preliminary pleasantries are over.

In many cases, of course, acting will explain these concepts much more quickly and accurately than words.

I   Words often confused

1 warned; intimidated; attacked; 2 threatened; intimidated; menacing (threatening); attacked; warning; threatened

J   Vocabulary expansion

1   1 edge; 2 rim; 3 border; 4 border; 5 border; 6 fringe; 7 edge; 8 frame; 9 frame (the whole thing), rim (round the lenses); 10 frame; 11 frame; 12 rim
2   Rodents – e.g. rats, rabbits, with prominent front teeth – **gnaw**; birds **peck**; wasps, bees **sting**.

Domestic Animals: The Dog that Bit People

K   Unfamiliar words

1 strongly and heavily built; 2 quick-tempered; 3 a room used for storing food; 4 ignoring, taking no notice of; 5 tried to bite or claw; 6 irritable; 7 in a silently bad-tempered manner; 8 a feeling of resentment, with a desire for revenge.

L   Interpretation of text

The writer's mother (1) thought the dog was sorry when it bit people; (2) believed the dog had bitten the Congressman because he was untrustworthy; (3) said it didn't hold a grudge; (4) thought it was not strong.
1   Because Muggs did not bite members of the family as often as he bit strangers; because Muggs did not recognise him as one of the family.
2   The fact that they were so confident that no one would hurt them that they came to greet her.
3   She thought his astrological signs made him untrustworthy; she persuaded herself that Muggs recognised these defects.
4   Because he was suspicious, and thought it might be an unpleasant joke.
5   The dog had eaten the newspaper he was going to read; she said the dog had a quick temper, but soon forgot about ill-treatment.
6   She thought the dog was not well (physically). The writer thought the dog was not well mentally, but was sure it was physically strong and dangerous.

M   Words often confused

1   1 neglected; 2 refused; 3 neglects (is neglecting), rejected; 4 denied, resist; 5 rejecting, denied, neglect, refuse, resist
2   1 scattered, spreading, spraying; 2 space, spray, scatter; 3 spread, distributed, scattered

8

Travel

(The corresponding unit in *Book 1*, Unit 10 Narrative: Travel, deals with the same subject.)

Introductory exercise

Here, students are asked to name the parts of a car, a train, a boat and an aircraft, filling in labels; obviously, the task lends itself to dividing the class into four groups.

The basic vocabulary to be taught is as follows:
car: wheel, tyre, steering wheel, windscreen, gears, accelerator, brake, boot
train: engine, carriage, compartment, railway lines, signal
boat: mast, funnel, hull, keel, rudder or wheel, deck, bridge, bow, stern, sail
aircraft: cockpit, cabin, fuselage, wings, engine, tail

A Wanderer in Europe

In view of the fact that *Book 1* contains some authentic accounts of journeys, I have preferred here to concentrate on less common variations – a walking tour across Europe here, and in the other passages holiday advertisements for comparison and a review of a travel book. The first passage, leading to questions on reading for gist, may at first be puzzling to students with little idea of geography, so there are some preliminary questions to be answered to aid understanding: the vocabulary is also more advanced than they have previously met, and I have therefore indicated that the section on unfamiliar words should be attempted first, contrary to the normal practice with passages of this type.

A   General understanding

1   The writer was in Austria.
2   He was staying with the Liechtenstein family. The number of servants in uniform (livery), the size of the car, the fact that the chauffeur did not expect him to tip like his employers.

3   On foot.
4   That he had an urgent appointment in Vienna; because he calls it 'a fiction that no one believed' and speaks of a 'phantom rendezvous'.
5   The previous night ('last night's folly'); because he could not afford it and the chauffeur did not expect it.

B   Unfamiliar words

1   **entangled**: by telling a complicated, untrue story, so he was caught in a complicated situation he had invented himself.
2   **snugly**: warmly and comfortably.
3   **phantom rendezvous**: because the person he was supposed to meet was an invention, and therefore unreal, like a phantom or ghost.
4   **cocooned**: because he was warmly, protectively wrapped up.
5   **swished**: because the car made that sound as it moved smoothly along the road.
6   **recrudescence of last night's folly**: he had made a mistake through inventing a story about going to Vienna, probably because of embarrassment and not knowing how to behave, and now was going to make another mistake for similar reasons.
7   **pressed them on**: by 'pressing' them in the chauffeur's hand, he almost obliged him to accept them.
8   **largesse**: because he could not afford to be generous, and was behaving like a rich man when he was very poor.
9   **coronetted**: like a light form of crown? More probably, it was an ordinary cap decorated with gold braid in the form of a coronet.
10   **slunk**: of having made a fool of himself, and confused the kindly chauffeur and station master.
11   **bemusedly**: in a very confused way.
12   **dwindling**: because it would look smaller to the station-master, the further he walked from the station.

C   Reading for gist

1 D; 2 B; 3 C; 4 C – it may well have been the custom for chauffeurs to receive tips (D); 5 D

D   Interpretation of text

1 Because he was wearing uniform (livery).
2 Because the writer did not intend to catch it.
3 Because they were not of great value to the chauffeur, but a source of embarrassment to the writer, who could not really spare them.
4 In the hope of getting out of the chauffeur's sight, to hide his embarrassment.
5 Because it could have meant greeting, but actually meant 'goodbye'.
6 Because he was so embarrassed and felt he had made a fool of himself.

E   Words often confused

1 noticed; advertising; advertising; advised; warned (advised); announced.
2 1 warning; 2 advertisement; 3 advice; 4 notice; 5 announcement; 6 advice, advertisement, notice, notice, warning (advice).

F   Vocabulary expansion

He was puzzled; he was (in fact) saying 'goodbye'. When you: 1 want to show it affection; 2 are sewing; 3 indicate agreement, *or* pass someone in the street and acknowledge the person formally; 4 meet someone; 5 show disagreement or are unable to answer, say 'no', etc.; 6 are indifferent to what you have seen or heard; 7 are trying to prevent yourself from crying out in pain *or* feel sorry for something you have just said; 8 very angry, frustrated

Holidays Abroad

Students should first decide on the purpose of the advertisements and give them a heading, giving their reasons.

Text A in fact is an American Express advertisement. It advertises the Pulitzer hotel, but its main purpose is to persuade people to use American Express cards, which will be welcome at such hotels. 'American Express cards make travel easy', or some such heading.

Text B advertises Holiday Club Pontinental. Its main purpose is to suggest that package holidays can be economical, but also provide everything the holidaymaker needs. 'HCP provides the whole, varied package, at no extra cost', etc..

Text C was placed by the Irish Tourist Board. Its purpose is to interest people in taking their holidays in Ireland. 'Come to Ireland for your Holidays', 'You'll receive a warm welcome in Ireland', etc.

G   Comparison of texts

1 C; 2 A (though B is also intended in the message); 3 A; 4 D; 5 B

Argument is possible in many cases here because of the use of words like 'primarily', 'main' and 'above all' in the stems of the questions. They are the favourite recourse of examiners at this level.

H   Use of language

1 The manager's image is presented as modern and international, the hotel's, in spite of the mention of 'modern comfort', emphasises its traditional, essentially Dutch background.
2 Because they would like to enjoy the feeling of staying in a house with a historic past that is 'typically Dutch', but would like the service to be entirely modern, with English-speaking manager and staff.
3 To create a feeling of tradition.
4 Free, because the intention is to convince readers that they will save money.
5 'Digging deep in your pocket', 'a grasping hand', 'dipping your hand in your wallet'.
6 An incredible variety; a nominal charge. This suggests you will find everything you can imagine, and will hardly have to pay anything.
7 'You'll get more for less'.
8 By mentioning a variety of countryside, activities, accommodation, etc.
9 a) C; b) B; c) C; d) A; e) B

Around the World in 80 Clichés

I   Unfamiliar words

1 Without pausing; 2 newspaper articles, tourist brochures, holiday snaps, etc. pasted into a scrapbook to remind one of the past; 3 b); 4 b); 5 backwards in time; 6 with such precision that part of a second matters; 7 b); 8 b); 9 time; in a very short time; 10 a)

J   Reading for gist

1 Because it does not provide details of the places visited, and so give the reader an accurate idea of them.
2 Because it takes very little to make Mr Heath happy – 'a good meal, a hot bath', etc.
3 Because what usually interests us are the difficulties encountered on journeys, because of the incidents involved, and Mr Heath had no difficulties.
4 He suggests that he was not sufficiently interested to find out, and did not make the opportunities for himself.
5 Because he seems to spend so much of his time on

his travels bathing, and because all his books seem to have one-word titles.

6 A; 7 D; 8 B; 9 C; 10 C in context, rather than D, because the second choice really indicates why he would call it *Swimming* rather than use a longer title for the same subject.

K   Use of language

1   We 'subject' people to disagreeable experiences, 'treat' them to agreeable ones.
2   Because he seems to pursue his hobbies with single-minded determination, as he is a bachelor, and therefore single, and because he describes them in titles using a single word.
3   Because the writer does not think it will be a privilege but something to be suffered.

4   Because it is assumed that as a bachelor his recreations do not involve the opposite sex, and because they apparently do not.
5   Because he does not provide particular details about the places he has visited; he is really using 'particularly' to mean 'very'. 'Agreeable' is a word expressing very little feeling, like 'nice', and sounds vague.

L   Words often confused

1   1 Memorial, memorial, commemoration, reminiscence, reminder; 2 memorandum, memoirs, reminiscences
2   1 recreation; 2 pastime; 3 hobby; 4 recreation; 5 hobby; 6 pastime
3   menu, course, dishes, recipe, plate

House and Home

(The corresponding unit in *Book 1*, Unit 11, Women in Society, has no direct connection with this.)

Introductory exercise

The exercise lends itself to the class being divided into four pairs, or groups.

1 *Rooms*: a) below the ground floor, for storing wine, coal; b) in the roof, probably for storing old furniture, papers, etc.; c) on the main living floor of the house, for entertaining visitors, watching TV, but not usually for eating; d) attached to the kitchen, for cleaning dishes, pots, and perhaps for doing the washing; e) probably on the main living floor of the house for reading, writing, etc.

2 *Furniture*: a) easily folded clothes, such as underwear, handkerchieves, socks, stockings, etc.; b) items of value, such as money, jewels, important documents; c) plates, glasses, etc.; d) suits, dresses, etc.; e) writing paper, documents, etc.

3 *Eating and Drinking*: a)/b) tea, coffee, etc.; c) water, wine, beer; d) beer or coffee, chocolate, etc. – the handle is the important point to note. A saucer is to hold cups so that liquid will not be spilt on the table.

4 *Receptacles*: bucket–water; can–petrol (in Britain, see below); flask–whisky; jar–marmalade; jug–milk; tin–corned beef; vase–flowers

  In the USA, people speak of a can of corned beef.

The Kitchen Sink

A Unfamiliar words

1 burdened, weighed down, with her arms full of purchases; 2 excessive quantities; 3 to provide nourishment; 4 with a series of raised lines on the surface, so that the water runs away more easily; 5 with small marks where the enamel has been broken off; 6 such things as tea leaves; 7 something that was not thought about until after the original design was made; 8 a fine network with holes between the metal threads.

B Reading for detail

1 A, in context. B cannot be considered a problem, and C and B have nothing to do with kitchens.
2 D. 'Double sinks are still the exception'. The others are specifically contradicted.
3 A. Because it is now possible to get hot running water. In most cases, D is still necessary.
4 B. This derives from the answer to 2.
5 B. It has not solved 'all' the housewife's problems, but it is an improvement.

C Interpretation of text

1 Medical authorities and paper manufacturers, the first to ensure that food does not become contaminated, the second for profit.
2 Hens, imprisoned in cages forming lines (a battery). Because they do not eat natural food, the eggs lose nutritional value and the marketing of the business means that they are no longer fresh.
3 'the March of Progress', 'actually runs hot', 'a hundred years of mental effort'.

D Words often confused

1 range; 2 extent; 3 margin; 4 scope; 5 range; 6 sweep; 7 extent; 8 sweep; 9 margin; 10 range

E Vocabulary expansion

1 **bag** cloth (handbag), paper or leather; **box** wood or metal or cardboard; **packet** paper or board; **sack** cloth, perhaps leather (in the USA, it can be used for a strong paper bag); **wallet** leather or plastic.
2 a) box (note also *packet*); b) wallet; c) sack; d) sack or bag (wholesale or retail); e) box; f) bag (*handbag*); g) bag; h) wallet
2 1 shattered; 2 a) fractured; b) chipped; c) shattered; d) cracked; e) flawed
3 1 refuse; 2 junk, scrap; 3 litter; 4 trash; 5 trash, junk

Three Rooms

Room A belongs to a composer, B to a writer/lawyer, C to a publisher.

F Comparison of texts

1 Room C, which is still partly used as a library, although it was originally two rooms; A was originally a garage, and B a barn.
2 Room A has been specially designed to aid the composer in producing different sound effects in different areas;
Room B, because it is large enough for the owner to store all his books, files, etc. and has no view to distract him from his work;
Room C is 'a suitably distinguished setting' for parties, large, etc., and is also appropriate for a publisher because it is a library.
3 Room C, because parties are held there comfortably.
4 The view does not distract the writer from his work.
5 Because it is used for parties, where a publisher entertains his guests.
6 To help the composer in his work by producing different sound effects.

G Reading for detail

This exercise is aimed primarily at reminding students to read carefully both on the first and second occasions when they go through a text. Students should check the statements against each passage in turn, first from memory and then by re-reading. They could suitably be divided into three groups, handling one passage each. The room is part of an old house and has a view of a beautiful garden (2A); It had been tidied up before the interviewer arrived (2C); It has a number of lights in the ceiling, and there are shelves on the walls (2C) – the first part does not apply to 2B, the second to 2A; There are a number of carpets on the floor (2C); The floor itself is made of tiles (2A); The room is essentially practical, designed for work rather than pleasure or entertaining people (2B or 2A). I have assumed to be false anything that is not directly stated, although, for example, there may be a number of lights in the ceiling in 2B.

H Words often confused

1 prolific; fertile; luxurious; lush; fertile; overgrown
2 1 inattentive; 2 careless; 3 preoccupied; 4 absent-minded; 5 indifferent

I Vocabulary expansion

This is the first of a series of exercises in which words that occur in passages are used as a basis for expanding vocabulary, not thematically, as has occurred in a number of the introductory exercises, but by exemplifying words that have some semantic connection, in this case verbs with the prefix *over*–. Pair work is the most suitable means of dealing with them. E.g. I will *overlook* your bad behaviour on this occasion.

1 overrule; 2 overrun; 3 overtake; 4 overthrew, overpowered; 5 overhauled; 6 overrated; 7 overlap; 8 overcome, overact

Lexical Progress Test 3

For interpretation of the statistics, please see the notes on Lexical Progress Test 1, on page 88.

Statistics for Test 3
Average score: 17·7/25 = 71·0%
Estimated Cambridge pass level = 19
Discrimination analysis = 0·35
Target score = 21
Note that this Test is in real terms a little easier than Test 2. The much higher average scores obtained are due to the fact that they represent those of students with a further 100 hours' tuition, compared to those attempting Tests 1 and 2.

On the basis of pretesting, the most difficult questions and awkward distractors are: 19 (resentment); 21 (pace, step); 24 (grip, hold).

Answers:
1 C; 2 A; 3 B; 4 B; 5 A; 6 D; 7 D; 8 C; 9 B; 10 B; 11 B; 12 C; 13 B; 14 A; 15 D; 16 A; 17 B; 18 C; 19 C; 20 B; 21 D; 22 A; 23 D; 24 A; 25 D

The Past

(Corresponding unit in *Book 1* – Unit 13 Description: The Past.)

Introductory exercise

1903 The first flight of the Wright brothers
1911 Roald Amundsen reaches the South Pole
1917 The Russian Revolution
1929 The Wall Street Crash
1933 Hitler takes power in Germany
1945 The end of the Second World War
1953 Mount Everest climbed for the first time
1963 The assassination of President Kennedy
1969 The first landing on the Moon
1974 Nixon resigns because of Watergate

The Generation Gap in the 1920s

A   Unfamiliar words

1 most important to consider; 2 making flat, straight and neat, and so removing the main problems; 3 apportioning, deciding who was to blame and who was not; 4 arguments used to make a special case in favour of one group or another, instead of considering the situation in general; 5 took place, happened; 6 celebrations; 7 represented and claimed to defend; 8 unwilling to believe, unconvinced; 9 division, break; 10 those who criticise by making fun of the seriousness of something; 11 confusion, mess; 12 exact copies; 13 killing

B   Reading for gist

1   They failed to prevent the Second World War and to remove economic inequality, and did not provide a proper system of social security.
2   Immediately after the First World War ended.
3   The fact that society was divided into two groups that could not understand one another, 'a deep cleavage of outlook'.
4   Because they seemed to have learned no lessons from the past, and to be intent on recreating

society as it was before the First World War.
5   Because they did not consider very closely how good intentions could be put into effect in practice, and how an international organisation could physically control nationalistic countries.
6   B. D is tempting, but what the writer says is that young people did not think it would be difficult to create such a society.
7   A. None of the others could have prevented war.
8   D. The writer specifically says so.
9   A. This was 'the most consistent error'.
10   C.

C   Words often confused

The first exercise depends primarily on verb forms and structural usage, rather than semantic distinctions. The models should be studied carefully, and students could also make sentences of their own before attempting the exercise, or afterwards.

1   1 inquire, seek, inquired, seeking, looking (searching); 2 inquire, search, search, looking (searching)
2   failed, failure, fault, blame, blame, failing
3   enforce, persuade, compel, urge, persuaded

D   Vocabulary expansion

1   1 outbreak; 2 outset, outcome; 3 output, outlay, outlet; 4 outfit, outing; 5 outcry, outrage, outburst; 6 outline; 7 outlaw; 8 outskirts, outpost
2   1 undermine; 2 underestimating, understood; 3 undertake; 4 underwent

Growing up in a Small Town

E   Unfamiliar words

1 One that pretended to imitate that of say, an opera house (Note that at that time cinemas were often called 'picture palaces'); 2 half of wood, and half of brick or stone (the ground floor); 3 made of stone, with a hard,

unattractive appearance; 4 a metal form of headgear worn to protect soldiers in battle; 5 large, flat-bottomed boats used on rivers and canals for transporting cargo; 6 a flower/vegetable bed, watercress being used as garnishing for salad; 7 small hills or mounds; 8 the fourth card from the top, counting an ace as the first in importance; 9 with effort, slowly (e.g. up a mountain); 10 containing small pieces of hard material (e.g. coal)

F   Reading for detail

1   A False. The market was in the square.
     B Correct. 'its broad dignity'.
     C False. The town, not the High Street, marked his future.
     D False. This applies to the cinema, which was not tasteful.
2   A False. His misapprehension applied to the film.
     B Correct. Otherwise, he would not have made the mistake.
     C False. He 'once allowed' them to go.
     D False. Although this may be true, the reference to his suspicion refers to his attitude after the Tarzan film.
3   A Correct. Such as weddings.
     B False. They were simply local people.
     C False. They only resembled oxen.
     D False. Wedding groups are taken outside the church, after the ceremony.
4   A False. B False. They were unsuccessful in their cunning.
     C Correct. They were 'individual' and he could 'recognise them anywhere in the world'.
     D The reason is pure imagination.
5   A They talked about the inn. False.
     B He imagined this. False.
     C Correct.
     D The name of the village suggests nothing of the kind. False.
6   B is correct. The rest are imagination.
7   A is correct – 'where the children would want to linger'.
     B is false. Commuters are not dangerous.
     C False. The dentist's would not seem sinister to the nurse.
     D False. This was not part of the route suggested.
8   Logically, since the station was reached by King's Road, and King's Road was a turning off the High Street, the only possible answer is D.

G   Words often confused

1   1 impression; 2 alarm; 3 name; 4 modesty; 5 faulty; 6 fallible; 7 false; 8 fallacious; 9 false
2   1 put up with; 2 bear; 3 underwent; 4 persevere with (in); 5 bear

H   Vocabulary expansion

1 ditch; 2 moats; 3 trenches; 4 gutter; 5 trough

Growing up in a Village

I   Reading for gist

1 D. 2 D – the villages may have been far apart, but were not deserted (C). 3 D. This does depend on an understanding of 'strokes and seizures'. but it is evident that the alternatives are wrong. 4 D. 5 D

J   Use of language

1   Because it suggests that they cared for them tenderly by hand, and felt it necessary to do so to keep them alive or healthy.
2   The idea that the motor-car corrupted the environment.
3   Because it was almost impossible to get away from it, as a result of the slowness of horses and the lack of other forms of transport.
4   Because they did not work very well, and made that sort of noise.
5   Because it took the motor-cycles two minutes to go up them.
6   Because they were always in need of repair, and the owners liked to experiment in the hope of improving their performance.

K   Unfamiliar words

1 with narrow tracks in them, especially those left by cartwheels; 2 helped; 3 food for animals, places where horses were shod, meadows where they were kept outdoors; 4 noisy; 5 crazy, maddened; 6 sudden heart attack

L   Words often confused

1 check-up; 2 revision, amendments; 3 repairs, adjustment; 4 revision, amendments

M   Vocabulary expansion

1 groan b) someone in pain; 2 howl a) a wolf; 3 squeak f) a mouse; 4 squawk g) an angry bird; 5 roar h) a lion, etc.; 6 sob e) someone crying bitterly; 7 wail d) someone mourning a person who is dead; 8 whine c) a child or dog wanting attention.
a) if you were divorced, and the court ruled that your ex-husband/wife(?) should pay it to keep you;
b) usually from a relative, to live on (e.g. while studying); c) an annual payment, usually interest on money deposited; d) any piece of paper stipulating how much is owed for goods or services; e) an extra payment made as a reward for good work, the company's success

(compare *commission*, a regular percentage payment);
f) tax on imported articles paid to the customers;
g) money paid for professional services (e.g. to a doctor,
lawyer, etc.); h) money paid by the state, usually to
maintain students while studying; i) a percentage
payment on a loan; j) money received from someone in
his or her will; k) money paid by divorced or separated
people, or by unmarried parents of children to keep
them, according to law (usually by ex-husband or

unmarried father to ex-wife/mother and child);
l) money paid by the state or a company on your
retirement; m) money paid to local government to
maintain the town, village, etc. and normally paid only
by householders and companies with business
premises; n) money paid to a landlord/landlady for
living in a house/flat belonging to them; o) money paid
to authors or inventors according to the sales of their
work

Computers

(Corresponding unit in *Book 1*, Unit 14 The future. Although there is no direct connection here, the themes are related.)

Introductory exercise

Open-ended discussion on this occasion.

The Case for Home Computers

A Reading for gist

If time permits, this passage should be handled on the same day as the second. 1 D, because the computer is 'so easy to understand'; 2 C; 3 A, although the others are hinted at. The main intention is to convince you that the computer will do what you want it to do; 4 B; 5 A, 'specifically for the family', 'you and your children . . .'.

B Use of language

1 It is not 'plain English', because it is jargon; it is/not 'gobbledy-gook' because it is easily understandable. It means the machine is friendly to the user, but implies, therefore, that it is easy for non-experts to use.
2 The image relates to dogs, which lick your hand if they are friendly, and suggests the machine is as friendly as a pet; it is used to create a comfortable, humanised atmosphere around the computer.
3 It is literally true because the resources of the computer are exploited through tapping the keys of the keyboard.
4 The advantage is that people without specialised experience will understand what the computer is saying.
5 It is important that the adventures are sufficiently challenging to test the mind, or intelligence, but also important that the user should be able to solve the problems presented.

C Words often confused

1 experience, experiences; experiment, experience, experimenting
2 1 vital; 2 requisite; 3 vital, viable; 4 living, vital, alive (living)

D Vocabulary expansion

1 specialist, consultant; 2 veteran; 3 connoisseur; 4 consultant; 5 veteran

The Invasion of the Space Invaders

E Unfamiliar words

1 Ghostly, but the implication here is of a building designed in a science-fiction world which seems unreal; 2 drew pictures and thought; 3 making a steady, repetitive noise as they move inexorably down the screen (any young student will know what is meant here); 4 moves (sideways) to avoid; 5 resting comfortably, as in a nest; 6 stomachs, but here in the part of the machine that collects the money; 7 edge, on the point of breaking through; 8 the constantly moving elements from which life eventually emerged; 9 highest points (cf. mountains); 10 dogs, allowed to move freely; 11 exciting (our emotions, interest)

F General understanding

1 D – 'sardine-can overcrowding', etc.; 2 C – it is important to note that they genuinely believe it, and are not 'pretending' (D); 3 B 'purity of spirit', but they do not really live in cells (D); 4 B – 'It is instructive . . .'; 5 D

G Words often confused

1 1 morale; 2 moral; 3 morality, morals
2 1 assure; 2 persuading, convinced; 3 converted

H Vocabulary expansion

A parcel; a suitcase; a villain, confidence trickster, someone pretending to be something other than what he/she really was.

Mary Poppins in the Chip

After the extreme points of view about computers represented by the previous two extracts, this passage, with its essential common-sense behind the humour, should be taught on a different day but not too long after the previous two.

I Unfamiliar words

1 Someone who enjoys spoiling others' pleasure (killing joy); 2 so full that things are likely to fall off, like a boat deep in water that is likely to sweep objects off the deck; 3 advertising information about a product (cf. books); 4 the writer has converted the word 'nit-picking' (making criticisms on points of minute, unimportant detail) into an invention of her own (testing one's intelligence, or 'wits'). (NOTE 'pick a lock'); 5 make sure that you know the whereabouts of; 6 household; 7 something that puts you off, causes you to lose interest – the phrase used is a recent Americanism; 8 throw away (i.e. into a ditch); 9 lively and cheerful, like a refreshing wind; 10 in a stupefied manner, overawed by the situation; 11 make them stick (like jam); 12 pull them off violently

J Interpretation of text

1 Because she is sent so many to write about, and readers expect comments on them when they are thinking of what to buy their children.
2 Because the three-year-old boy flushed some of the counters down the lavatory.
3 They are most of them valuable or difficult to replace at short notice, causing his mother, etc. a lot of trouble.

4 Because the name put her off, as she does not feel happy about technological subjects; a call from the lady marketing it.
5 Because the writer is astonished that computers can be handled by such young children; *it* means technological progress (especially as designed for the young).
6 She was so used to her young son destroying games by flushing them down the lavatory that she thought the journey would not be worthwhile if he would be capable of destroying this in the same way.
7 The lady pays children to open bottles she cannot open herself, which are supposed to be too difficult for children to open; children find it much easier to operate the Talking Computer than adults like the writer.
8 Mary Poppins sounded like a kindly nurse (with an insufferably maternal voice) and it is a joke that a computer, with no personality of its own, should sound like her.
9 Seven years of work by average men.
10 Because it is made in Hong Kong, where it is not necessary to pay the workers social security and the workers do not pay income tax at British rates.
11 He was about to flush them down the lavatory; the word 'antique' indicates their age, and therefore, value.
12 Astonishment.

K Words often confused

1 discharged from; 2 dispense with, replaced; 3 laid off; 4 rejected; 5 discard, replaced, substituted; 6 written off; 7 discharged from; 8 rejected, discarded

Pay special attention to the problem of 'substitute A for B', 'replace A with B', and ask for sentences to confirm that the class recognise the difference. The passive, 'B was replaced by A', is much simpler than 'B was substituted for by A'.

Education

(The corresponding unit in *Book 1*, Unit 15 Discussion: Education, is directly relevant, and the summary to be attempted in *Book 3*, Unit 15, also deals with the subject.

Introductory exercise

This consists of open-ended questions.

The Royal College of Music

A   Unfamiliar words

1 Moves to focus on; 2 playing music for the customers to listen to; 3 three musicians playing in a teashop; 4 confused, loud noise; 5 found everywhere; 6 to prevent music in one room being heard in another, or outside; 7 having too much ornamentation; 8 wind instruments, those that are blown, such as clarinets, but not normally such as trumpets, which are made of metal and are called brass instruments; 9 a musical academy; 10 someone who has been attacked by rivals, because of envy.

B   Reading for gist

1   A person who has a complex emotional life and is probably a little mad.
2   One of hard work and 'unco-ordinated noise'.
3   He would prefer them to come later, but accepts them, 'rather than see them go elsewhere'.
4   Because they normally realise that they have not made enough progress to have hopes of succeeding, and make their own decision.
5   The majority continue with musical careers, but not as concert performers – as teachers, assistants, secondary singers, etc.
6 D; 7 D – 'keen students' would not be upset by A; 8 B; 9 D; 10 B

C   Words often confused

1   1 healthy, fit, sane, sound; 2 sound; 3 fit

2   1 temper, humour; 2 mood, temperament; 3 tendency, moods, humour, temper

D   Vocabulary expansion

1   1 outgrown, outnumber; 2 outclassed; 3 outweigh; 4 outlive
2   1 abdicate, renounce; 2 seceded; 3 give up, forsake (desert); 4 deserted; 5 part with; 6 withdraw; 7 vacate; 8 withdraw

Footsteps to Fame

E   Unfamiliar words

1 Collector of insects, especially butterflies, etc.; 2 traditional working dress and hat of girls in the country in previous centuries; 3 ornamental edges to dress; 4 are attracted to it; 5 fascinated by the idea of a career on the stage; 6 with quick steps and jumps (most easily demonstrated); 7 bring to land, catch; 8 designed the dancing steps; 9 magic stick; 10 self-conscious modesty, to attract attention; 11 falsely amused, to attract attention; 12 formed a line; 13 to establish the force of personality; 14 moving, in an emotional way

F   Interpretation of text

1   Because she admits that she lied when she said 'How lovely!'.
2   Because she was 'like a milk churn in build' (square).
3   Because she was about to perform on stage.
4   Because it indicates that Victoria was heavily built, with the result that she would not be graceful when dancing.
5   She has no natural grace at all, and resembles a miner digging coal.
6   Because she was very big, but dressed in clothes which were edged with frills, like a doily.
7   Because she thought they were 'shameless', the reason being that young children behaved as if

they were stars in the theatre.

8 The 'strain on her face', and the obvious effort implied by her trying to catch the fish for three minutes.

9 Because by this time the audience were accustomed to the sea as a setting for the dancing.

10 Because the tree was so heavy.

11 She was behaving artificially, like a professional actress on stage; because they would like to delude themselves that young children they know are like great stars; because 'shameless' implies not being ashamed of what one should be ashamed of.

12 Because she will be successful there, and not have to come back.

G Use of language

1 'lied' – expressing the writer's real feelings;

2 'wielding', 'heaving' – both suggest carrying a heavy object requiring great muscular strength, which is hardly appropriate for a little girl with a butterfly net; 3 'piled into' – suggesting that the car was overloaded and the occupants on top of one another, as in a pile; 4 'clamoured' – begged noisily and persistently, suggesting the parents gave in for the sake of peace and quiet; 5 'simpering' – smiling in a silly, unnatural way; 6 'strutting' – walking in an affected, self-satisfied way; 7 'tore into' – started playing in an aggressively lively way, as if she was going to tear the music to pieces.

H Vocabulary expansion

1 a serious (i.e. criminal) law case; 2 a football match; 3 to judge a book, film, etc.; 4 to decide on the value, sound construction of a house, etc.; 5 a tennis match

Lexical Progress Test 4

For interpretation of the statistics, please see the notes on Lexical Progress Test 1, on page 88.

Statistics for Test 4
Average score: $17 \cdot 1/25 = 68 \cdot 6\%$
Estimated Cambridge pass level = 19
Discrimination analysis = 0·27
Target score = 21

On the basis of pretesting, the most difficult questions and awkward distractors are: 10 (overbalanced); 11 (failure, fault, miss); 16 (moral); 19 (dispensed).

Answers:
1 C; 2 B; 3 C; 4 D; 5 B; 6 C; 7 C; 8 B; 9 A; 10 C; 11 A; 12 D; 13 B; 14 B; 15 C; 16 C; 17 D; 18 C; 19 D; 20 D; 21 A; 22 D; 23 D; 24 B; 25 A

Advertising

(There is no direct relationship with the themes of the units in *Book 1*, but it is increasingly important for students beginning the final stage of their preparation for the Proficiency examination to be aware of the ways in which words are manipulated in English, and advertising provides one of the most obvious sources for such manipulation.)

Introductory exercise

The fifteen slogans are related as follows, with a completely subjective assessment of their aims.

1 insurance policies – pleasure, freedom from worry.
2 home computers – family pride, concern for the children's education.
3 home computers – fear of the unknown, technological ignorance.
4 insurance policies – greed, security.
5 cars – *machismo* associated with good social position.
6 insurance policies – greed.
7 insurance policies – fear of old age, retirement.
8 home computers – fear of children's future because of inadequate education.
9 cars – aggression, *machismo*.
10 cars – adventure, pleasure, excitement.
11 insurance policies – greed.
12 cars – speed, endurance, retention of (sexual) energy.
13 home computers – fear of children's future, technological and educational ignorance.
14 cars – size for family man needing car for holiday.
15 home computers – saving money.

In general, the advertisements for cars emphasise aggression and *machismo* (because men buy most cars, and secretly may use them as a substitute for deficiencies elsewhere, perhaps giving themselves a feeling of power); those for home computers play on parents' fears for their children's future in an increasingly technological world, and also on their own lack of such knowledge; those for insurance policies on greed (the chance of making money) and fear of old age, with the accompanying promise of security.

Changes in the Art of Persuasion

A Unfamiliar words

1 Growing upward and outward, and so expanding in quantity and range; 2 a story popularly believed to be true, or believed within the profession, with no basis in fact; 3 temporarily try out alternatives to our usual preferences, like a married person making advances to someone else; 4 strong, and consistently found (in this case); 5 mothers who care about their children's hygiene and health; 6 caused to flow out of them; 7 people conducting surveys; 8 between one party and another, inconsistent in voting patterns; 9 a hopeless quest or search; 10 produced, as if by magic but actually by a trick.

B Reading for gist

1 The aim was to convince us that we should always rely on the same brand; the idea of brand loyalty was subsequently exposed as a 'myth', because people like a change now and then.
2 The new advertisements were more sophisticated.
3 They were full of information about the product, on the grounds that people bought things in a rational manner.
4 Advertisers assumed that while the majority are loyal to a party, or product, the important minority are influenced to change their minds because of unconscious motivations, and even the majority base their choice mainly on habit and emotion.
5 It means that the consumer is now treated as if he had no mind of his own, and is at the mercy of the advertiser. It is not clear whether this is really true, because we do not know how effective advertisements are. The writer appears to be sceptical of such a transformation really having taken place.

6 D (note the use of 'never') in A); 7 C – it did not 'prove' the original assumption was correct (A); 8 C; 9 A; 10 B

C. Words often confused

1 1 adopted; 2 adopted; 3 decided, designate, elected; 4 designated, decided
2 1 exhibited; 2 exposed, revealing; 3 detect
3 1 detection; 2 exposure; 3 exhibition; 4 revelations, disclosure
4 1 resign; 2 relax (rest), stay, rest; 3 compose; 4 rests; 5 stay, relax, resigned
5 1 long-standing; 2 inveterate; 3 deep-seated; 4 durable; 5 chronic; 6 immemorial

D Vocabulary expansion

1 shrink; 2 evaporate; 3 wane; 4 slump; 5 set; 6 ebb

Television Advertising

E Unfamiliar words

1 obligatory; 2 unhurried, casual; 3 check the validity of, approve or censor; 4 here, films shown; 5 increased; 6 incongruous, inconsistent

F Reading for detail

1 A. The first sentence is important. The Act did not stipulate B or C, and D occurred as a result of the regulation, not intentionally.
2 D – 'the leisurely operation of "self-discipline"'. They are not scrutinized unless complaints are made, in fact.
3 C. ('Under the Television Act . . .')
4 A. The separate companies joined forces to set it up.
5 A. 'To impose a single standard of interpretation'.

G Words often confused

1 1 inspect; scrutinised; 2 kept under observation; 3 explore; 4 scan, observed; 5 explored, take stock of; 6 investigating, inspected
2 1 obligatory; 2 inquisitive; 3 authoritative; 4 requisite; 5 demanding, obligatory, requisite
3 1 applied, submit; 2 resigned, submit; 3 appealed, resigned, surrendered; 4 submit, apply, appeal
4 1 whole, bulk; 2 majority; 3 whole, majority, bulk

Advertising Standards

H Unfamiliar words

1 making a solemn promise; 2 similar; 3 standard of measurement; 4 reliable measure; 5 without meaning

to; 6 check; 7 support; 8 goes against, breaks; 9 tax (imposed within the profession); 10 shortened

I Reading for gist

1 C; 2 D; 3 D, and not A, which is clearly contradicted; 4 D – 'he will find it hard, if not impossible, to have it published'; 5 C

J Use of language

1 Because the context has to do with claims to make weak people strong and muscular; it means 'demonstrating our potential strength'.
2 'An extraordinary profusion of different colours' (quantity plus variety); because it is unlikely that the flowers would bloom in such a short time.
3 Ornamented and full of extravagant statements; because it is making exaggerated claims. The choice of metaphor is obviously influenced by the subject, an advertisement for seeds.
4 When you do not want to speak to them any longer; because the use of words makes false claims.
5 Because although the Authority try to protect the public by monitoring advertisements, they rely on the public in turn to inform them of any that are misleading.
6 'Breaching' means 'breaking' (but is deliberately chosen so that the action does not sound quite so serious) – cf. 'breaching an agreement' (doing something that is not in accordance with it) and 'breaking an agreement' (tearing it up); 'bending' means taking advantage of any vagueness in the wording of the rules to break them in spirit, but not necessarily in the letter of the law.
7 Because two negatives in English do not quite make a positive, and the phrase therefore does not give away how strong the suspicion of people in this case might be. Compare 'It is not altogether surprising that . . .' to 'Obviously, . . .'.
8 Because the verb should be singular in sentences beginning with 'neither' (cf. 'none'), the sentence is correct. But few English native speakers observe this rule in speech.

K Words often confused

1 alleged, testify; 2 certifying, entitled, reclaim; claim, (allege), stipulated; 3 entitled; 4 attributed; 5 claims, entitled, stipulated

L Vocabulary expansion

1 batch; 2 herd; 3 shoal; 4 bunch, bouquet (if specially prepared and carried/presented on a formal occasion); 5 quota; 6 quorum; 7 flock; 8 squad; 9 gang; 10 clump

Adventure Then and Now

(There is some overlap here with the corresponding unit in *Book 1*, Unit 18 Narrative: Turning Points.)

Introductory exercise

The first person to reach the North Pole was Commodore Peary in 1909; Roald Amundsen reached the South Pole in 1911; John Hanning Speke reached the source of the Nile in 1858; Sir Edmund Hillary and Norgay Tenzing climbed Mount Everest in 1953; Armstrong and Aldrin set foot on the Moon in 1969.

Sturt's Exploration in Central Australia (1845)

This passage should read in contrast to the one that follows, so that the two should be dealt with as soon after one another as time permits.

A Unfamiliar words

1 dirty; 2 lively and cheerful; 3 skilled; 4 shell fish; 5 weapons used by primitive people and thrown at the enemy; 6 sea birds; 7 swelling out; 8 here, long, shallow containers (cf. a horse *trough*); 9 destroyed completely; 10 low-lying land, partly under water

B Reading for detail

1 D. 'thought that man and beast were one creature'; 2 by process of elimination, D – 'a much more vigorous breed', 'many . . . were handsome'; they did not grow the *nardoo* plants (B) and had only lost their front teeth (C); 3 B 'There were indeed great stretches of water further to the east', but the party did not see them (D); 4 C 'no bulging stomachs' – the other characteristics were also evident among one or all of the previous tribes encountered; 5 A – because of what they told him.

C Interpretation of text

1 Because they offered them their wives, who were dirty and in any case it was an offer they were morally obliged to refuse.
2 They would have predicted the weather accurately and their sight and sense of smell would have pointed out things that were useful or dangerous.
3 We do not know. Because he felt sorry for them.
4 Because bulging stomachs among primitive peoples, in particular, are a sign of malnutrition.
5 That there were unfortunately no prospects for farmers because of the lack of water. This is, in fact, what he said, quite correctly.

D Words often confused

1 1 foreigners; 2 freaks; 3 scarcity; 4 exception; 5 stranger, rarity, foreigner; freak; exception, scarcity
2 1 foreign, rare; 2 strange, exceptional; 3 scarce
3 1 arrive, (reach), meet; 2 contact (reach), find; 3 encountered, meet, found
4 1 opportunity (chance), circumstances; 2 reason, chance, occasion; 3 circumstances, event, chance; 4 chance (opportunity), occasion, occasion, circumstances, reason

E Vocabulary expansion

1 1 breed; 2 clan; 3 sect; 4 tribe; 5 caste
2 1 chop; 2 split; 3 carve; 4 crack; 5 split; 6 divide; 7 crack; 8 divide

A Modern Crossing of Australia

F Unfamiliar words

1 difficult choice; 2 slower and easier-going; 3 here, physical endurance, toughness; 4 sunset (strictly speaking, twilight); 5 smell, but here hint, sign; 6 very funny; 7 in quantity and in quick succession; 8 single mass of stone (normally used of pillars); 9 fear and respect; 10 cattle stations

G Reading for detail

1 D, which is why this area is defined as 'the empty places'; 2 B, because it is a 'more leisurely' safari. C is not true because he would have flown to the centre to begin it; 3 A – 'the most hospitable country on earth'. C is false, because they have clubs; 4 D – 'tradition' required it; 5 B. We assume that there were still birds from the mention of the kookaburra in the first paragraph.

An Early Balloon Voyage

As in the case of the previous two passages, this passage is linked to the one that follows and should be read in conjunction with it.

H Unfamiliar words

1 At 1.40 (or at twenty (minutes) to two); 2 in the middle (midst) of; 3 the cheers, applause; 4 crowd; 5 air; 6 deserved; 7 greatest; 8 spectator, onlooker; 9 immediately, without delay; 10 pulled; 11 height; 12 bad (stormy)

I Reading for detail

1 A – 'so as to be distinctly seen in every part of the town'. It disappeared from sight but was afterwards seen again; 2 B – 'apprehensive that the corn would be injured' by the crowd approaching; 3 B – since he was assisted by shepherds; 4 C – 'to that place' refers to 'his home at Kilnwick Percy'; 5 C

J Words often confused

1 1 performed, fulfil; 2 fulfilled, discharging;
   3 carrying out; 4 discharged, carrying out;
   5 perform, discharge, fulfilling; 6 carry out
2 1 rose, aroused, raise; 2 arisen, raise, aroused;
   3 raised, rise; 4 raise, arisen
3 1 crowded; 2 flocked; 3 gathered; 4 assemble
4 1 crowd; 2 flock; 3 gathering; 4 congregation;
   5 assembly

Ballooning for Fun

K Interpretation of text

By pretending that it is difficult for her to get up early; by being overcome with admiration on meeting the handsome pilot; by assuming that the balloon would go wherever she wanted it to; by being terrified of what might go wrong.

1 She did not like the idea of getting up so early, and thought that nothing enjoyable could take place at that time of day.

2 Because they looked prettier. It confirms the general impression that she is a helpless, superficial young girl who judges the balloon by its colour, etc., rather than by design, safety, capability, etc.

3 To imitate the way in which the pilot spoke very slowly and clearly.

4 Being unable to control where the balloon was going, and so for example flying into a mountain, drifting out to sea, etc.; hitting electrical power lines, and exploding, crashing to the ground; drifting into space reserved for aircraft, and colliding with one.

5 Because he was trying to get in touch with his girl-friend via the radio in her Range Rover, and kept getting other car radios instead.

6 Inflate the balloon, with a fan; by heating the air in the balloon; not much, since it is blown by the prevailing wind; a considerable amount; because it used a gas burner, which hissed, and made a different noise when the flame was turned up, and because it was equipped with radio.

7 The risks have increased because there is more likelihood of colliding with something in the air or coming down in a populated area; they have decreased because it is easier to keep in touch with people on the ground and inform them of the situation. A matter of opinion, but it seems a rather romantic expression to use. In fact, he is deliberately looking for an adventurous experience when it is not necessary, but on the other hand he is supported by people on the ground and not entirely dependent on his own resources, courage, etc.

8 An open question, but the differences are that 200 years ago, balloonists had the novelty and received the admiration we have given to the first astronauts, while we regard balloonists simply as people with an interesting, perhaps dangerous hobby and probably underestimate the skill and danger. They are really quite different because at that time any form of flight seemed wonderful, whereas we see balloonists nowadays as people who deliberately choose to fly in a primitive way to enjoy themselves.

L Words often confused

1 contradict; 2 obstructing; 3 protested, refused; 4 resist, contradict, object, refusing; 5 oppose, protesting, obstruct; 6 opposed, refused; 7 protested, obstructed; 8 opposing, resist

Language

(This unit is closely related to the corresponding unit in *Book 1*, Unit 19 Discussion: Sociology in the sense that that unit explores the use of language in argument, and this one concentrates on ways in which language can be used and misused to create false impressions in readers' minds. Both units emphasise how important it is in reading one's own language as well as a foreign language to weigh words carefully, and how easy it is for language to become deformed by clichés.)

Introductory exercise

This exercise has the value of drawing students' attention to the problem mentioned above in a practical way. Incidentally, though perhaps it would be counterproductive to tell students this, every sentence here is built around a lexical item included in a past Cambridge Proficiency paper, showing the extent to which these depend on customary associations between words, and in effect, on cliché and the recognition of it. Suggested answers:

1   Students who have been doing the preliminary English course, which lasts two years, should have no difficulty in following this one.
2   This bank does not usually lend customers money for long periods unless they can provide proof of being able to repay it.
3   I am out of work at present because I have not found a job that suits me.
4   The local authority knows quite well that it must provide satisfactorily for old people in planning its prospective housing programme (or include enough houses for old people in its programme).
5   As I was walking along Charing Cross Road, as usual, I saw someone behaving suspiciously and arrested him when he would not tell me what he was doing outside the bank.
6   The fact that we failed to win the election again this time is not due to the voters feeling our policies have failed but has happened because the world situation is getting worse.
7   As the owners of the school are not prepared to consider giving teachers better annual rises, many of them will have to take private classes in order to earn more.
8   I know people may think it is strange that I don't want to explain why I have resigned.

The Decline of the English Language

I consider this passage to be a model for students to follow in their own compositions; it is a perfect example of how to argue clearly and concisely, giving examples of what is meant throughout.

A   Unfamiliar words

1 wrong use; 2 old-fashioned idea; 3 for ever, with no foreseeable end; 4 become a drunkard, alcoholic; 5 ugliness and carelessness; 6 capable of being reversed, of being sent in the opposite direction; 7 unimportant and not serious; 8 sticking, joining; 9 pleasant-sounding; 10 to be more solemn and important than it really is, to convince people that it is important because it sounds important

B   Reading for gist

1   They say that language has become decadent because our civilisation is decadent, and that language is a natural growth which cannot be altered by human effort.
2   If we think foolishly, we express ourselves foolishly; if our means of expression are clumsy and inaccurate, our thoughts will be clumsy and inaccurate.
3   One can take the trouble to think clearly and learn how to express oneself clearly. It is everyone's responsibility.
4   If people thought more clearly and knew what the words they heard and read really meant, they would be more aware politically and presumably choose better governments.
5   Because it is easier, and involves less thought and effort.
6 A; 7 C; 8 C; 9 B; 10 B

C Words often confused

1 annulled; 2 disallowed; 3 cancelled; 4 demolished; 5 exterminate (get rid of) (do away with); 6 dispose of; 7 cancelled; 8 abolish (do away with); 9 executed, exterminated; 10 do away with

D Vocabulary expansion

1 flat; 2 polluted; 3 rusty; 4 old-fashioned; 5 contaminated; 6 mouldy, stale; 7 rotten

The Effect of Language on Juries

E Unfamiliar words

1 pictures, like rapidly taken photographs; 2 those who put the theory forward; 3 mistaken, false; 4 failures to do justice, cases in which the wrong verdict is reached; 5 put, set, asked; 6 calling forth a reaction, usually an emotional one; 7 called (officially); 8 less strongly worded

F Reading for detail

1 C–D is a trap, because it suggests that the human eye's main job is to take photographs; 2 D–A and C are false because each group heard only one question, and some heard the basic form without emotional language; 3 B. Again, C and D are wrong because only one question was asked of any one person; 4 C – 'some subjects were asked nothing at all about the speed of the cars'; 5 A – the inventions occur afterwards (B), and there is no evidence they had changed their minds (C).

G Words often confused

1 resemble, characteristics; 2 impersonation, resemblance; 3 impersonate, characterises, personification; 4 characteristics, resembled, personified, resemblance

Language and Censorship

This passage relates to the previous two in the sense that the first (Orwell) indicates the dangers that arise from the misuse of language; the second (Nicholson) shows how people's minds can be influenced by a choice of phrase; the third demonstrates how language can be habitually misused to the point where the user and perhaps his readers are unconscious of the manipulation, the point that Orwell was making with the invention of Newspeak in his novel *1984*.

H Synonyms

1 notion; 2 innocuous; 3 trivial; 4 advocates; 5 remove; 6 tedious; 7 alarmingly; 8 dictate

I Use of language

This exercise is of importance in that students are frequently unaware of the defects in the writing they may read in English.
1 My subject is books *or* Books are what concern me.
2 The real meaning of his local community and its present state.
3 Discovering and learning things for oneself without being presented with definite answers to problems.
4 Trying to introduce people to culture because of your love for humanity in a gentle manner.
5 Not likely to be very enjoyable.

Draw students' attention to Mr Harrison's word order in the phrase pointed out and criticised in their book.

J Interpretation of text

1 *indispensable* – the writer thinks the *Assistant Librarian* is a journal no one would miss. Its correspondence columns are full of letters from people who are by inference noisy and violent. *magnificent* – used in association with 'mental sludge' (rubbish). *innocuous* – used correctly in association with the title, but concealing very dangerous content, in the writer's view; he has already said that the article itself is rubbish.
2 To indicate that Mr Harrison writes in a clumsy manner, and so is not competent to comment on the English language.
3 Because it is clear that Mr Harrison is not impartial.
4 Because he despises it.
5 This is not entirely clear from the context, but the terminology indicates that he belongs to the radical left, and because of his dislike of tradition, 'formal education', etc., would only accept political views agreeing with his own.
6 'Nor is this a trivial point; I have rarely . . .' (line 36)
7 The writer defines impartiality as being prepared to listen to what both sides in a discussion, or the side one is opposed to, has to say; Mr Harrison regards it as weak-minded and therefore liable to corrupt. Mr Harrison thinks that impartiality is only suitable for those who do not believe strongly in anything; the writer thinks that in order to be impartial it is essential to believe strongly that the other side have a right to be heard.
8 (d) – 'promulgating tedious literary worth' suggests that the end of the creative writer is a matter of style.
9 He believes that the public are too ignorant, or persuadable, to be trusted to weigh up knowledge

for themselves and reach open-ended conclusions of their own.

10   He also believes that librarians cannot be trusted to choose books for the readers since knowledge of their content is not an adequate criterion for making a choice.

K   Words often confused

1   1 disapprove, ban, advised, remonstrated, disagree, react, disagree, disapprove, banned
2   1 prescribed, cure, prescription; 2 redress; 3 make amends, cure, redress

Lexical Progress Test 5

For interpretation of the statistics, please see the notes on Lexical Progress Test 1, on page 88.

Statistics for Test 5
Average score: 18·1/25 = 72·3%
Estimated Cambridge pass level = 18
Discrimination analysis = 0·21
Target score = 21
This test, and the following Progress Test, was attempted by students not long before they were due to take the Cambridge Proficiency examination. On the basis of pretesting, the most difficult questions and awkward distractors are: 2 (visualises);

9 (circumstance); 19 (suitable); 22 (assistance).

Answers:
1 A; 2 C; 3 A; 4 C; 5 D; 6 A; 7 A; 8 C; 9 D; 10 A; 11 C; 12 A; 13 C; 14 B; 15 C; 16 B; 17 C; 18 B; 19 C; 20 C; 21 C; 22 D; 23 A; 24 C; 25 B

Consequently, in contrast to previous results obtained with students at a much earlier stage in preparation, the average scores were equivalent to Cambridge pass level. The Test itself is about 2 points (or 8%) easier than an average Cambridge Proficiency examination Lexical Test.

Finance

(There is no direct correlation with units in *Book 1*.)

The topic, like Work in Unit 2, may seem boring to younger students. A study of the lexical items in context in previous Cambridge Proficiency examinations, however, reveals that the three areas from which they are most often drawn are business. finance and the law (see Unit 18). This was my main reason for including the topics here. The specialised lexis relating to finance, however, is so dense that I have replaced the normal thematic introductory exercise with two that aim to teach students or remind them of the principal terms used in connection with banking and the stock exchange.

Introductory exercise

Banks: 1 rates; 2 current; 3 interest; 4 charges; 5 demand; 6 deposit; 7 loans; 8 commission; 9 cheques; 10 balance; 11 statement; 12 account; 13 credit; 14 black; 15 red
The Stock Exchange: 1 shares; 2 investment; 3 bonds; 4 expenditure; 5 rate; 6 currency; 7 investors; 8 stockbrokers; 9 profits; 10 speculative; 11 bid; 12 price; 13 Capital; 14 dividend; 15 Trusts; 16 profitable

Prospects for a National Economy

A Unfamiliar words

1 Recovery from a poor economic position; 2 a slump, so prospects have improved, a period when the economy remained in a low state; 3 altered to show increases and improvements on the original forecast because things look better; 4 through growing in terms of production, earnings and profit, or the opposite; 5 growth in the quantity of goods produced in the country, in this case for domestic consumption (i.e. within Norway); 6 it can make it float on the surface, instead of its sinking – again, the idea of a graph rising and falling explains this idea; 7 lack of

movement and consequent decline; 8 a powerful, rapid one like a wave; 9 is more brilliant than, in the sense that its contribution is now noticeably greater and proceeding better; 10 improving, showing signs of rising

B Reading for gist

1   That it is improving at a moderate rate, and so prospects for the future seem better than they did.
2   Much better.
3   The importance of oil activities, which dominate the economy to such an extent that it is difficult to obtain a balanced picture.
4   Because it is the only way in which employment can be maintained (since the oil industry, although profitable, employs relatively few people).
5   Export industries can feel confident, while those protected against imports (sheltered sectors) and producing entirely for the home market, often in competition with foreign firms, have less reason for optimism. The shipbuilding industry for home consumption is in great trouble.
6 C; 7 A (4·3% a year); 8 C; 9 D; 10 B

C Words often confused

1   1 carry out; 2 achieved, performed; 3 carrying out, succeeded, brings about, succeeds; 4 perform (carry out), achieved (succeeded)
2   1 explain (account for), attributed; 2 derives, assigned; 3 derived, attributed, explain; 4 assigned, explained, accounting for Local Authority Bonds

E Unfamiliar words

1 Without deductions (e.g. for tax); 2 taken away; 3 competing; 4 business deal; 5 committed, and therefore cannot be withdrawn

F Reading for detail

Some teachers find questions of this kind, requiring

calculations, as difficult as students do, so I have therefore included a full explanation.

1 A is Correct. Half of 8% for half a year. 'Interest is paid gross . . . on bonds with lives of less than one year', so there is no tax to be deducted. B is False. There are no sales charges. C. That is 8%. D is a combination of two wrong answers.

2 'The biggest bonds with the longest life are the best payers', so if you were prepared to invest for a long period you would buy one requiring £10,000 plus. C is correct.

3 B is correct, for the same reason as 1A above. 'Some bonds with lives of less than one year even offer monthly payments', but this means that it is not usual (D).

4 C is correct. 'To find out which bonds best meet your needs, ring . . .'

5 D is correct. Second half of first paragraph and last paragraph. A would be true if you put it in a safe with no interest at all. B is false. C is false, because nothing is free from risk in financial terms, and the money might be worth much less after a period of time. It would be true to say that they are 'comparatively free from risk'.

G Use of language

1 To obtain.
2 The difference between the money they can obtain through rates and grants and what they need to spend; because they have to borrow money, or else fail to meet the needs of the community.
3 Because you can buy them in an office on the spot, like stamps over a counter, for example.
4 Longer, more than five years.
5 A single sum of money, paid together, as against periodic payments of interest. In this case, the accumulated interest would be paid in the total sum at the end.

H Words often confused

1 1 cost, debt; 2 charge, debt, costs, price, cost(s), bills (debts), price, bill, prices, charge; 3 cost price
2 1 subject (by law), (liable – it may be charged, and in practice, it is); 2 likely, (probable); 3 subject; 4 likely, (liable); 5 bound, likely, (probable); 6 likely; 7 subject, liable; 8 subject (liable to catch cold), likely
3 1 deduct, reduce; 2 subtract; 3 reduce, 4 diminished (reduced), reduced,
4 1 ensure (guarantee), assure; 2 confirm;

3 guaranteed, insured; 4 guaranteed, reassured, confirming; 5 guarantee, assure, reassured

Money Problems

This form of comparison is of the type most likely to be included in a Proficiency examination, so the passage should not be omitted.

I Unfamiliar words

1 loan; 2 taxes (in fact, customs duty); 3 having to do with the tax authorities; 4 no longer accepted as currency in transactions (technically, as *legal tender*) because they have been replaced or their value has become too small; 5 of practical use for its purposes; 6 take the goods or good things you are offering; 7 take advantage of the best moment to do something, get your work done (from farmers taking advantage of fine weather to gather hay and make it into haystacks before it rains); 8 traps, difficulties in the path; 9 unsuspecting and unaware; 10 bitterness; 11 old, retired people; 12 leading industrialists

J Reading for gist

1 C. Tax relief means you pay less tax, not avoid it altogether (D); 2 D; 3 C. The Royal Mint is not a bank. It is to be assumed that students will realise it is the Government authority for minting or making money (physically!); 4 C. None of the other actions is essential; 5 B, on 1 December. OAPs are liable to tax, and the first £5,300 is tax free.

K Comparison of texts

1 C
2 D
3 Correspondent 3 is certainly not trying to save money, and neither is Correspondent 4, except by avoiding lawyers, but he has presumably made that decision already. My answer is C, but students who justify B with the argument about number 4 given above, should have the benefit of the doubt.
4 C – 1, 2 and 5.
5 This question is hardly scientific, but 2, whose father lives in Switzerland, is unlikely to be older than 5, who is an old-age pensioner. 1 and 4 could be the same age, but 4 is thinking of making his will. Putting the two together, the most likely answer is that 5 is the oldest, 2 the youngest, and the correct combination is D.

17

Human Relationships

Introductory exercise

1 The second pair are officially engaged. A couple. In Britain, the signs would be that the girl wears an engagement ring.
2 The bridegroom and bride; the best man and bridesmaid(s); husband and wife.
3 a) someone you know, but not very well; b) someone who works with you; c) someone who is serving with you in the armed forces, or someone politically aligned with you (on the left); d) someone who passes the time with you (particularly, someone employed to accompany you (usually a woman) on journeys, etc.); e) someone who plays with you as a child; f) someone who works with you (usually in a factory, as distinct from colleague, which normally implies a professional association); g) someone who plays in the same team; h) someone legally associated with you in business, professionally, or someone playing with you in certain games (e.g. tennis, golf); i) someone involved in the joint production of a piece of work, but also someone who assists the enemy of his/her country in war; j) someone who assists a person in a criminal act

Making Friends

A Unfamiliar words

1 witty answer; 2 attractive; 3 small pieces of information (gossip in most contexts); 4 noticeably different; 5 married partners of either sex

B Reading for gist

1 A; 2 D; 3 C 'physically attractive individuals are preferred as friends'; 4 C 'we judge them to be more like us than they are'; 5 A 'similarity of attitudes was a good predictor...'

C Use of language

'Too many cooks spoil the broth' (A project in which a number of people see themselves as leaders is likely to end in disaster); 'Many hands make light work' (The more people working together on a project, the quicker the work will be done and the easier it will be); 'Birds of a feather flock together' (We seek the company of those like ourselves). 1 We can only judge the success of something by results; 2 it is dangerous to upset or antagonise anyone who provides you with a source of profit, and makes life easy for you; 3 a moderate advantage already within one's reach is better than what one might eventually obtain in due course, even though in theory the gain would be twice as much; 4 people who are separated (by circumstances) grow more affectionate towards each other; 5 those who get married without thinking about the consequences will have plenty of time to be sorry about it afterwards; 6 if you have once been tricked or badly treated in certain circumstances, you will be doubly careful in future; 7 you begin to despise people or things you have become accustomed to; 8 do not trust entirely in any one person or project; 9 if you try to do things in a hurry, you will probably find that your mistakes take up more time than you would have taken if you had done them more calmly; 10 your real friends are those who show their friendship when you are really in need of it

D Words often confused

1 1 fun; 2 enjoyment; 3 joke, amusement, joke; 4 entertainment; 5 entertainment; 6 fun, jokes, amusement, fun, jokes.
2 1 inaugural, primary, original, principal, initial; 2 original, primary; 3 initial, original, principal

E Vocabulary expansion

1 soldiers; 2 people on holiday, rich people; 3 poor

people; 4 people on a journey; 5 students, people without enough money to buy a home of their own, people staying temporarily in a place; 6 rich people in the country; 7 people in a poor district of a city; 8 people living outside the city in a building they had built for themselves, or had found; 9 people in the desert, or on a camping holiday; 10 Red Indians.

Matchmakers

F Unfamiliar words

1 in process of disappearing; 2 carrying (with difficulty); 3 buckets; 4 went out with (in a formal way); 5 implying an unofficial engagement; treacherous quicksands, unreliable bases, because modern marriages are not built on secure conditions; 6 have a serious effect on, cause it to be less attractive or respected; 7 advertisements from lonely people looking for partners to share their lives; 8 a go-between, acting as an aid to the man and woman thinking of marriage; 9 suffer a loss of self-respect; 10 a dishonest business

G Reading for detail

1 B 'because she judged the peasant's life too hard'; 2 C, whatever other people might think!; 3 B 'the test of a ritualised courtship'; 4 A 'releases on to the remarriage market...'; 5 D.

H Words often confused

1 uncommon, intrinsic; 2 characteristic, peculiar, distinctive; 3 intrinsic, uncommon, characteristic, distinctive, peculiar

Divorce

I Unfamiliar words

1 with a shabby, uncared-for appearance; 2 the symptoms, such as a headache, which are the result of drinking too much; 3 retort, quick answer; 4 the side of the harbour where passengers disembark; 5 shout in a vulgar way; 6 coming in like a storm; 7 the mass of soap formed for shaving by special kinds of soap; 8 here, rubbish, with the implication that it is dirty; 9 tensed; 10 stolen; 11 hairs

J Interpretation of text

Up to now, direct questions have been asked about this sort of passage, but if it occurred in an examination they would be in multiple-choice format. I have therefore adapted to that in view of the fact that students by this time would be reading the passage not long before attempting the examination.
1 B. It would only be A if the couple were a good deal more stupid than the writer and his wife; 2 D. The origin of the quarrel was that the wife felt bound to shout for a porter because her husband had no hope of getting one without being more active; 3 D, because they would have been divorced and possibly remarried; 4 B. The implication is surely that one is a bachelor from birth until marriage, not from some specific time at which one would be legally allowed to marry; 5 B. If used, there is a lot of friction on his skin, trying to produce a lather, but no lather results. Of course he is playing on the double meaning of *friction*, as rubbing two surfaces against one another and disagreement, causing tension between the two people; 6 D; 7 A 'switch of targets'.

K Vocabulary expansion

1 cheered; 2 screamed; 3 groaning; 4 sobbed; 5 booed

18

Crime and the Law

As in the case of *Unit 16*, the abundance of technical terms and the precision with which they are used makes it necessary to precede the unit with an exercise reminding students of them and teaching any that may be unfamiliar.

Introductory exercise

1 *Crime*
accused, arrested, charged, tried, convicted, sent to prison
a) if the jury found him/her not guilty; b) if there was some evidence that the trial had not been properly conducted, or further evidence had appeared; c) if the court considered that he/she could be relied on to appear in court for the trial, bail being the money paid to guarantee the appearance; bail is not normally granted in cases where the court considers the accused person is likely to leave the country because he or she is guilty and faces a long term of imprisonment; d) if he or she had been sentenced to death, and the death sentence was revoked, or commuted to a term of imprisonment

2 *Trials*
The *defendant* is the person accused of the crime; the *defending counsel* is the lawyer presenting the defendant's case; the *judge* conducts the trial and advises the jury on points of law; the *jury* (12 members of the public) decide whether the defendant is guilty or not; the *prosecuting counsel* presents the case against the defendant; the *plaintiff* (usually in civil cases) is the person bringing the legal action against another (in criminal cases, the plaintiff is the Crown (or Government) acting through the police); the *witnesses* give evidence for or against the defendant.
a) The defending or prosecuting counsel; b) the defendant; c) the witnesses (and the defendant, in some cases); d) the judge; e) the jury; f) the judge; g) the judge; h) the defending or prosecuting counsel
a) before the trial takes place; b) at the beginning of the trial; c) during the trial, after the opening speeches of the counsel; d) at any point in the trial, but in particular before they retire to consider their verdict;

e) when all the evidence has been heard; f) when the jury have given their verdict; g) when the verdict was 'Not Guilty'; h) in the closing speeches before the judge instructs the jury.
It will be evident from this that the most difficult thing for students is to remember the verbs used in association with nouns at different stages in the process. If time permits, students could be asked to take roles, at least in the sense of explaining what they would normally do in a trial, and other students could decide on the order of events, asking them 'what would you do now, at this point?'.

Judging

A Unfamiliar words

1 prejudices making it difficult to be impartial;
2 interesting little stories; 3 guessing; 4 records of what was said; 5 as compensation for injury suffered;
6 enlarged, making the sum much greater; 7 things of little importance, with no rational basis; 8 vital areas of human characteristics; 9 trials that are not real but imitate real court procedure; 10 small

B Reading for gist

1 A; 2 B; 3 C is presented as more dangerous than A, which also exists as a risk; 4 B; 5 D

C Words often confused

1   1 engaged; 2 appointed; 3 enlisted; 4 hired, engaged; 5 appointed, engaged; 6 engage, enlist, recruit, appointed, hire
2   1 competent (qualified); 2 qualified; 3 effective, qualified, capable, efficient (perhaps effective), competent; 4 qualified, capable

The Law

D Unfamiliar words

1 piece; 2 a dead body; 3 with maggots or worms; 4 like

a duck; 5 spiders make cobwebs and they are most often found in houses that are old and not cared for; 6 raising his eyebrows in surprise or frowning; 7 levels of authority; 8 those who take cases of all kinds, instead of specialising in a particular branch of the law; 9 tied to a desk, and therefore working in an office all the time; 10 those who hope to be, prospective

E   Reading for detail

1 D. It is full of activity, if not very efficient (C); 2 D – 'absurdly theatrical and archaic'; 3 C. They consult lawyers if they have been accused of a serious crime, but not necessarily when they are under arrest, awaiting trial (D); 4 B; 5 D

F   Words often confused

1 retract, perjured, deceive; 2 belied (disguised); 3 disguising, misunderstand, deceiving; 4 belied, disguise, misunderstood

G   Vocabulary expansion

1 vibrates; 2 undulating; 3 fluctuates; 4 waved; 5 waved; 6 fluctuated; 7 fluctuate, swayed; 8 swaying, vibrate, waving

Murder in an English Country House

As indicated, this passage should be read in conjunction with the one that follows. The questions relate to the two passages together.

H   Unfamiliar words

Passage A: 1 in a lying position; 2 handle; 3 sweating; 4 expressionless; 5 altered (for dishonest purposes); 6 rang. Passage B: 7 the person; 8 noises like those made by a baby sleeping; 9 noises made by e.g. an angry bull, a pig; 10 as if he had fur in his throat, thick and not clear.

I   Comparison of texts

1 A – in both cases the victim was stabbed in the back of the neck; We do not know the motive (B); the first victim was sitting in an armchair, the second lying on a couch (C); a dagger was used in the first case, an ice-pick in the second (D).
2 The first narrator clearly knew the victim well, and had just seen him (first sentence); the second

narrator did not know the victim well, but had collected the keys from him and returned them. Therefore C is correct.
3 The narrator in the second story shows no sign of emotion or shock. He simply informs the police. All the people in the first story are either horrified (the butler, Raymond), or sorry (the police inspector) except the narrator, who acts calmly, and makes sure that the police are informed. Therefore B is correct.
4 Neither disturbed the position of the body; neither handled the murder weapon – the second narrator moved the blanket, but did not touch the ice-pick; both informed the police; but in the second case the narrator left the scene of the crime – D.
5 The first narrator noticed that 'the blue envelope containing Mrs Ferrars' letter had disappeared'; the second narrator did not notice anything missing, but he knew where the register was, although he did not know the contents of the desk; no motive is given in either case. The answer is C.

J   Reading for detail

1 C – 'I thought I detected signs of emotion beneath the stolid mask', and not B; 2 C – 'Good evening, gentlemen'. He expresses his sorrow quite naturally, assuming none of them is connected with the crime; 3 B – 'the party on the couch seemed enough explanation for that', and he is assumed at this point to be drunk; 4 A – because it was 'not accidental'; 5 D – since he not only leaves the house but also the district before reporting the murder, and does not give his name. It was a neighbourhood where it was not unusual to find an accountant armed with a gun and a knife. B may be true, but it is pure supposition – in fact, it is not true.

K   Words often confused

1 1 informed of, communicated to; 2 acquaint himself with, confide in, dropped . . . a hint; 3 informed, communication with, confided (dropped a hint), communicated to
2 1 disturb; 2 upset; 3 interfere with, trouble; 4 overturned (upset); 5 trouble, interfere in, embarrass; 6 disturbed, overturned
3 1 accidental; 2 incidental; 3 unintentional; 4 random; 5 casual; 6 casual, incidental
4 1 folded; 2 wrinkled; 3 bent; 4 creased; 5 folded; 6 bent

Lexical Progress Test 6

For interpretation of the statistics, please see the notes on Lexical Progress Test 1, on page 88.

Statistics for Test 6

Average score: $16.9/25 = 67.4\%$
Estimated Cambridge pass level = 17
Discrimination analysis = 0·29
Target score = 21
This Test is about one point (or 4%) easier than Cambridge Proficiency Test level. On the basis of pretesting, the most difficult questions and awkward distractors are: 4 (worried); 6 (hopeful, will-be, willing); 7 (supplementary); 11 (broken down).

Answers:

1 B; 2 D; 3 B; 4 B; 5 A; 6 B; 7 A; 8 D; 9 B; 10 A; 11 C; 12 B; 13 B; 14 B; 15 B; 16 C; 17 C; 18 B; 19 D; 20 C; 21 C; 22 A; 23 B; 24 A; 25 D

Test Papers

The three test papers follow the new Cambridge format. There are 25 lexical items, followed by five multiple-choice questions on each of three passages, one of which concentrates on understanding gist, one on detail, and one either depends on the appreciation of nuance and register and stylistic effects or else asks students to compare advertisements or letters to derive the correct information.

Lexical Tests

In order to construct the lexical tests I have chosen items from the overall bank based on what has been taught in the exercises in this book. About 70 per cent of the items are new to students in this form, while the other 30 per cent employ the same choices as in previous tests, but not with the same sentences, and not necessarily with the same correct answers. The items have been ordered so that each test is exactly equal in difficulty and has the same discrimination analysis figure (0·41). The average score for students on each test is 16·0, constituting Cambridge pass level. Within the tests, the items have been presented in order of difficulty according to pretesting so that problems are most likely to occur towards the end of each test.

If these test papers are attempted when less than 20 hours' tuition remain before the examination, they will accurately predict students' results, but at the same time doubtful candidates can be helped by explanation of items, which, because of their high discrimination value, are likely to appear in examinations. At the same time, it must be made clear that a student's result on an individual test can vary by up to plus or minus 2. For maximum predictability, students should therefore attempt all three tests and the assessment be made on the combined scores.

The estimated Cambridge level on any one of these tests is 16. If all three tests are taken together, a student scoring 50 out of 75 could be confident of passing this section of the examination. Those with scores between 45 and 50 are marginal passes. A score of 55–60 would almost certainly reach B level in the examination, and scores of over 60 out of 75 would be A.

Multiple-choice Comprehension Tests

This form of test has been notoriously unreliable in Cambridge examinations for many years. It is to be hoped that its reliability will increase with the new format, and that students who have learnt the techniques for dealing with the different kinds of comprehension passage in the course of studying this book will approach it with more confidence and be less susceptible to making mistakes for other than linguistic reasons. The marking for each of the tests here is to award two marks for each correct answer. It is therefore possible for a student to obtain a maximum score of 30 out of 30 for each series of three passages. If students, as suggested, attempt all three papers, 90 marks are possible. A guide to Cambridge Proficiency pass level is that students should answer at least 10 out of 15 questions correctly in each series, giving 20 out of 30, and a combined total of 60. Coupling these scores to what has been said above about lexical tests, the pass mark for any one test paper is 36/55, and a student totalling 110 out of 165 on the three papers taken together would have a reliable chance of passing. As a rough guide, because scores on multiple-choice comprehension tests cannot be computed as accurately as those on lexical tests, a total of 100/165 represents marginal cases, 110/165 a C pass, 120/165 a B and 130/165 a potential A.

How to conduct the Tests

Many students fail to produce their best levels of performance in tests because they have no sense of time, and panic. They are convinced that they will not complete the paper and answer too soon. It is therefore important that tests or parts of them should be conducted according to the time limits allowed in the examination. It is also true that the time limits for this paper are rather more demanding than in others, so that while the principle of 'More haste, less speed' applies as a motto, students cannot afford to spend too long on any one question. In total, the time allowed for this paper is one hour, and students are likely to do best if they allot fifteen minutes to each part (i.e. on Section A and on each of the three passages in Section B).

The best results I have had from students in allaying their fears and training them to take note of time have been as follows. They should attempt Section A first, using as far as possible the principle of recognition rather than logic; since most of the items are presented in the form of clichés, it is better to rely on the memory of having seen or heard the phrase than on any similarity with their first language, which will almost certainly be a trap. It is even advisable to repeat phrases, including each choice in turn, silently, unless the correct answer is immediately obvious, until one reaches a conclusion. Students should not spend too long over any one item. It is better to turn to the reading passages after fifteen minutes, and return to the few gaps that may be left later.

The comprehension passages should be read twice before students even look at the questions. Above all, they should never attempt to work from the questions to the text, which is fatal. Different strategies have been recommended throughout the book for different kinds of comprehension test. In questions that deal with the gist of the passage, it should be possible to recognise the correct answer as a summary or paraphrase of the content of a paragraph; in questions dealing with detail, it is advisable to test every statement, true/false. It may occur that two statements appear to be correct. In these circumstances, apart from checking on the use of the words in the stem or distractors such as 'most', 'always', 'often', 'only', etc., students must eventually decide on the basis that one answer is unarguably right in every circumstance, while the other may in some way be questionable, and choose the former. Questions relating to style or register are a matter of recognising the writer's intentions. Here, no special technique can be recommended, but the experience of the passages in this book should have made students aware of the kind of variation from a normal mode of expression likely to be adopted by a writer for, for example, humorous or ironic intent; passages involving comparison are largely a matter of attention to detail, and reading everything with the utmost care.

Students must attempt to complete each passage within 15 minutes, and above all not leave themselves without time to read the last one properly. They should then return to the gaps they may have left in the lexical part of the test, and complete them. Some students are prone to leave blanks, which is foolish. A wild guess has a 25% chance of being right, and in general a 50% chance, because students are usually capable of eliminating more than one of the distractors and are in doubt only between the two that remain.

While the results will give teachers an accurate prediction of what is likely to happen in individual cases in this part of the examination, it is not too late to use these tests for teaching purposes. The explanation of why wrong answers are wrong still has value, even at this late stage.

NEW PROFICIENCY ENGLISH
Book 3
Use of English

Introduction

Relationship with the course as a whole

While this book can be used independently of the others in the course, it is more closely related to *Book 1* than the rest; apart from training students in the skills required to deal with all the forms of question set in the Use of English paper and providing practice exercises, it also has a large number of remedial exercises reminding students of structures they should already know. These exercises are intended to aid teachers in the re-presentation of structures necessary for the successful completion of tasks in *Book 1*, wherever this proves necessary, or for straightforward remedial work to correct persistent errors.

The book is made up of sections that relate to different forms of question in the examination and teachers could follow through any given section from the beginning as far as they chose, but if the book is used in conjunction with *Book 1*, the chart at the back of this *Teacher's Guide* should be referred to in order to provide a varied group of exercises appropriate to students' level. It must be remembered that most Proficiency courses are of long duration, and I have therefore endeavoured to grade the introduction of structural elements on a scale that ranges from the level of students soon after passing the Cambridge First Certificate examination up to that of the Proficiency examination itself. Throughout the student's book, exercises have a number of their own for easy reference but there is also a reference in square brackets to the corresponding unit of *Book 1*, where the structure referred to has first been emphasised in connection with a composition task. Teachers wishing to use remedial exercises as part of their re-presentation of structures for *Book 1* should refer to the notes on *Book 1* units earlier in this *Teacher's Guide*, where the cross-reference is given to remedial and other related exercises in *Book 3*.

Types of exercise. Purpose and forms of presentation

Paper 3 of the revised Proficiency examination consists of two sections; the first is made up of grammatical questions of four kinds – selective cloze, structural conversion, completion of sentences and rewriting of sentences, using a given word – while the second requires students to answer open-ended questions on a passage and also write a summary of all or part of it. In the following paragraphs, I have explained how each of these potential forms of question is handled in the book and also what I consider to be the most effective way of presenting the exercises in the classroom. Teachers will note straight away, however, that the sections do not correspond in order of presentation with the examination. In particular, the selective cloze section, which comes first in the examination paper, is last in this book before the test papers. As explained below, reordering of this kind is intentional, since I am concerned not to provide a series of test papers, imitating the examination, but to teach students all that they need to know in order to pass such tests according to the system that has worked best for me in the classroom over the past seven years in which I have been using the predecessor to this book. *Proficiency English Book 3*.

In making reference to that book, I should point out that I have retained some elements of it, in particular the majority of the passages for summary (Section 2) and the questions on them, but have considerably amplified the notes both for students and teachers; elsewhere almost all the material is new or completely reshaped – not because of changes in the examination, which has not in fact varied in standard or content apart from the transfer of Section C (guided composition) to the composition paper, but as a result of the extensive pretesting carried out.

Section 1: Structural revision

The first section of the book consists of structural revision exercises related to the content of parallel units in *Book 1*. As already stated, the notes for *Book 1* units in this *Teacher's Guide* indicate points at which the exercises could best be introduced as part of the re-presentation of structures, but it must be emphasised that there is no obligation to complete all the exercises.

Logically, there are far more exercises relating to the early units, which would normally be attempted by students soon after passing the First Certificate examination, and relatively few in the later stages. The index at the back of the student's book, however, can always be used for quick reference when a specific remedial exercise is required. It should also be noted that in some cases the remedial practice is most suitably handled in the form of a comparison between structures, and in these cases, therefore, an exercise in structural conversion from Section 3 would be the most appropriate; these exercises are also listed in the index, and reference is made to them in the notes for *Book 1* units where they are relevant.

The majority of the exercises consist of a number of examples, though there are some in continuous prose form. I strongly advocate one of two ways of going through them in the classroom. Once you have drawn attention to the examples at the head of an exercise and ensured by brief oral practice and further examples of your own that students understand the problem involved, you should either allot one example to each student or ask the class to work in pairs on all the examples. The first method, which is the quickest, means that students all have one minute to decide on the right answer, and time is not lost, which happens when students are picked at random to answer each question; in that way, too, they pay more attention to each others' answers. Pair work ensures that students do more examples, but at this level it is again important not to waste time by going through everyone's work in detail. Ask each pair to provide an answer and invite others to raise alternatives if they disagree.

The point I aim to establish here, above all, is that in advanced classes grammatical problems of this kind must be treated as difficulties for the class as a whole to analyse and solve and not in any way as tests of individual knowledge.

Section 2: Passages for comprehension and summary

I have placed this second because it is the most important section of all for students and demands the most work and also because the remaining sections have the intention of extending the students' awareness of usage and derive out of the first two, rather than having a justification in their own right. If teachers follow the order of presentation of sections, work will also be more varied and the purely grammatical sections will be separated from each other.

There are twelve passages for comprehension and summary. If used in conjunction with *Book 1*, they appear in connection with every third and fourth unit in the six sections of that book, and in many cases there is an overlap in terms of theme. The student's book contains advice on how to answer questions and how to attempt a summary, all of which is given together with the first set of questions on the first passage, 'A Space in the Country'. In the notes accompanying this section in the *Teacher's Guide*, I have provided specimen answers to all the questions and also given a list of points that I think should be included in a good summary, which taken together, make up a summary themselves within the number of words permitted in the examination. Needless to say, neither the answers nor the 'summaries' are definitive and teachers will frequently

find more satisfactory versions of their own, but at least they provide a point of reference for discussion.

The initial advice on the open-ended questions indicates to students the different types that are used. It also suggests that students should get used to answering in complete sentences even though Cambridge do not insist on it, simply making reference to 'coherent and relevant answers'. While it is not necessary for students to rewrite the questions in full in producing written answers, it seems to me that they should at least be capable of saying 'It means that. . .' or 'The phrase refers to. . .'. There is nothing in the Cambridge instructions that prevents students from quoting from the original passage in their answers, but if they do so, they should use quotation marks to indicate to the examiner that they have quoted deliberately and not chosen a phrase that seemed a good guess. On the other hand, the general standard of their English and the quality of summaries will be improved if they get used to rewording the original content in answers, using simpler terms, instead of hoping to find a phrase in the text which exactly meets their needs.

If possible, passages should be read before students come to class but in any case not very much help should be given, except to explain any cultural items of information. The level of English required for comprehension is not as high as for reading passages in *Book 2* of this course and in most cases the only phrases that would trouble students are precisely those they are asked to comment on in the questions. I have found that the most satisfactory way of dealing with questions in the classroom is to divide the class into four groups and give each twenty minutes to answer three or four questions, excluding the summary. For each passage, I have indicated in the notes the most convenient way of dividing up the questions among four groups, taking into account the complexity and probable length of the answers required. Groups should report back after twenty minutes, and you should, of course, be careful to point out inaccuracies in the form of the answers as well as in the content.

I have suggested that summaries should eventually be done as homework, following the classroom group work on the questions. Initially, however, students should study the explanation of techniques (given on pages 40–41 of the students' book, in connection with the passage 'A Space in the Country') and I suggest that the second summary should be done as group work in class to check that students can put these techniques into practice. It may be necessary to revert to this group work procedure with later summaries from time to time if students continue to find it hard to adapt to what may be a fresh skill, even in their own language.

In my view, there are two essential criteria for the correction of summaries. One is that the summary should be written clearly in good English and contain as many of the points that are relevant in a coherent form; the wrong way to attempt a summary is to string together a series of quotations from the text. For this reason, rewording of answers to the open-ended questions is an aid both to picking out relevant points and to expressing them clearly and simply. The second criterion is that the summary must be kept within the lengths prescribed. Excessive length derives mainly from an inability to recognise that details must in almost all cases be omitted, or replaced by short general statements. The examples given both in the student's book and the *Teacher's Guide* should help in this respect. I have deliberately avoided using structures and short-cuts in my own versions of the summaries that would only be available to a native speaker.

Section 3: Structural conversion

This section has always been included in the Proficiency examination and I have practised in the book over 90 per cent of the conversions employed in recent years; as stated above, some of these are used for purposes of general revision and are related to the exercises in Section 1. Consequently, for example, the revision of comparative forms in Exercise 2 of Section 1 is related to the first group of exercises (67) of Section 3 on alternative forms of making comparisons. In general, my approach would be to use revision exercises as part of the grammatical presentation of the unit in *Book 1*, and to turn to structural conversion exercises to confirm points a few days later. If structural conversion forms a useful basis for presentation, however, I have indicated this in the notes on the *Book 1* units in this *Teacher's Guide*.

Structural conversion exercises are best done in pairs, once the initial examples have been studied. Students should read the sentences to each other in the correctly converted form, taking it in turns, and only asking for help in cases where they disagree. It should then be possible, by asking pairs at random what they said for any given question, to make sure that the class as a whole has fully understood the point at issue. Exercises of this kind are necessary but can easily become boring in advanced classes if they take longer than about 15 minutes.

As an individual check on students' progress in this area, I have included five progress tests at intervals throughout the book. Each test contains 20 questions, and all the items are based on conversions that have previously been practised. In constructing the tests and determining the order of the exercises, I pretested all the items extensively, with over 500 students, at three different stages of preparation for the Proficiency examination. The notes on the tests in this *Guide* show

the results of this pretesting, and contain a discrimination analysis as an indication of the validity of the test. They also give a calculation of its difficulty as compared with Cambridge Proficiency, and a target pass mark for students to aim at. The target takes into account the fact that the students using this book will have done the preparatory exercises, unlike the groups who took part in the pretesting, and should consequently score more highly. In marking tests, it is important to discover which questions still cause problems so that the appropriate exercises can be referred to once again. In terms of general revision, it should be noted that the last four units of the book contain no new structural conversions; instead, each has a revision exercise of 10 separate items.

Section 4: Rephrasing

The third and fourth groups of questions in the examination paper ask students to complete sentences and to rewrite them, using a given word. Whereas it is possible to analyse and pretest all the kinds of structural conversion Cambridge have employed, there is virtually no limit to the range of items that could be used as a basis for these groups. The first, in general, demands a knowledge of verb forms, tenses and modals, etc., but it can include any other structure students may have encountered. The second, though it depends considerably on rephrasing either through employing a phrasal verb or an expression involving a noun and preposition instead of a verb (e.g. **have an effect on** instead of **affect**), can hardly be covered completely in a text book. What I have therefore tried to do is to provide a varied sequence of exercises, based on the content of previous examination papers and containing as much information as possible. The student's book also contains an appendix for general reference, which lists the most common expressions employing a verb, or a verb + noun, and a preposition. The kind of approach students should adopt to questions of this type is described on page 81 in the student's book. The types of exercise included are as follows:

Rephrasing

In the examination, students are asked to rewrite a sentence, using a given word and altering the structure accordingly. To prepare students for this type of exercise, I have begun by providing alternative sentences with the same meaning, so that the student can work out which words are missing in the second sentence and, at the same time, become aware of two ways of saying the same thing and the structural and other differences this may involve. From Unit 17 onwards, I have adopted the Cambridge format of supplying one word which must be included in the rephrased sentence.

Phrasal verbs

Each unit contains an exercise on phrasal verbs. As it is not possible to provide texts containing large numbers of phrasal verbs correctly used in a coherent manner, I have preferred to concentrate on one common verb at a time, so that the first exercise contains eight sentences in which the verb or phrase in italics must be replaced by a phrase using **turn** and the appropriate preposition. In this way, students learn the meaning of the phrasal verb in context and realise that it is an alternative to another way of saying the same thing.

Comparative verb structure

These exercises, which occur in a number of units, draw attention to a common form of rewording exercise in which a verb with a different structure must be used in place of the verb given (e.g. **succeeded in doing** must replace **managed to do**).

Other forms of exercise

In a few cases, I have included exercises relating common verbs to nouns (e.g. **make an attack on** as an alternative to **attack**). I have used the same technique here as with phrasal verbs, supplying a sentence with the same meaning, which must be rewritten as directed.

Sentence completion

This form of test item, which is normally placed third in the examination, is in some ways the most difficult for students, and a number of variations are often possible. I have not introduced these exercises until Unit 17, and have helped students by grouping the items into those involving a knowledge of tenses, those employing modals, etc. so that at least they know what sort of thing is missing.

As a general rule, this section of the book is probably the one of most interest to students because it provides them with a variety of new forms and lexical items. It is therefore best dealt with in class on the same lines as the structural revision work, assigning one question in advance to each student, or letting them work in pairs. At the same time, because examination items are less predictable here than elsewhere, it is the section that can most easily be missed out if you are short of time.

Section 5: Selective cloze

This forms the first part of Section A in the examination, but I have deliberately placed it last for two reasons. One is that it is the most convenient check on the students' general awareness of problems of usage, and so can be used as a kind of mini-progress test either in individual terms or for the class as a whole. The other is that as far as possible I have linked the cloze test for each unit to the themes of corresponding units in *Book 1*, or else, where there are passages for summary in the unit in *Book 3*, have based the test on part of the passage. To this extent, each of these tests becomes a test of recognition in terms of the way in which paragraphs are formed. Familiarity with the content of the passage has the advantage of overcoming the students' main problem with them in examinations, where they are frequently confused by the content in itself; at the same time, the original passage is not reproduced word for word, so it would be impossible to score highly from memory alone.

I have begun with two exercises aimed at showing students how to approach cloze tests. What is, of course, essential is that they should read through the text, at least twice, to understand the gist of it, before they attempt to fill the gaps, and then they must also decide what sort of word is likely to fill a gap. Subsequent exercises can be done either as tests, allowing 20 minutes for completion, or as pair work or in groups of three. To avoid spending too long over them, it is advisable to give each group a section of the text to concentrate on, containing about five blanks, but to ask them to record sources of disagreement. The most valuable information to be gained from tests of this kind is to learn what misconceptions about usage still exist in the students' minds. Each unit ends with a cloze test, which includes several gaps where the item being tested has recently been learnt.

Section 6: Test papers

There are three test papers following the Cambridge format to be attempted just before the Proficiency examination. All of them have been pretested, and are devised to be as close as possible to Cambridge standards of difficulty, with maximum discrimination. Two hours should be allowed for the tests as a whole, though they can be conveniently split into three sections to fit in with class times, if necessary. If so, 45 minutes should be allowed for Section A, 30 minutes for the questions on the passage in Section B, and 45 minutes for the summary. In the examination itself, I would advise students to attempt as many questions from Section A as possible within 40 minutes, and then to turn to Section B, attempting to complete it within an hour or so, in order to spend the last 15 minutes checking through their work and completing any items from Section A they have not done. It is above all important to leave sufficient time for reading the passage and planning and writing the summary. Full instructions for marking and assessing the tests are given in the notes on the test papers.

133

Section 1: Structural revision

| 1 She had a **bright green** dress on.
2 A **pretty little** girl opened the door.
3 She lives in a **lovely, old country** house.
4 He seems an **intelligent young** man.
5 Have you done the **first four** questions yet?
6 A **great big black** dog stood watching us.
7 For his birthday, I bought him a **lovely Indian** chess set, with **carved ivory** chessmen.
8 His portrait didn't flatter him. The artist gave him a **long lined** face and **thick red** lips.
9 He's bought a **new yellow German sports** car.
10 The game is played with a set of **three round grooved metal** balls and a **little wooden** ball you have to aim at.

2 A 1 the most embarrassing
2 an older
3 quicker
4 more intelligent
5 oldest
6 redder
7 redder
8 worst
9 more embarrassed
10 slightest
11 more quick-thinking
12 better mannered
13 the most absent-minded
14 older
15 more
16 easier

B 1 busiest, more patient
2 heavier, more thickset, curlier, more pleasant
3 friendlier, more relaxed
4 more grateful, more willing
5 most stupid/stupidest, narrowest, angrier, more awkward, more careful

C 1 bigger, harder
2 fatter, more liable
3 more, cleaner
4 longer, sleepier
5 older, more irritable, less, worse
6 A longer, more impatient, more
B more, less likely

D There are a variety of possible answers.

3 A 1 Jack works in Christie's Cement Factory, **which** belongs to his father-in-law.
2 He married Jane Christie, **who** used to live next door to us.
3 It came as quite a shock to Jack to meet old Mr Christie, **whom** he had never spoken to before. (. . . to **whom** he had never spoken . . .)

4 To encourage the young people, Mr Christie gave them the house opposite, **which** he had built himself.
5 On the whole, this was an advantage to Jack, **whose** parents were opposed to the wedding.
6 The young couple get on quite well with Mr Christie, **whose** money they borrow whenever it suits them.

B 1 The girl you were speaking to is my cousin Mary.
My cousin Mary, **who** you were speaking to just now, has a great admiration for your work.
2 This house, **which** was built over a hundred years ago, is still occupied by the same family.
The house my grandfather built over a hundred years ago is still standing.
3 His faithful comrade, Frank Martin, with **whom** he had been associated all his life, eventually succeeded him as leader of the party.
His faithful comrade, Frank Martin, the man he had been most closely associated with all his life, eventually succeeded him as leader of the party.
4 Sally is the girl **whose** horse I was telling you about.
Sally, **whose** horse won the race last Saturday, is thinking of entering for the Derby.

C 1 His daughter applied to enter the university **where** he had studied.
His daughter applied to enter the University of Cambridge, **where** he had studied himself.
2 **When** I met her, she was an artist.
At that time, **when** I first met her, she was an artist.
3 I expect employees to give me a reason **why** they are late.
I was late because of the bus strike, **which** made it necessary for me to come by underground.
4 The town **where** I grew up has changed in recent years.
Farley, **where** I grew up, has changed in recent years.

5 In 1957, **when** my brother was **born,** I was still living there.
I was still living there **when** my brother was born.

D Dear Sir,
My father, who works in an office in London, says the country is going to the dogs. I think he means that there are too many places like the greyhound stadium that is near our house, where my Uncle Bert goes every Wednesday. My mother, who is a teacher, says 'going to the dogs' is just an expression, which means that it is a phrase people use when they cannot think of the precise words. She says my father means there are too many people in the country like my Uncle Bert, who doesn't go to work. My sister Jenny, who reads your column every day, says you are the sort of person that can solve my problem, because she has read letters from people whose questions you answered. Do you think my father means there are too many people who go to greyhound races, or there are too many people who don't work? My Uncle Bert fits into both categories.

Bath owes its name to the fact that it grew up around the Roman baths, (1) **which** were among the largest in the Roman Empire. The city, (2) **which** now has a population over 80,000 people, still has centres (3) **that/which** treat people with rheumatic diseases with the mineral waters (4) **that/which** first attracted the Romans to the spot.
The main attraction of Bath today, however, is its architecture, much of (5) **which** dates from the eighteenth century, (6) **when** it became a fashionable centre for aristocratic visitors, (7) **whose** overeating and drinking caused them to suffer from gout. John Wood the Elder designed the Circus, (8) **which** was begun in 1754, and John Wood the Younger was responsible for Royal Crescent, (9) **which** faces a sloping lawn (10) **that/which** runs down towards a park. The Pump Room, (11) **which** is mentioned in the novels of Jane Austen, (12) **who** lived in Bath at the beginning of the nineteenth century, is also worth a visit.
At the time (13) **when** Jane Austen lived there, the Assembly Rooms, (14) **which** now house one of the finest costume museums in the world, were the place (15) **where** people met for dances, as their name suggests. The feature (16) **that/which** makes them particularly attractive today is that sections of streets have been recreated with life-size figures, all of (17) **which** are dressed in the costume of the period.
The main sporting attraction of Bath is its

rugby team, (18) **which** is among the best in the country, but there are also two golf courses nearby, both of (19) **which** are open to the public, and there are plenty of courts in the parks, (20) **where** visitors can play tennis. Those (21) **who** are interested in football should go to Bristol, (22) **which** is only a short drive away, (23) **where** there are two professional teams.
Bath is one of the most beautiful places (24) I have visited in England and is certainly a city (25) **where** visitors from abroad are always welcome.

4 1 a) non-defining
    b) coordinate
  2 a) coordinate
    b) non-defining
  3 a) non-defining
    b) coordinate
  4 a) non-defining
    b) coordinate
  5 a) non-defining
    b) coordinate

5 (1) live
  (2) get up
  (3) is not working
  (4) comes
  (5) think
  (6) choose/want
  (7) finds
  (8) is working
  (9) goes/travels
  (10) go
  (11) rent
  (12) is
  (13) remember
  (14) know
  (15) does not like
  (16) is singing/is performing
  (17) wants
  (18) asks
  (19) refuse
  (20) does not mean
  (21) am
  (22) feel
  (23) Don't you think
  (24) do you think
  (25) is just doing

6 (1) lived,
    ... had several ...
  (2) got up,
    ... was a pop-singer ...
  (3) was not working
  (4) came
  (5) thought
  (6) chose/wanted
  (7) found
  (8) was working
  (9) went, travelled
  (10) went
  (11) rented
  (12) was
  (13) remembered, had been
  (14) knew
  (15) didn't like,
    ... they were always ...
  (16) was singing/was performing
  (17) wanted
  (18) asked
  (19) refused
  (20) did not mean
  (21) was
  (22) felt
    ... I was happy ...
  (23) Don't you think
    ... I made ...
  (24) Do you think
  (25) just did

7 (1) looked
  (2) had already finished
  (3) noticed
  (8) had been going
  (9) had been reading
  (10) had not got

(4) had just left   (11) said
(5) had been   (12) had had
(6) had not noticed   (13) had been/
(7) met   happened

8 1 **It is clear** that he didn't work very hard.
2 **It is difficult for me to understand** why he took the job.
3 **It is dangerous for them to work** in such conditions.
4 **It is likely** that the factory will be closed soon.
5 **It is expensive for him to travel** to work by train.
6 **It is lucky** you didn't take the job they offered you.
7 **It is easy for them to criticise**. . .But **it is curious** they didn't say anything at the outset.
8 **It is true** we haven't had a very successful year so far, although **it is not necessary for us** to worry about it.

9 1 like
2 as
3 as, like
4 as, like
5 as, as

10 (1) have always thought   (11) arrived
(2) have met   (12) did
(3) have come   (13) did not seem
(4) spent   (14) have been getting
(5) was   (15) said
(6) has changed   (16) have been riding
(7) have never forgotten (17) have never lived
(8) was   (18) have always had
(9) fell   (19) said
(10) was   (20) have never had

11 Some of the adverbs in this exercise are not adverbs of frequency and are therefore *not* necessarily bound by the same rules.
1 When I worked in London, the trains were not **always** late. They **occasionally** arrived on time. What I can **never** forget is the voice that **always** greeted us when we arrived at Victoria. I think it was a record that was **always** put on in the mornings of a woman who **always** sounded bored: 'We are sorry your train is late. This is due to circumstances beyond our control.' They may **sometimes** have changed the record as the excuses were **occasionally** different, and it has **sometimes** occurred to me that the woman's voice may **actually** have been real.
2 If I had not **just** seen it with my own eyes, I would **never** have believed it.
3 He would **never** have been convinced, although he has **frequently** been told about it, if you had not taken him to see it for himself.
4 How could you **ever** have imagined it?

5 He must **often** have wondered if he would **ever** have been given the job if the boss had not been an old friend of the family.

12 1 **Such** famous country houses **as** Chatsworth, Blenheim Palace and Castle Howard were built in the eighteenth century.
A number of famous country houses, **such as** Chatsworth, Blenheim Palace and Castle Howard, were built in the eighteenth century.
2 Castle Howard was used for the television series, 'Brideshead Revisited', in which **such** famous actors **as** Jeremy Irons, Laurence Olivier and John Gielgud took part.
. . . in which famous actors, **such as** Jeremy Irons, Laurence Olivier and John Gielgud, took part.
3 The last two stars . . . with other well-known actors, **such as** Richard Burton, Vanessa Redgrave and Ralph Richardson.
. . . with **such** well-known actors **as** Richard Burton, Vanessa Redgrave and Ralph Richardson.
4 A lot of great composers, **such as** Mozart, Beethoven and Chopin, led interesting lives.

13 1 Someone once defined fox-hunting as the unspeakable in pursuit of the uneatable.
2 King Edward VII was known as 'the Peacemaker'.
3 I regard his last book as the best of his novels.
4 The blurb describes it as tragic, but I would class it as black comedy.
5 He treats his staff as equals, unlike his predecessor, who treated them like slaves. Of course, his predecessor never accepted anyone as his equal.

14 A 1 I could ride a bicycle when I was eight years old.
2 Could you swim when you were a child?
3 He could speak several languages at the age of ten.
4 He could run 100m in 10 seconds at his peak.
5 Could you beat your father at tennis when you were at school?
B 1 I'll be able to ride a bicycle. . .
2 Will you be able to swim. . .?
3 He'll be able to speak several languages. . .
4 He'll be able to run 100m in 10 seconds. . .
5 Will you be able to beat your father at tennis. . .?
6 No, I've never been able to afford it.
7 No, I've never been able to face the idea.
8 No, I've never been able to find the time.
9 No, I've never been able to understand it.
10 No, I've never been able to sing in tune.

C 1 ...I finally succeeded in getting a ticket.
...I was finally able to get a ticket.

2 ...they eventually managed to persuade the workers to return to work.
...they eventually succeeded in persuading the workers to return to work.

3 ...but he was eventually able to swim to the shore.
...but he eventually managed to swim to the shore.

4 ...we finally managed to find out what had happened to the parcels.
...we finally succeeded in finding out what had happened to the parcels.

5 ...he was eventually able to find a cure.
...he eventually succeeded in finding a cure.

D 1 (1) may   (3) may/might
    (2) can   (4) might

  2 (1) may   (4) may
    (2) might   (5) might
    (3) can

E Here are some possibilities:
Harry **may have** phoned while I was out.
He **might have** had an accident.
He **can't have** had so much extra work.

15 1 had better
    2 ought to/should
    3 had better
    4 ought to/should
    5 had better not
    6 shouldn't/ought not to
    7 shouldn't/ought not to
    8 had better not

16 A 1 a It's for playing badminton.
        b To play badminton with.
        c Because I'm going to play badminton.
     2 a It's for taking pictures underwater.
        b To take underwater pictures with.
        c Because I'm going to take some pictures.
     3 a It's for doing statistical calculations.
        b To do statistical calculations with.
        c Because I'm going to do some calculations.

  B 1 He came in quietly **so as not to/in order not to** wake his wife.
    2 They bought some champagne **to/so as to/in order to** celebrate the end of the course.
    3 **In order to/So as to/To** explain the situation to the public, the Government put a special programme on television.
    4 He booked a ticket for the performance **to/in order to/so as to** be sure of getting in.
    5 He booked a ticket for the performance **in**

order not to/so as not to have to stand in a queue.

6 **So as not to/In order not to** stand in a queue, he booked a ticket for the performance.

7 **So as to/In order to/To** make sure of a seat at the performance, you are advised to book in advance.

8 **So as not to/In order not to** bore you, I'll make this the last sentence in the exercise.

C 1 He sent them to university **to** give them a good education.

2 He sent them to university **so that/in order that** they would get a good education.

3 He sent them to the university **in order that/so that** they could put their names down for the entrance examination.

4 I've left her a note **to** tell her where to meet us.

5 I've left her a note **in order that/so that** she knows where to meet us.

6 He's sold his house **to** pay his brother's debts.

7 He's sold his house **so that/in order that** his brother can pay his debts.

8 He's given his brother some money **so that/in order that** he can pay his debts.

9 He's employed a nurse **so that/in order that** his mother is/will be looked after.

10 He's employed a nurse **to** look after his mother.

17 (1) must have started   (8) must have changed
   (2) had to admit
   (3) had to do   (9) had to do
   (4) must have enjoyed   (10) had to work
   (5) must have been   (11) must have made
   (6) had to climb   (12) must have regarded
   (7) had to think

18 1 The Headmaster is angry, **it seems**.
     The Headmaster **seems** angry.
   2 You're a stranger here, **it appears**.
     You **appear** to be a stranger here.
   3 They **appear** to have been waiting a long time.
     It appears that they've been waiting for a long time.
   4 **It turned out** that they hadn't made any preparations for our visit.
     They turned out not to have made any preparations for our visit.
   5 **He seems** not to care whether he upsets people or not.
     He doesn't care whether he upsets people or not, **it seems**.
   6 **It appears** that you don't know who I am.

You don't know who I am, **it appears**.

7   **It appears** they haven't played this game before.

    They appear not to have played this game before.

8   **They turned out** not to have been told we were coming.

    They hadn't been told we were coming, **it turned out**.

19 1 enjoyed myself
    2 be ashamed of yourself
    3 introduce myself
    4 feeling sorry for himself
    5 weighs herself
    6 kill himself, drown himself, shoot himself
    7 blame yourself
    8 consider ourselves

20 1 a) had to get up   4 a) had to drive
       b) should have got up   b) should have driven
    2 a) had to renew
       b) should have renewed   5 a) had to sell
                    b) should have sold
    3 a) should have got
       b) had to get

21   1 She said she hadn't seen them since the previous year.
     2 He said he wasn't going to do that till the following week.
     3 She said she hadn't expected to see me there.
     4 He said he couldn't deal with that until the day after.
     5 She said the Browns might know where it was.
     6 He said he would have to go to the doctor's the following week.
     7 They said that by the time they got there, the train would have left.
     8 She said that if I had seen him the previous night at 10 o'clock, he couldn't have gone very far.
     9 He said that when I had spoken to them the day before, they might not have understood how important the problem was.
    10 She said I should have told her where she could find it. In that case, she would not have spent hours looking for it.

22 A (1) some   (5) one
        (2) it   (6) ones
        (3) it   (7) one
        (4) some
   B (1) one   (9) That
        (2) These   (10) one
        (3) this   (11) those
        (4) one   (12) those
        (5) That   (13) that

        (6) one   (14) one
        (7) these   (15) one
        (8) ones
   C (1) one   (6) ones
        (2) ones   (7) ours
        (3) ones   (8) yours
        (4) one   (9) ones
        (5) yours   (10) yours

23 A 1 It's the time you spend in airports that annoys me.
           What annoys me is the time you spend in airports.
       2 The thing that upsets me is the rudeness of the employees.
         It's the rudeness of the employees that upsets me.
       3 What gets me down is the inefficiency of the service.
         The thing that gets me down is the inefficiency of the service.
       4 What I really can't stand is the so-called shuttle service.
         It's the so-called shuttle service that I really can't stand.
       5 What annoyed me most was the smile on his face.
         It was the smile on his face that annoyed me most.
       6 What causes the trouble is the fact that nearly all the planes leave from Madrid.
         The thing that causes the trouble is the fact that nearly all the planes leave from Madrid.
   B 1 It's in New York that the real action takes place.
         The place where the real action takes place is New York.
       2 The place where he made his name was London.
         It was in London that he made his name.
       3 It's in Ireland that they breed the best racehorses.
         The place where they breed the best racehorses is Ireland.
       4 It was only in his native village that he was truly content.
         The only place where he was truly content was in his native village.
       5 The place where it becomes a great river is at Khartoum.
         It is in Khartoum that it becomes a great river.
   C 1 It's in autumn that we have to be on the watch.
       2 It's in August that most of them come.

3 It was in middle age that he wrote them.
4 It was on 14th July, 1789 that the storming of the Bastille took place.
5 It is on July 4th that they celebrate Independence Day.

24 1 He sounds **as if/as though** he knows what he's talking about.
2 He speaks **as if/as though** he had a plum in his mouth.
3 The tourist asked me if I came from London, England, **as if/as though** I did not know where London was.
4 It looks **as if/as though** he is tired of arguing with the rest of the managers.
5 You talk **as if/as though** you were the boss.
6 He looks so pleased with himself **as if/as though** he had said something clever instead of confusing the issue.
7 Of course we have. You talk **as if/as though** we lived in the jungle.
8 At her wedding yesterday, the actress remarked, 'This is the love of my life,' **as if/as though** she had not been married six times before.

25 1 If you happen to come across. . .
2 If we had been consulted. . .
3 If they try to prevent you. . .
4 If they protested. . .
5 If I told you. . .
6 If he speaks to you. . .
7 If the Headmaster heard about it. . .
8 If they had given us. . .
9 If you receive. . .
10 If I had been brought up. . .

26 1 He travels to London by train every day.
2 He listened carefully outside the door for a few moments.
3 I'll read the report in detail in my office after lunch.
4 They're coming to the office for a meeting tomorrow.
5 They're planning to get married quietly next week at St Mary's Church.
6 Ten minutes before the service was due to begin, the bride arrived at the church in a Rolls Royce.
7 We'll decide the matter democratically at the meeting next week.
8 As soon as the officers came in sight, the guard stood smartly to attention.
9 All through the night they celebrated their victory joyfully in the streets.
10 For the first time since he had got married, he ate his lunch alone in the kitchen.

27 B 1 smoking
2 to smoke
3 learning
4 to learn
5 walking/to walk
6 working
7 interrupting
8 to work
9 playing
10 to get up
11 to play
12 to hit, to try
13 riding
14 ride
15 to tell
16 telling
17 seeing
18 to give, to tell, to speak
19 talking
20 to talk
21 to give up, smoking, to give up
22 to see, go, saying, worrying

28 1 resign myself to
2 given to
3 am opposed to
4 dedicated to
5 amounts to
6 object to
7 looking forward to
8 came near to

29 1 You can't imagine what a wonderful time we had.
2 You'll never guess what a beautiful present he's given me.
3 It's incredible how much income tax I have to pay.
4 You can imagine how pleased I was.
5 I can't begin to tell you what a boring party it was.
6 He soon realised how inefficient the whole organisation was.
7 It's unbelievable how greedy some people are.
8 It's remarkable how little the holiday cost us.

30 1 To get her hair cut. She's having her hair cut.
2 To get his eyes tested. He's having his eyes tested.
3 To have a suit made. He's having a suit made.
4 To get her shoes repaired. She's having her shoes repaired.
5 To have a tooth out. He's having a tooth out.
6 To have the house decorated. She's having the house decorated.
7 To get some photocopying done. She's having some photocopying done.
8 To have his photograph taken. He's having his photograph taken.

31 Lie detectors are widely used in the United States to find out whether a person (1) is telling the truth or not. Polygraphers, the people who operate them, (2) claim that they can establish guilt by detecting physiological changes that accompany emotional stress. Whether they will ever be adopted in Britain (3) is a matter of opinion. Most people, if they were given the chance to solve crimes simply by this method, (4) would probably think it was

valuable, but recent research not only raises doubts about how lie detectors (5) should be used but also asks whether **they** (6) should be used at all. The reason, it seems, (7) is that the tests, apart from many of the polygraphers being unqualified, (8) are themselves capable of making mistakes. Perfectly innocent people, with nothing to be afraid of, (9) often blush when a customs officer asks them questions. Fear, which produces a heightened electrical response on the lie detector, (10) does not always establish guilt. It depends on whether the subject (11) is afraid of being found out or (12) is afraid of being wrongfully convicted. But a person whose past experience (13) has prepared him for such tests (14) can confuse the lie detector by reacting violently to neutral questions. So the lie detector, although it may prove some people guilty, (15) will not always catch the criminal and (16) may place innocent people under suspicion. It seems surprising that a much more effective way of using lie detectors, which (17) has been suggested by an American psychologist, (18) has not been put into practice more often. The method (19) consists in asking the subject to read aloud certain statements about the crime when **he** (20) is connected to the lie detector. Anyone who is unaware of the true facts (21) would make no distinction between saying 'the thieves used a red car' and 'the thieves used a blue car'. But a person who was involved in the crime, although he tried to disguise his reaction, (22) might give himself away. That an innocent person could be convicted because of the evidence of a machine (23) is the most serious accusation that can be made against lie detectors and this possibility, if the psychologist's method were used, (24) would be avoided.

32
1 used to play
2 was used to giving
3 used to live
4 would (often) visit
5 would remark, were used to breathing, would look
6 used to work
7 was used to, used to work
8 used to say, would make, used to get

33
1 Last week, I went to Amsterdam, (1) **where** there is a superb collection of pictures by Van Gogh. The museum (2) **where** the pictures are housed has a lot of interesting information about the houses (3) **where** he lived, the area (4) **where** he worked as a kind of worker priest, and the South of France, (5) **where** he died.
2 He found it difficult to find a publisher for his first novel, (6) **which** he was very proud **of**.

The company (7) **where** he sent it asked to see him, however. They wanted to know if the places (8) he had written **about**, and in particular his native village, (9) **where** most of his novel took place, were the only topics (10) he could deal **with**. 'The point is,' said the publisher, 'that this company, (11) **which** I am the manager **of**, is interested in the American market, (12) **where** books with an English background are not so popular.'

34
1 will have been married
2 will be waiting
3 have finished
4 will have drunk
5 has done
6 will have forgotten

35
1 someone, whoever
2 Anyone, someone
3 some, whatever, any
4 Anyone, someone, whoever
5 any, anything, some
6 any, whoever, some, Any, some, Whoever, whatever

36 A
1 Harold insisted that they should stay until they had seen the photographs.
2 Paula suggested that they should see them the next time they came.
3 The shop steward demanded that the workers should get a pay rise of 12%/The shop steward demanded a pay rise of 12% for the workers.
4 The chairman suggested that they should take the matter to arbitration/The chairman suggested taking the matter to arbitration.
5 The accountant proposed that everyone should keep calm.

B
1 Alice asked her mother to let her stay up and watch the horror film.
2 The official authorised him to leave the country.
3 The manager urged the players to keep trying.
4 The old soldier commanded his comrades not to shoot until they could see the whites of their eyes.
5 The clerk required me to sign it in triplicate.
6 The colonel ordered the jailers to treat the prisoners well.

37 A
1 Is it really necessary for him to work so hard?
2 Does he really need to spend so much money?
3 Is it really necessary for you to take so many clothes with you?
4 It isn't necessary for them to pay immediately.
5 We don't need to book in advance.
6 It isn't necessary for you to come if you

don't want to.

B 1 You needn't have paid so much for the house.

2 In the end, I didn't need to ring him because he called to see me.

3 You needn't have brought so much bread.

4 It was a good thing I didn't need to go shopping.

5 They had already arranged to spend the night at a friend's house, so we didn't need to put them up.

6 The food wasn't very good, but he needn't have made such a fuss about it.

38 A 1 quite, rather 5 quite
2 quite, rather 6 rather
3 quite 7 quite, rather
4 rather 8 rather, rather, quite
B 1 fairly 5 rather
2 rather 6 Quite
3 fairly 7 rather
4 rather
C 1 quite, rather 4 quite, rather, rather
2 quite, rather 5 quite, rather, rather
3 rather, rather
D 1 quite 5 fairly, quite
2 fairly 6 fairly, quite
3 quite 7 quite, fairly
4 fairly, quite 8 fairly, quite

39 1 especially
2 especially
3 specially, specially, especially
4 especially, specially, especially
5 specially, especially

40 C
(1) –	(19) the	(37) –
(2) the	(20) –	(38) –
(3) the	(21) the	(39) the
(4) –	(22) –	(40) the
(5) the	(23) the	(41) the
(6) –	(24) the	(42) the
(7) –	(25) –	(43) –
(8) the	(26) the	(44) the
(9) –	(27) the	(45) –
(10) –	(28) the	(46) –
(11) –	(29) the	(47) –

(12) –	(30) the	(48) –
(13) The	(31) the	(49) the
(14) –	(32) the	(50) the
(15) the	(33) –	(51) the
(16) the	(34) the	(52) –
(17) The	(35) –	(53) –
(18) –	(36) the	

41 1 a Only the person who wears the shoe knows if it fits him.
   b Only by wearing a shoe do you know if it fits you.
2 a Only his closest friends knew what had happened.
   b Only by asking his closest friends did he discover what had happened.
3 a Only when Sarah grew up did she realise how important the meeting had been.
   b Only Sarah understood how important the meeting had been.
4 a Only a first-class writer could have written this novel.
   b Only as the novel develops do we discover what its real meaning is.
5 a Only northerners speak like that.
   b Only in the north do people speak like that.

42 1 No sooner had I received your telegram than I contacted the agency.
   As soon as I received your telegram, I contacted the agency.
2 I had no sooner completed one book than I had to begin another.
   As soon as I (had) completed one book, I had to begin another.
3 No sooner had the money been paid than the prisoner was released.
   The money had no sooner been paid than the prisoner was released.
4 No sooner had I arrived at the beach than it started to rain.
   As soon as I (had) arrived at the beach it started to rain.
5 They had no sooner sold the house than they were offered a better price for it.
   As soon as they (had) sold the house, they were offered a better price for it.

Section 2: Passages for comprehension and summary

A Space in the Country

There is an explanation in this unit of the student's book both of the kinds of question set for comprehension and the most suitable ways of approaching them and also of the summary, where the techniques advocated are demonstrated in depth. I provide suggested answers to the questions here and in the following units; in subsequent units, I list the points that should be included in a satisfactory summary.

When the passage has been read in class and any points of vocabulary (other than those included in the questions) cleared up, it is a good idea to go through the instructions given in the student's book and invite the class to provide answers. Subsequently, I recommend that questions are best answered as group work (see Introduction to *Book 2*, page 76).

In the same way, it is advisable to talk students through the stages suggested in writing a summary. The second summary, Cost and Compassion, page 42, ought to be done in class in groups of three to ensure that students put into practice the techniques they have been shown. I recommend that subsequent summaries should be done at home individually, but the advice given in the student's book should always be used for reference.

43
Suggested answers:

1 'A green revolution' means a change taking place in the countryside because country parks have been established.
2 This phrase means that the emphasis in country parks is on providing facilities for people to enjoy themselves rather than on preserving the countryside.
3 'In the pipeline' means 'being planned'.
4 It is likely because they may disturb the countryman's work or cause him more work by lighting fires, leaving litter, etc.
5 'It' refers to 'A good country park'.
6 You should check whether the park is open or not.
7 'Setting out' means 'starting out on a journey'.
8 'Bygone' means 'former'. At one time the park belonged to an ancestral estate.
9 There is no truly typical country park because country parks have been created in many different places with different surroundings.
10 'Their' refers to 'country parks'.
11 The Countryside Commission have helped the scheme with money (to reclaim sites such as mineral workings and transform them into parks).
12 This was necessary because in many cases the sites would have been unsuitable and dangerous for visitors.
13 This phrase means that the prospects for country parks are favourable.
14 The evidence is that a large number of people visit the parks (so there is justification for planning more of them).
15 It means that country parks have proved popular and are therefore unlikely to disappear in the future.

44
This exercise is fully worked out in the student's book.

Cost and Compassion

As suggested above, the most satisfactory way of handling the questions here is to divide the class into groups; a fair variety of questions for each group will be obtained with four groups answering questions 1–4, 5–8, 9–12 and 13–15 respectively.

45
Suggested answers:

1 The Government is proposing to offer disabled people either an allowance for travelling expenses every week or some form of modified four-wheel car. This is because the three-wheeled vehicles previously provided have proved dangerous.
2 The significance of the use of 'already' is that people who already suffered from some physical handicap were further handicapped by being given dangerous vehicles.
3 The 'list' referred to can be closed because it was a list of deaths and injuries caused to people driving three-wheeled vehicles, and these will no longer be issued.
4 'They' refers to 'The arguments. . .more

independent lives'. (The whole phrase should be supplied.)

5   'Admit' means 'accept, agree that it has'.

6   'Pending' means that the claims for compensation have not yet been paid, or dealt with.

7   'This latter decision' refers to (c), the decision withdrawing the right of the disabled to a tricycle. (Note that, strictly speaking, the author should have written 'This last decision', referring to the last of three, not the second of two.)

8   Various governments have changed their minds because they did not know how to solve the problem, (so they first pretended it did not exist, then admitted it existed but there was no alternative, and finally decided to withdraw the vehicles).

9   'Adequate funds' means 'enough money for the purpose'.

10   'This' refers to the fact that 'the low number of drivers. . .benefits of mass production'.

11   The connection is that there are few disabled people, and so it would not be economical to make a car specially for them by mass-production methods. The writer thinks a mass-produced car could be made for the general market which would have some optional variations so that it could be adapted for disabled people.

12   'Along these lines' means 'of this kind', 'designed in this way'.

13   Designers could make ordinary cars suitable for disabled people if they incorporated certain variations, such as doors hinged at the bottom and variomatic drive. This would make it easier for a disabled driver to get in and out of the car, and would mean that the driver would not have to change gear.

14   'A weekly grant' means money paid by the authorities every week (as a travel allowance).

15   The writer calls it this because it will cost the government a lot of money, yet will not be enough to cover the expenses of handicapped people, and will not satisfy them (because they will not be able to travel freely from their own homes, as they could with their own vehicles).

46

The points that should be made in the summary are as follows. As previously indicated, it is advisable for groups of three to work on this summary together and to check that they are following the procedures suggested in association with the previous one.

1   The Government has withdrawn the right of disabled people to three-wheeled cars because they proved dangerous.

2   It must now decide whether to give these people a weekly travel allowance or provide a four-wheeled vehicle suitable for them.

3   The writer thinks that a travel allowance would be a bad solution because it will cost too much but not meet the needs of handicapped people.

4   The objection to a four-wheeled car is that it could not be mass-produced, but he argues that a conventional car with certain modifications could be adapted for disabled drivers, and so would not be too expensive. (100 words)

Paragraph 2 is not relevant to the question, and paragraphs 3 and 4 are only valuable for background information.

How Safe are British Dams?

47

The most convenient allocation of questions for group work is 1–4, 5–7, 8–11 and 12–15, using four groups. Suggested answers:

1   'Which' refers to 'the American Teton dam failure'.

2   The connection between the events and the Reservoir Act is that disasters abroad caused by dam failures occurred at a time when the Act had not yet been put into effect and there were doubts about the safety of British dams.

3   The phrase means 'an accident that is so unlikely to occur that its occurrence would be hardly believable'.

4   The factor of uncertainty is the frequency of floods of a certain power; it is not as important as it seems because although such a flood may not happen again for thousands of years, it could still happen immediately after the dam was built.

5   The 'event' referred to is the collapse of a dam.

6   British dams are older than those in other countries and in many cases there are no records of the construction or subsequent behaviour.

7   A dam is most likely to collapse soon after it is built, or after a long period of uneventful operation.

8   'The stage' referred to is the stage when British dams have been in operation for a long time without failures.

9   'The trend' is the increasing number of incidents that may lead to a major collapse.

10   'Which' refers to 'the relatively good safety record of British dams'.

11   The main reasons are 'sound engineering practice and administration', 'luck' and 'an equable climate'.

12   'An equable climate' is one that does not show strong or sudden changes.

143

13 The law has been inadequate because people have rarely been prosecuted for failing to rectify a defective dam, and even when they have, the penalties have been light.

14 'Penalties' means the fines paid by those who have failed to rectify a defective dam.

15 The division of responsibilities is not satisfactory because it places enforcement of the law in the hands of so many different local authorities that standards of safety could vary widely.

48
Points to be raised in the summary should be as follows:

1 The writer is concerned about British dams because most of them are old and some are below present standards of safety, so the risk of a dam failure is increased.

2 Dams tend to fail either soon after construction or after a long period of operation, the stage British dams have reached.

3 The Reservoirs Act will provide legislation to remedy defective dams and ensure that dams are inspected, which has not previously been done properly.

4 The defect of the Act is that it places the responsibility in the hands of local authorities, and the safety standard could vary, causing a disaster. (100 words).

The Sun Sinks Slowly on the Western

The most convenient allocation of questions for group work is 1–4, 5–8, 9–11, 12–15, using four groups.

49
Suggested answers:

1 'Its' refers to 'Hollywood'.

2 Television networks followed Hollywood's lead by thinking that westerns were a certain means of success, (and so they made their own series, bought old Hollywood films, etc.).

3 The writers thinks westerns are like a house slipper because they are something the public has grown used to and feels comfortable with (because people know what to expect, etc.).

4 'Those few' refers to westerns made in the 1970s.

5 'Debunk' means to criticise and make fun of (the myths by showing them as less serious and important than they were believed to be).

6 Recent westerns are not as successful as *High Noon* or *The Wild Bunch* because they lack 'a clear vision of an alternative version of the west'.

7 'One' refers to 'an alternative version of the west'.

8 'The nadir' means 'the lowest point' (of popularity).

9 The laws about horses prevent film companies from ill-treating them, and this makes western films more expensive to make.

10 It implies a conspiracy theory because it suggests that investors and producers join together to decide whether audiences should see western films or not, so the audiences are at their mercy.

11 'Ideological productions' means that films fit the ideology of the public, and so they will be popular when they reflect the way the public thinks.

12 'The crucial variable' is the vital factor varying from one film to another.

13 'A passive receptacle' is something – here, the audience – that accepts whatever is put into it without protest.

14 'It' refers to 'the audience'.

15 The writer thinks that audiences influence film makers by showing that they prefer films with an ideology that reflects their social experience; as this experience changes, some kinds of film become more or less popular, and film makers, in order to make money, try to follow the popular trend.

50
The points that should be made in the summary are as follows.

1 For a long time both Hollywood and the television networks relied on the western as a genre that was always popular.

2 The films and television series repeated familiar characters and types and the public accepted this and liked it because they were used to it.

3 During the 1970s, however, westerns suffered a decline in quality and popularity. Fewer films were made and television westerns were replaced by detective series.

4 A number of explanations have been given for this decline, but the author thinks the real reason is that the western no longer reflected the social experiences of the audience. (99 words).

Chemical Threat to Lake Nakuru

The most convenient allocation of questions for group work is 1–4, 5–7, 8–11, 12–15, using four groups.

51
Suggested answers:

1 They are urging it because Copal's activities are almost certain to destroy the wildlife of Lake Nakuru.

2 'Its' refers to 'Lake Nakuru'.

3 'This' refers to the fact that Lake Nakuru is 'an occasional home for . . . up and down the valley'.

4 The government's attitude is inconsistent because

it accepted a grant from the World Wildlife Fund on condition that wildlife in the lake would not be threatened by man-made hazards, but it permits Copal's operations, which have this effect.

5 The result of this has been that the World Wildlife Fund has suspended new financial support for Kenya.

6 The algae are important to birds like flamingoes because they form the basis of their food chain (since they feed the fish on which the flamingoes live).

7 'The edge of destruction' means the point where destruction is almost inevitable.

8 The level of copper in the lake water is so high because the water flowing into the lake from agricultural lands is polluted by the spillage of copper oxychloride from the Copal factory.

9 'The lethal level' means the level at which the algae would be killed.

10 The reason for the flamingoes leaving Lake Nakuru is that the lake is one of several temporary homes they use.

11 'They' refers to 'copper levels'.

12 The writer would consider the destruction of the lake justified if it provided Kenya with great economic benefits.

13 The reasons given are that Copal's products are not competitive on the world market because its prices are too high, as it is forced to use pure copper instead of scrap, and the transport costs are also high, because the factory is such a long way from the coast.

14 'That' refers to 'the price offered by a chemical company in a copper-producing company'.

15 'It' refers to 'time to prevent the damage from becoming irreparable'.

52

The points that should be made in the summary are as follows.

1 Copal manufactures copper oxychloride on the shores of Lake Nakuru, which is famous for its wild life.

2 The World Wildlife Fund, which helped the Kenyan government to set up the area as a national park, believes the toxic products of the factory will soon destroy the ecology of the lake.

3 The copper levels in the lake are already threatening the algae that form the basis of its food chain.

4 The writer believes Copal's licence to manufacture should be withdrawn not only because of the ecological damage it causes, but also because its activities are uneconomical and its products uncompetitive. (100 words).

Price of Living in the High Alps

The most convenient allocation of questions for group work is 1–4, 5–8, 9–12, 13–15, using four groups.

53

Suggested answers:

1 The connection is that these districts are being developed for tourism. The building crane represents the construction of hotels, ski-lifts, etc. and these will alter the mountain landscape.

2 'So' means 'that is what'. In other words, Swiss planners and officials believe construction will raise the standard of living in mountain areas.

3 'Come out ahead' means 'show higher figures'.

4 The main differences are that the mountain districts are more agricultural, while the rest of the country enjoys higher incomes, better services, more employment opportunities and a growing population.

5 'Which' refers to 'topographical and weather conditions'.

6 The majority of farmers in the Rhone Valley work in factories in the valley and travel from their farms in the mountains daily.

7 'The rule' means 'the norm', 'what is normally the case'.

8 'They contribute . . .'; 'they preserve the landscape'; 'they represent the Switzerland . . . holiday dreams'.

9 'Which' refers to 'a country' (i.e. Switzerland).

10 Goats are mainly found in the mountain areas, but only 20 per cent of the pigs live there.

11 Farmers contribute to the mountain landscape by caring for the woods, buildings and land, and their animals fertilise the land.

12 They help tourism by maintaining the picture of the Swiss landscape that tourists are attracted by (the alpine horn, the cow bells, etc.).

13 It means that the farmers form an essential part of the picture of Switzerland that tourists imagine.

14 It is written like this because it is doubtful whether the 'benefits' farmers are aware of in city life are really advantages.

15 The Swiss government thinks that other kinds of employment, apart from farming, must be emphasised in mountain districts; Andreas Werthemann thinks that if tourism is allowed to spread too far, farming will disappear.

54

The points that should be made in the summary are as follows.

1 Mountain farmers are necessary to Switzerland because the country produces less than half of its food requirements.

2 Apart from supplying food, the farmers care for the landscape and preserve the Switzerland that attracts tourists.

3 Their existence is threatened because their life is hard and the cities appear to offer them many advantages and because the growth of tourism in the mountain areas may affect their lives.

4 While the government believes that more tourism will raise the standard of living, there is a risk that farmers will then disappear altogether and the reasons for tourism will disappear with them. (98 words).

Liberty v Equality

The most convenient allocation of questions for group work is 1–4, 5–8, 9–12, 13–15.

55
Suggested answers:

1 Reformers have always thought the two things went together.

2 'Under-privileged' means 'not having had the advantages that the majority of people have had'.

3 'This' refers to 'some loss of liberty'.

4 Such laws can inhibit liberty either because it becomes necessary to prohibit activities that would lead to inequality or because the laws are interpreted in such a way that people are dealt with in broad categories.

5 It means that teachers did not stay long in the school and so there were continual changes in the staff (so that the children constantly had to get used to new teachers).

6 'The whole effect' refers to the results of 'the segregation of children according to merit after the Second World War'.

7 Officials are likely to be more polite towards those who have more upper-class accents and so a system of education that reinforces class divisions will make it difficult for people to receive the same treatment as citizens.

8 The argument is that it is unjust because some children have all the advantages and others all the disadvantages at school and it is also a bad thing socially because it reinforces class divisions.

9 Equality would be satisfactorily served in this case because all the children in the area went to the same school.

10 It means 'nearby', 'within easy travelling distance'.

11 It means 'the area very close to the school'.

12 This means a form of education in which discipline is not so strictly enforced and children have more freedom.

13 They are not allowed to choose because

segregation would result, either on class lines or according to ability, and this is considered harmful for the young and for society.

14 'It follows' means 'it is a logical consequence'.

15 The writer thinks that it is wrong for local authorities (in their anxiety to prevent segregation of children along class lines or according to ability) to prohibit parents from all choice in cases where social considerations would not be affected (i.e. in cases where the only difference between schools was the emphasis on certain kinds of education).

56
The points that should be made in the summary are as follows.

1 When the State passes laws aimed at producing greater equality, it may limit individual freedom, either by prohibiting activities which increase inequality or by treating people in broad categories.

2 In education, many local authorities try to counteract the effects of segregating children on class lines or according to ability by giving parents no choice of school.

3 The writer agrees that all children should go to the same kind of school but if schools in the same area specialise in different subjects, local authorities should allow parents some freedom of choice. (94 words).

Middlesex

The most convenient allocation of questions for group work is 1–4, 5–8, 9–11, 12–15.

57
Suggested answers:

1 Middlesex should no longer exist because it is officially part of London; it still exists in the sense that it has an individual character, very different from that of the city.

2 We suppose it had an 'insatiable appetite' for more land to administer, and so for power.

3 This phrase means that officials declared that Middlesex was dead because its administrative functions were taken over by the Greater London Concil.

4 London depends on Middlesex for people because most of the inhabitants of Middlesex work there (its inhabitants supply much of London's labour force).

5 'Densest dormitory' means the area that the largest proportion of people use to live and sleep in, although they travel to work in the city.

6 'So' refers to 'monotonous'.

7 The advantages were that the houses in Middlesex were comfortable, had gardens, and provided an

element of privacy.

8 The writer thinks the critics are mistaken because they assume that life in the suburbs must be as dull and uniform as the houses.

9 They are more to blame because they have renamed areas and not allowed them to preserve their individuality.

10 They show themselves to be romantic because giving the house a name and preferring to call a street an avenue are attempts to preserve individuality, and the names chosen suggest the houses are old or in the country, and not part of monotonous suburbs.

11 The example the writer gives of this is the tomb J. C. Loudon erected for his parents. It was grand because of its size and shape.

12 It influenced the development of Middlesex because the people who lived there wanted houses and gardens and were prepared to travel to London every day, so the county became a residential area for workers in the city.

13 'Along the lines' means 'in the form'.

14 It is a mistake because it has a personality of its own, which is separate from that of the city.

15 It refers to 'the city' and 'the county'.

58

The summary is less a matter of including specific points than the previous ones have been; the following is what I think a good answer should contain.

1 Officially, Middlesex no longer exists, because it is now part of Greater London for administrative purposes, but it still has its own personality, different from that of the city.

2 The personality is provided by the people, most of whom live in suburban houses with gardens and work in London.

3 Middlesex is essentially a dormitory for these people and has developed to meet their needs.

4 Although this suburban area is monotonous architecturally, the inhabitants try to emphasise its country origins by naming their houses.

5 It is a pity that the council in contrast, integrates areas instead of preserving their individuality. (99 words).

Walking

The most convenient allocation of questions for group work is 1–4, 5–8, 9–12, 13–15, using four groups.

59

Suggested answers:

1 It means, in this case, 'at the moment when you are about to bump into one another'.

2 'A second impasse' is a situation where it is once again impossible for the two people to move forward, because they are again facing each other in the same way.

3 The situation begins to resemble a dance routine because the two people seem to be following each other's steps at the same moment, like dancers.

4 The evidence is that parents regard a baby's first steps as next in importance to its first words.

5 This phrase means a 'significant stage in the child's development'.

6 It means 'intentionally staying close to each other' (while walking along).

7 'This' refers to 'deliberately maintained proximity'.

8 They make it plain by staying together and 'adjusting their pace to re-establish contact' on turning corners, etc.

9 It is embarrassing because the person walking alongside may think we have bad intentions; we avoid it by walking faster or slower, or crossing the street.

10 'On the surface' means 'superficially', 'apparently'.

11 It is a gesture made in public to indicate to everyone that the person who makes it thinks he has done something foolish.

12 'On display' means being watched by the other people in the street, as if they were in a shop window.

13 They discovered that men and women behave quite differently when passing someone coming the other way. 'Men tend to face . . . turn their backs on them.'

14 'They' are the 'estimated five million Britons who treat walking as a recreation'.

15 They were made for walking. (Even though students may be too young to remember the words of this song, the idea should be clear in the context.)

60

The points that should be made in the summary are as follows.

1 People adopt a number of conventions when walking.

2 In order to avoid collisions, they must first decide who is walking with others.

3 People walking alone must go round a group unless it is very large.

4 It is easy to distinguish people walking together because they stay together and wait for each other, but important to avoid walking next to strangers by accident since they might misunderstand our attentions.

5 The most curious conventions discovered are that

walkers feel others are watching them and behave unnaturally if they mistake their destination, and that men and women on crossings adopt quite different behaviour. (99 words).

Showing the Flag

61

The most convenient allocation of questions for group work is 1–4, 5–9, 10–12, 13–15.

Suggested answers:

1   They either avoid them, or buy a flag to avoid embarrassment.
2   They do this because of complaints from people asked to contribute to too many charities.
3   'They' are 'local authorities'.
4   It means that in being generous, we should first consider those nearest to us. It is relevant here because local authorities give preference to local charities on flag days.
5   She did this because she got the idea from a Danish priest who sold artifical roses in aid of charity.
6   'Society ladies' means ladies belonging to the upper classes and mentioned in the society pages of newspapers, etc.
7   'Which' refers to 'linen roses'.
8   'The enterprise' referred to was Mrs George's idea of selling flags in aid of the Prince of Wales's National Relief Fund.
9   Silk flags were expected to produce a more lavish contribution because they were made of more expensive material.
10 The main reasons for changes in the design of flags were the shortage of raw materials (in the First World War) and economy and ease of production since then.
11 'The pinned variety' means the kind of flag that was fixed with a pin.
12 New regulations were introduced in 1915 because of the rapid growth of flag days. The regulations prohibited children and animals from being used for collections and only granted permits to societies, not to individuals.
13 The objection to children being employed was that they were being exploited (and were probably missing lessons at school).
14 Oxfam's way of collecting money is different because it has established shops and sells direct to the public.
15 It is ironic because the emblems were originally sold cheaply for charity and have now been sold again for charity, but at much higher prices because they are now collectors' items.

62

The points that should be made in the summary are as follows.

1   Flag days began in Britain in 1912, when Queen Alexandra organised the sale of emblems for charity.
2   During the First World War flag days developed so rapidly that it was necessary to make regulations to control them.
3   Since then, further regulations have been introduced to limit the number of collections per year.
4   The emblems were originally made of a variety of materials, but are now usually made of sticky paper, which is cheaper and easier to produce.
5   In recent years, charities have introduced new methods of collecting money, particularly by establishing shops to sell direct to the public. (98 words).

Greenwich Newly Observed

The most convenient allocation of questions for group work is 1–3, 4–6, 7–10 and 11–15, using four groups.

63

Suggested answers:

1   It is landlocked because it is housed in a concrete dock, (and so 'locked' to the land).
2   The writer is referring to the arrival of visitors from all over Europe (which will prove that Greenwich has 'come up' at last) and saying that it is about time they did.
3   The suggestion is that the people who live in Greenwich now do not belong to the upper classes, as they did in Victoria's time.
4   It means that it was not a long journey to travel every day to work in the City of London.
5   'It' refers to Greenwich entering its second golden age.
6   They moved because they were disappointed with Islington and Hampstead and those districts were becoming too expensive.
7   Residents are not pleased because the area is becoming a tourist area and shops are being replaced by souvenir shops and boutiques.
8   'The boutique syndrome' means the tendency for shops that sell household necessities to be replaced by those that sell luxuries and tourist items.
9   'Staple items' are everyday objects that people regularly buy.
10 The phrase refers to established shops which are likely to change their stock in trade and become tourist shops.
11 He suggests the money is being wasted because

they will soon be dirty again (unless something is done about the traffic passing by).

12 'Under cover' means protected from bad weather by a roof'.

13 'Red tape' means 'bureaucratic formalities and restrictions'.

14 'That' refers to the improved service to London offered by the hydrofoils.

15 'Any amount of' means 'a limitless quantity'.

64

The points that should be made in the summary are as follows.

1 Despite its attractions for tourists, people have been waiting for a long time for Greenwich to regain its former prosperity.

2 Tourism has certainly brought more visitors, so that shops to serve them are replacing the traditional ones, though this does not please the residents, many of whom are young professional people who have recently moved there.

3 The GLC have modernised the pier and there is now an excellent hydrofoil service to London for the benefit of commuters and visitors.

4 But the money spent on improving Greenwich's appearance and reviving the town centre will be wasted unless its traffic problems are solved. (100 words).

An Unromantic Artist

The most convenient allocation of questions for group work is 1–4, 5–8, 9–11, 12–15, using four groups.

65

Suggested answers:

1 It means 'a long way from', 'very different from'.

2 Constable was very different from Haydon because he was much calmer in temperament and less ambitious.

3 He was different from most of his contemporaries in regarding painting as a profession and concentrating on accuracy, instead of having a romantic attitude to it and feeling inspired.

4 'This confrontation' refers to the argument between Constable and Blake.

5 The writer means that the paintings Constable

sent to exhibitions were different from the sketches he left in his studio (so that it was as if he were two artists).

6 'It' refers to 'this division among nineteenth-century artists'.

7 'That' refers to 'the difference . . . between the public and the private self'.

8 The problem that faced most Romantic artists was that they knew that what the public liked was not as good as what they could paint for themselves, but were obliged to please the public to make a living.

9 It tells us that in the writer's opinion Constable compromised his original paintings to please the public too often (for the good of his art).

10 He was largely indifferent to it, except to the money it brought him.

11 'It' refers to 'this success'.

12 He was 'thoroughly insular' because he never crossed the Channel, and 'thoroughly anti-Bohemian' because he was mainly concerned with providing for his family and being respected socially.

13 'On the brink' means 'on the point' of succeeding.

14 'Pulled them off' means 'achieved them successfully'.

15 It is ironic because Constable was never accepted by the art experts of his time.

66

The points that should be made in the summary are as follows.

1 Unlike the majority of Romantic artists, Constable did not believe in inspiration. He believed that it was enough to paint what he saw.

2 In temperament, he was calm and his main ambition was to provide for his family and achieve social respectability.

3 He was indifferent to the success of his paintings abroad, apart from the money it brought him.

4 Like other Romantic artists, he was obliged to compromise to please the public, and so his paintings in exhibitions were different from his sketches.

5 We may regret this, but he himself seems not to have been concerned very much by praise or criticism. (95 words).

Section 3: Structural conversion

67 A 1 I am not **as old as** my brother Alex.
2 He is **taller than** I am.
3 He has a **more aggressive** personality **than** I have.
4 I haven't **such** a violent temper as he has.
5 I am not **as good** at mathematics **as** he is.
6 He has **more** friends **than** I have.
7 I don't work **as hard as** he does.
8 My ideas are **more straightforward than** his.

B 1 The hotel does not seem **the same as** it used to be.
2 The entrance is **different from** what it was before.
3 In what way is it **different from** what you expected?
4 It just doesn't give me the **same impression as** the one I had last year.
5 Five years ago, the situation was not **the same as** it is now.
6 The people you meet at university will be **different from** the ones/those you are used to in the village.

C 1 You should have booked your tickets in advance, **as** I did/have.
2 They're going to Brighton for their holidays, **like** us.
3 They all had a good time at the party, **like** you.
4 I study hard, **as** he does.
5 I wish I could go away on holiday whenever I felt like it, **as** she does.
6 He plays football, **like** his father.

D 1 He **not only** keeps everyone up at night with his noisy parties, **but** he **also** wakes us up the next morning by playing the piano.
2 **Apart from playing** to win, he insults his opponents.
3 **Apart from writing** to him, I've also tried to contact him by phone on several occasions.
4 He **not only** spends all his own money, **but** he **also** borrows it from his sister.
5 I **not only** find the scheme expensive **but** I **also** find it unattractive.
6 **Apart from making** a complaint, they threatened to call the police.

E 1 **The longer** the game went on, the **more exhausted** the players became.
2 **The more** I go on thinking about the situation, the **more despondent** I feel.
3 **The longer** time goes on, the **clearer** the situation is bound to become.
4 **The more** you go on eating so much, the **fatter** you'll get.
5 **The faster** you drive, the **more likely** you are to have an accident.
6 **The better** a child is brought up, the **better** he will behave.

F 1 I've **never** seen **such a** good film.
2 It's **the most difficult** job I've **ever** had to do.
3 It's **the worst** service I've **ever** experienced.
4 I've **never** visited **such a** beautiful country.
5 I've **never** had **such an** enjoyable holiday.
6 It's **the most interesting** book I've **ever** read.

68 1 What a wonderful time we had at the party!
2 It's such a beautiful present!
3 How rude he is!
4 What a rude man he is!
5 They've made such an awful mess!
6 She was so calm in the middle of that crowd!
7 What a tiring journey we've had!
8 I was so lucky to see you there!

69 A 1 **Unless** they pay the rent by Saturday, I'll throw them out.
2 You can't take the examination **if** you **don't** pay the fee.
3 You shouldn't make accusations like that **unless** you're sure of the facts.
4 **If** you **don't** apologise, I'll ring my lawyer.
5 **Unless** he tells us who he is, we won't let him in.
6 I think we've lost our way, **if** that **isn't** the path over there.

B 1 **Unless** you're busy, I'd like to ask you some questions.
2 **Provided (that)** you **don't** object, we'll interview the next candidate now.
3 I'm prepared to go on with the project, **unless** you disagree.
4 We should have a good time, **as long as we don't** get bad weather.
5 I won't be able to make the arrangements, **unless** you let me know in advance.
6 We'll meet on Saturday, **so long as** I **don't** hear otherwise from you.

150

70　1　He was dressed in black for the funeral.
　　2　He had a black tie on for the funeral.
　　3　The bride had a white dress on.
　　4　She was also wearing a white veil.
　　5　The bridesmaids were dressed in blue.
　　6　The bride's mother had a diamond necklace on.

71　1　**Walking** on railway lines **is** dangerous.
　　2　**It is** unhealthy **to stay** indoors all the time.
　　3　**Playing** tennis at the weekend **is** a pleasant form of relaxation.
　　4　**It is** a depressing experience **to work** for people who don't appreciate your efforts.
　　5　**Living** in a hotel **is** more expensive than living in a flat.
　　6　**It is** illogical **to expect** other people to do what you would not do yourself.
　　7　**It is** better **to marry** for love than for money.
　　8　**It is** always a pleasure **to meet** interesting people.

72　1　**He had** no one to talk to.
　　2　**There are** plenty of assistants to help her.
　　3　**There haven't been** any letters **for her** today.
　　4　**I have** several patients in my ward.
　　5　**She should have** other children to play with.
　　6　**There are** always long queues of people waiting to see him.
　　7　**There won't be** anywhere **for us** to stay.
　　8　**There is** no reason **for them** to complain.

73　1　She took the child's toys away from him, which was unkind.
　　2　It was stupid of him to make a fuss about nothing.
　　3　It was clever of him to solve the puzzle in five minutes.
　　4　It is extremely annoying of him to ring me up in the middle of the night.
　　5　They didn't take your advice, which was foolish of them.
　　6　It was hurtful of them not to invite her to dinner.

74　A　1　I haven't played tennis since December.
　　　2　They haven't won the election since 1974.
　　　3　The last time I voted in an election was in 1970.
　　　4　The last time he made a speech on television was at Christmas.
　　　5　She hasn't travelled by air since March.
　　　6　We last heard from them on 1st August.
　　B　1　I haven't played tennis for nine months.
　　　2　They haven't won the election for eleven years.
　　　3　He last paid the rent five weeks ago.

　　　4　I last heard from her some time ago.
　　　5　The last time they made a profit was ages ago.
　　　6　He last went to see his mother ages ago.
　　C　1　It's several months since I last played tennis.
　　　2　They haven't won the election for eleven years.
　　　3　They haven't written to us for a long time.
　　　4　It's a long time since I worked as hard as this.
　　　5　It's six weeks since he last attended school.
　　　6　We haven't met for many years.

75　1　It's the first time I've ever spoken to him.
　　2　I've never flown before.
　　3　He was worried, because it was the first time she had ever been late.
　　4　We were surprised, because they had never invited us to lunch before.
　　5　He said 'no' very brusquely, although I had never asked hm for money before.
　　6　It's the first time you've ever made a complaint about it.

76　A　1　In spite of the rise in food production, there are still too many people who are hungry.
　　　2　Even though notices have been put up everywhere, people still spoil the park with their litter.
　　　3　They weren't able to get into the cinema, though they queued for an hour.
　　　4　We went on playing, despite the rain.
　　　5　Although we have increased production, we have not made a profit.
　　　6　They hope the students will continue to pay despite the rise in fees.
　　B　1　I'm not going to employ him, whoever he is and wherever he studied.
　　　2　I don't trust her, however polite she is.
　　　3　She never listens, whatever you tell her, or however often you tell her.
　　　4　I don't want it in the house, however much you paid for it.
　　　5　I'm going to speak to him, whoever he is.
　　　6　Wherever he has gone, he'll come back.

77　1　The lawyer came to see him because he complained.
　　2　The first performance of the play was postponed because the leading actor was ill.
　　3　He deserves his success because of his hard work.
　　4　They refused to fly because of the fog.
　　5　They have made him redundant because of his age.
　　6　Because of the rise in the cost of living, they have asked for more money.

78 1 The pilot is thought to have lost his way in the fog.
2 It is expected that the Prime Minister will mention the subject in the House of Commons this afternoon.
3 She is reported to be planning to resign – in the year 2000!
4 A foreign team is understood to be negotiating his transfer for £2 million.
5 They are believed to have discovered the cause of his illness.
6 It's said that she knows everyone worth knowing around here.

79 1 The reason for the food shortage at present is quite clear.
2 Can you give me any reason why you were absent yesterday?
3 The reason for the Government's decision to stop providing tricycles for disabled people was that they were unsafe.
4 Is there any reason for taxes to be increased?
5 The reasons why I am resigning are private.
6 I am afraid I can't offer any logical reason for your son's failure in the examination.

80 1 She may not have received our letter.
2 His train may be late.
3 He might not be able to come tomorrow.
4 He may not have realised how important it was.
5 They may have got tired and gone home.
6 They might be waiting for you to ring her.
7 They may not have understood the instructions.
8 He might not be aware that we are looking for him.

81 1 Cambridge are so fond of this structure that they put it in every examination.
2 He was so distressed by the news of her resignation that he had to take the rest of the week off.
3 She not only managed to upset most of her colleagues but she also had a row with her boss.
4 She felt so strongly about the matter that she never spoke to him again.
5 Not only did he leave the hotel without paying, but he also took the television set from his room.
6 So quickly did the tide come in that they were in danger of being cut off.

Progress Test 1

All of the items included have been practised in previous exercises. This must be borne in mind in interpreting the statistics given below, where the items were attempted by students at this level, some 50 hours of tuition time after passing the Cambridge First Certificate, but without the benefit of the exercises provided here. The scores obtained therefore represent the average difficulty of an item for students at this level. They are accompanied by the discrimination analysis, where 0·30 indicates a reliable test, showing that the top 20% of students scored 30% better on the items than the bottom 20%.

The scores are also compared to an estimate of the standard a student would need to have reached in order to obtain Cambridge Proficiency level in this kind of test, and there is a target pass mark to be aimed at, which assumes the advantage students should have gained from doing the exercises in this book. The target score is logically always higher than the results obtained from students without this advantage, and in some cases may reach or surpass the levels given for Proficiency itself, although it is equally clear that a score on a given progress test reaching this level would not in itself be an indication that the student would be ready to pass the examination, since the points tested, fresh in the students' minds, form only a part of the total battery from which the examination items would be devised.

Together with the statistics, I have also indicated acceptable alternative answers and comments on doubtful answers and common sources of error.

The time allowed for the test and for all subsequent Structural Conversion Progress Tests, should be 20 minutes.

Statistics: Structural Conversion Progress Test 1
Average score: 14·2/20 = 70·8%
Estimated Cambridge pass level = 18
Discrimination analysis = 0·42
Target score = 17

Answers:

1 You can't have broken them all, (surely)!
2 A cousin of mine is spending the weekend with us.
3 His idea is not as (so) sensible as yours/His idea is less sensible than yours.
4 In spite of the rain (In spite of the fact that it was raining) (In spite of its raining), they went on playing.
5 She is regarded as the outstanding painter of her generation.
6 He's likely to arrive late.
7 He'll never forget her, whatever she says. (NOTE: The inversion of the two main clauses is not

152

acceptable, since a full stop or semicolon would.be required.)

8 Apart from being intelligent, (Apart from his intelligence), he was also very handsome.

9 I've never met such an unpleasant man (so unpleasant a man) (a man who was so unpleasant). (NOTE: I do not advocate teaching the second alternative unless students raise it themselves, since it is likely to confuse the majority.)

10 As soon as she came in, she went into the kitchen.

11 The older I get, the more irritable I become.

12 The children are easy to amuse (are easily amused).

13 It's very kind of you to say such things.

14 Unless he pays the rent by Saturday, he'll have to go. (NOTE: Students who understand the structure but omit the *s* from the third-person singular must be ruthlessly penalised.)

15 They have been accustomed to such disasters for a long time.

16 Because of his injury (his being injured) (the fact that he was injured), he wasn't able to play. (NOTE: The last possibility, though just about acceptable, is very clumsy.)

17 She had a blue dress on (She had put a blue dress on).

18 Such famous singers as Placido Domingo and Montserrat Caballé have sung here. (NOTE: A comma after 'singers' should be penalised, since it suggests uncertainty about the difference between 'as' and 'like'.)

19 He may not have realised what we had to do at first.

20 He last came here (visited the place) at the end of June. (NOTE: It is important to penalise the wrong word order of 'He last was here' and the use of any other preposition but 'at'.)

82
1 Handicapped people are going to be given a new form of car.

2 Her application for the job is being considered.

3 The tickets can be paid for by cheque or in cash.

4 Your application form should not be posted later than 10th August.

5 The contribution he made will never be forgotten.

6 A copy of the contract was not sent to him.

7 He was not sent a copy of the contract.

8 This form will have to be filled in before a reduction in income tax can be obtained.

9 Your request cannot reasonably be granted unless more information is provided.

10 The family portraits were being sold to pay their debts.

11 Further economies may already have been thought of.

12 The goods have already been paid for.

13 You have already been paid for the goods.

14 He must have been highly thought of, since he was given such a good reference.

15 He must have been highly thought of to have been given such a good reference.

83
1 . . . Nor is this the only cause for disagreement with their conclusions.

2 . . . Nor is this the only reason why they dislike it.

3 Nor is it easier for foreign students to understand than *The Times*.

4 Nor will we beat Haiti, if it comes to that.

5 Nor do they usually use inverted forms in their sentences!

84
1 Neither my father nor my mother was born in London.

2 Neither in the big cities nor in the holiday resorts will you find so many friendly people.

3 Neither your qualifications nor your previous experience make you a suitable candidate.

4 Neither as a politician nor as a lawyer did he distinguish himself.

5 Neither in the *Guardian* nor in the *Sun* did I find any reference to the events.

6 Neither the *Guardian* nor the *Sun* paid any attention to the events.

85
1 Everything comes to an end, sooner or later.

2 Everyone who knows him likes him.

3 Everyone in the village looks forward to the festival.

4 Have you bought everything I asked you to buy?

5 At my time of life, everyone I have met and everything I have seen have become a distant memory.

86
1 I asked her if/whether she had seen John the previous day.

2 She asked me why I wasn't going to the party the next day.

3 She asked them if/whether it would be ready by the day after.

4 They asked her how she could expect them to complete the job by the following week when they had not been told how to do it.

5 He asked the clerk how much longer he would have to wait before someone took some/any notice of him.

6 She asked him if/whether he thought they might have lost their way.

7 She wondered if she would ever feel the same as she had a week before.

8　He asked her if she could imagine how long it had taken them to get there the previous night.

9　She asked him how he thought she had felt when she had been told that he would not be arriving until the following day.

10　She asked him if they should not thank Betty and Steve for the lovely party they had given before they went home.

87　1　She asked me not to tell him where she was.

2　He told the students to finish the exercise they had been doing the previous day.

3　He told them not to open their books until he told them to.

4　She asked the candidates to hand their papers to the examiner when they went out.

5　The sergeant told the recruits not to shoot until he said 'Shoot!'

88　1　His tastes are not so luxurious as those of his grandfather.

2　The new law is not as far-reaching as that of the previous government.

3　Our production is greater than that of the Soviet Union.

4　The people here are rather taller than those of other islands.

5　His general intelligence is higher than that of the average person.

6　His essays show more imagination than those of most students.

89　1　His classes are full, not only in the mornings but also in the evenings.

2　Both the Government and the Opposition voted in favour of the proposal.

3　His success depends not only on hard work, but also on good business sense.

4　He has always been a good speaker, not only in private gatherings but also in front of large audiences.

5　The tragedy is that both the films and the negatives were destroyed in the fire.

90　1　He fell in love with her both because of her beauty and because of her personality.

2　Not only did he write to the Prime Minister, but he also obtained an interview with him.

3　Not only does he speak Spanish, but he also speaks Catalan.

4　He speaks both Spanish and Catalan.

5　He has the ability to please both the audience and the critics.

6　We find evidence of his preoccupation with forms both in his early work and in his most recent novels.

Progress Test 2

Statistics: (for their interpretation, see the note accompanying Structural Progress Test 1, page 152).
Average score: 13·3/20 = 66·4%
Estimated Cambridge pass level = 17
Discrimination analysis = 0·38
Target score = 16

Answers:

1　I'll mend it later if (provided) you leave it here.

2　Even if you offer(ed) me more money, it won't (wouldn't) change my decision *or* I won't change . . .

3　He wondered if he would ever see her again.

4　I finally succeeded in convincing him of its value.

5　She asked me not to do it (that) again.

6　He asked if anyone knew the way to the station.

7　We still didn't get in, in spite of having queued up (queuing) for hours.

8　A new bridge is being built across the river. (NOTE: Though odd, the word order: 'across the river is being built' could conceivably be used.)

9　Neither she nor I knew where it was.

10　Their English is certain to improve in time or . . . will certainly improve in time. (NOTE: But not 'surely improve', which doesn't mean the same thing.)

11　She must have come by bus.

12　The owner of the car couldn't be traced (by the police).

13　Did he explain why he behaved (had behaved) like that (in that way)?

14　There's no reason for you to come, if you don't want to. (NOTE: 'for you coming' is not acceptable.)

15　You had better do it again.

16　The Prime Minister is believed to be planning to resign.

17　There is no one who (that) works harder than he does.

18　You should do something about it, rather than sit there grumbling.

19　The policeman asked them what they had been doing the night before (the previous night). (NOTE: The time reference is indispensable.)

20　It was unfair of him to blame me for his mistakes. (It was unfair that he should have blamed me . . .) (NOTE: The second alternative, in my view, should not be taught, but only accepted if students raise it, since it could be confusing.)

91　(1)　you tend
(2)　you would be
(3)　you came
(4)　you are
(5)　your
(6)　you are making
(10)　one's been brought up
(11)　can one?
(12)　one's
(13)　one
(14)　one finds

(7)	yourself	(15)	oneself
(8)	you	(16)	your
(9)	your	(17)	you're
		(18)	you've swallowed

92 A 1 I wish/If only we could go to the beach.
    2 I wish/If only you earned more money.
    3 I wish/If only there were something interesting on television this evening.
    4 I wish/If only that dress didn't cost so much.
    5 I wish/If only you didn't have to work so hard, and we had a chance to go out and enjoy ourselves.

  B 1 I wish they had invited more people.
    2 I wish we hadn't made up our minds so quickly.
    3 I wish I had taken your advice.
    4 I wish you could have come with me.
    5 I wish we hadn't lost contact with them.

  C 1 I wish you would pay attention to what I'm saying!
    2 I wish you wouldn't keep reminding me of my mistakes!
    3 I wish you would be more careful!
    4 I wish you wouldn't always blame me when things go wrong!
    5 I wish the Government would do something about unemployment!

93 1 I must get my hair cut.
   2 The piano needs tuning.
   3 The house needs redecorating.
   4 I must get these calculations checked.
   5 You must get your shoes mended.
   6 My suit needs cleaning.
   7 I must get the central heating serviced.
   8 Before he gets a good part in a film, he must get his nose straightened.
   9 I must get my racket restrung.
 10 Your teeth need seeing to.

94 1 Let's ask him what he thinks about it.
   2 Let's get married tomorrow.
   3 Let's not make up our minds too soon.
   4 Let's go to the cinema this evening.
   5 Let's not sell it.

95 A 1 I haven't often seen a more beautiful landscape.
      I have hardly ever seen a more beautiful landscape.
    2 I seldom travel by train these days.
      I hardly ever travel by train these days.
    3 We seldom have the opportunity to play tennis.
      We don't often have the opportunity to play tennis.

    4 He seldom came to the office after his retirement.
      He didn't often come to the office after his retirement.
    5 She hardly ever writes to us nowadays.
      She seldom writes to us nowadays.

  B 1 Not often do we have the opportunity . . .
    2 Hardly ever again in his life would he encounter . . .
    3 Seldom have the great writers of the past employed . . .
    4 Not often do I see . . .
    5 Seldom will you come across . . .

96 A

1	explain	8	refuse	15	invite
2	admit	9	accuse	16	apologise
3	agree	10	deny	17	regret
4	beg	11	promise	18	complain
5	order	12	prefer	19	advise
6	warn	13	remind	20	suggest
7	wonder	14	offer		

  B The following are suggested answers.
    1 'I'm not going to/I won't pay the rent.'
    2 'I didn't have anything to do with it!'
    3 'I'll repair the typewriter for you next Saturday.'
    4 'You robbed the bank, didn't you?'
    5 'Whatever's going to happen to me in the end?'
    6 'I'd rather not make up my mind straight away.'
    7 'Remember to post those letters on the way to work.'
    8 'This is the meaning of the word.'
    9 'Don't cross the road without looking to the right and left.'
  10 'I think your suggestion is a sensible one.'
  11 'Please, please don't tell my father about it!'
  12 'Don't fire!'
  13 'I'm afraid I made a mistake.'
  14 'Would you like to come to dinner?'
  15 'Would you like me to look after the children while you're out?'
  16 'I'm terribly sorry I'm late!'
  17 'I wish you wouldn't spend so much money on silly things.'
  18 'I wish I had had the chance to go to university.'
  19 'Why don't we go out to dinner?'
  20 'You really ought to give up smoking.'

97 1 She is not nearly as old as her husband is.
   2 The hotel where we stayed last year was much more expensive than the one where we are staying now.

3   His sister did much better in the exam than he did.
4   We spent much more money last year than we have this year.
5   This series was not nearly so interesting as the last one.
6   It was much hotter last week than it is now.
7   They didn't play nearly so well in the final as they did in the first match.
8   Strangely enough, I get far more work done at home than I do in the office.

Progress Test 3

Statistics: (for their interpretation, see the note accompanying Structural Progress Test 1, page 152).
Average score: 12·6/20 = 62·8% (Note that in comparison with the previous two structural conversion progress tests, these results were obtained with students who had had 100 further hours of tuition, so that the test is considerably more difficult.)
Estimated Cambridge pass level = 15
Discrimination analysis = 0·49
Target score = 16 (Note that this is above Cambridge level, but the score is attainable if students have fully comprehended the previous exercises.)

Answers:

1   He isn't very fond of apples.
2   He begged me not to tell anyone about it.
3   This is the procedure that every student has to follow.
4   The inspector accused Jones of having killed (of killing) her or accused Jones of her murder.
5   I must get my suit cleaned.
6   She apologised for not having rung me (for not ringing me) (for having failed to ring me) (for failing to ring me).
7   They both worked hard but Sheila was the only one that passed the examination.
8   I wish I had thought of that at the time.
9   He was not allowed to play with other children (by his parents) or He was forbidden to play with other children . . .
10 He came in quietly so as not to wake his wife.
11 He may not have been working here long, but he's already impressed the manager.
12 We would have crashed if I had not braked.
13 It was thanks to her (kindness) that I recovered.
14 Those wires must not be touched in any circumstances.
15 I consider it (to be) the best book I've ever read or I consider it is the best book . . .
16 Let's not argue about it or Let's avoid an argument about it (avoid arguing about it).
17 She regretted having been so rude to them.

18 He would rather travel by train than fly.
19 One never knows what's going to happen, does one? (NOTE: Mixtures partly including 'you' forms cannot be accepted.)
20 The flood water makes it difficult to reach them or The flood water is the reason why it is difficult to reach them (reason for it(s) being difficult to reach them.)

98 1 Being a teacher, he has often come across problems like this.
   2 As/Since you are so tall, you'll have no difficulty in reaching the top shelf.
   3 Mary's father being so rich, she inherited a lot of money when he died.
   4 As/Since Mary's uncle was as rich as her father, he left her a lot of money, too.
   5 As/Since she is so rich, she has never had to worry about money.
   6 Being the oldest person present, she felt she should take the initiative.

Progress Test 4

Statistics: (for their interpretation, see the note accompanying Structural Progress Test 1, page 152)
Average score: 11·3/20 = 56·4%
Estimated Cambridge pass level = 14
Discrimination analysis = 0·43
Target score = 15 (As in the previous test, this is above Cambridge level, but the score is attainable if students have fully comprehended the previous exercises.)

Answers:

1   Do you think we are alike? or Do you think we resemble each other (one another)?
2   He encouraged the child to swim across the pool.
3   I agree that we haven't done as much as we could (have done) to help.
4   A number of other people are thought to be involved in the affair.
5   So absurd was the proposal that it was greeted with laughter.
6   He raised his hand and, in doing so, knocked the lamp over.
7   He said angrily: 'You should have looked where you were going.' (NOTE: The present forms are not acceptable.)
8   I am very interested in antiques, but what interests me most (above all) is silverware (what I am most interested in is . . .).
9   Nothing less than the full amount will satisfy him.
10 Whether he should go or not is something he must decide himself (something for him to decide (himself)).
11 Fred suggested that we should go. (NOTE: I find 'suggested our/us going' unnatural here. In

American English, the form would be: 'Fred suggested that we go.')

12　I'll never forget what a terrible state she was in.

13　The heavy rain caused the roof to collapse (made the roof collapse) (was the cause of the roof collapsing (the collapse of the roof)).

14　I don't know what gave you the idea (what put the idea in your head) that I'm rich.

15　It's the first time (that) I've ever seen anything like this.

16　I hardly ever watch that programme. (NOTE: The 'ever' is essential.)

17　It is not until last Wednesday that they had (any) news of his whereabouts.

18　There's no reason why he should complain.

19　While Jane was on holiday, she did a lot of work *or* While she . . ., Jane did . . . (NOTE: A main source of error here in pretesting was 'on holidays', which is not acceptable).

20　Five years ago, the situation was different from what it is now (was not the same as it is now).

99　1　Take an umbrella in case it rains.

　　2　You'd better write this down in case you forget it.

　　3　He has taken out an insurance policy in case he has an accident.

　　4　He took out an insurance policy in case he had an accident.

　　5　I have taken the precaution of informing the Minister, in case he thinks we are acting independently.

　　6　You'd better offer them an alternative date, in case they can't come on Sunday.

　　7　I suggested that he should give them an alternative date in case they couldn't come on Sunday.

　　8　He advised those present to consider his political record, in case any of them doubted the honesty of his motives.

100　A　1　If it hadn't been for his example, they would all have run away.

　　　　2　But for the nurse's presence of mind, the hospital would have been burnt down.

　　　　3　If it hadn't been for his prompt intervention, a fight would have broken out.

　　　　4　But for his retirement, I would never have become managing director.

　　　　5　If it hadn't been for their assistance, we would all have been in trouble.

　　B　1　However hard you looked, you would never find it.

　　　　2　However much money you had offered him he would not have sold it to you.

　　　　3　However badly he had behaved, they would never have disqualified him from the tournament.

　　　　4　Whoever he had as a secretary , he would still find fault with her.
　　　　　　However efficient a secretary we found him he would still find fault with her.

　　　　5　However efficient a proposal you had made him, he would still have turned it down.

101　1　Excellent though the performance was, I think it could have been improved.

　　2　Strange though it may appear, there are still plenty of people who prefer taking risks to leading a quiet life.

　　3　Although it may have seemed amusing to you, it was no joke as far as we were concerned.

　　4　Understandable though it may be, I don't think his attitude is justified.

　　5　Although this construction is rare in modern English, the examiners seem to be fond of it.

102　**Seldom has it** been my privilege to address such a distinguished company of men and women. I would go so far as to say that **not only is it** an exceptional gathering in my experience, but **rarely has a gathering** of so many outstanding personalities from all walks of life taken place, and **hardly would it** be possible anywhere else in the world. In saying this, I am not flattering you. **Not only am I** perfectly sincere in what I say but I will go further. **Nowhere could we** find a more beautiful collection of ladies. **Neither would it** be possible for us to encounter a more intelligent group of people. **Rarely has one** the opportunity to take part in a historic event of this nature, and **never did I imagine**, when I was invited, that I would be so honoured as to be asked to make the welcoming speech . . .
—Have you ever heard such pompous rubbish?
—No. If I wanted to imitate him, I'd say: **Never have I heard** such a lot of nonsense in my life.

103　1　It may seem irritating to you that you have to do so meaningless an exercise.

　　2　I would certainly not teach so old-fashioned a form in my classes.

　　3　The only reason I have included so misleading a structure is that it is often found in examination papers.

　　4　I call it misleading because it cannot be substituted for so common an expression as 'such a pity', where there is no adjective.

　　5　It cannot be used, either with uncountables like 'such nonsense', which is so appropriate an expression to end the exercise with that no more needs to be said.

104
1. It's time they gave their papers in.
2. It's time for me to be on my way.
3. It's time she took her medicine.
4. Political events made it clear that it was time they called an election.
5. They had done so well at the casino that they realised it was time for them to pocket their winnings.
6. It's time you made up your mind about your future.

105
1. . . . I'd rather you stayed until 5 o'clock.
2. . . . I'd prefer you not to mention his health when you see him.
3. . . . I'd rather you didn't get mixed up with him, that's all.
4. . . . Yes, but I'd prefer you to get down to some serious work.
5. . . . No, but I'd rather you showed it to me after dinner.

Progress Test 5

Statistics: (for their interpretation, see the note accompanying Structural Progress Test 1, page 152). Average score: 10·3/20 = 51·5%. (This test was attempted by students who had had a further 100 hours' tuition, compared to those attempting tests 3 and 4, and were preparing to attempt the Cambridge Proficiency examination a short time afterwards. It is in fact more difficult than Cambridge Proficiency, because it includes all the items Cambridge have used in previous years which I consider to be variations of little direct value to students in their own production of the language and which I have therefore held back until the final stages of the book.)
Estimated Cambridge pass level = 11 (where an average Cambridge test would have a pass mark of 13). Discrimination analysis = 0·47
Target score = 15, four more than Cambridge, because of previous preparation.

Answers:

1. Nowhere had he ever met such hospitable people.
2. Provided you let me know (tell me) what you need in advance, I can arrange everything.
3. It was clear to everyone that he had been responsible for the crime.
4. Sarah is the only one of her friends (that) I know.
5. She insured her life, in case she had an accident.
6. Under no circumstances will I ever consent to the marriage.
7. I'm in no hurry. Herbert is the one (the man, person) who's pressing for a decision.
8. Despite having worked hard (his hard work), he could not finish the job.
9. Should she feel worse during the night, give her these tablets.
10. Were the painting to prove valuable, it would be a pity . . .
11. She never visited Farley without remembering the happy times . . .
12. His honesty, more than anything else (his other qualities) is what I like most about him.
13. You'd still have lost, however well you'd played.
14. Susan hasn't written to me (rung me) recently.
15. Only when there was no hope of victory did they surrender.
16. He must have been thought of as an important man to have been so well treated (treated so well) *or* for them to have treated him so well.
17. I'd rather you signed the cheque now.
18. But for my respect for you, I would have hit him. *or* But for the respect I have for you, I . . .
19. Brilliant though he is as a speaker *or* Brilliant speaker though he is, he really doesn't know much about the subject.
20. No sooner had I shut the door than I realised I had left my keys behind.

106
1. The plane must have been late taking off from London.
2. He would rather play tennis than study.
3. I suggested that he shouldn't work so hard.
4. She regretted not having applied for the job.
5. I have hardly ever seen a more interesting film.
6. He has been considered the greatest living novelist for a long time.
7. I insisted on paying for the lunch.
8. The policeman asked him where he had been at 11 o'clock the previous night.
9. I last saw her at the end of May.
10. She would have been upset if you had told her.

107
1. They have no reason to complain.
2. Are you going to do any work while you are on holiday?
3. What marvellous weather we have had since we arrived!
4. They looked for the manager everywhere, but he couldn't be found.
5. They are unlikely to argue about it.
6. Neither Joan nor I saw him.
7. Since he was a father himself, William could understand the parents' concern.
8. Did they explain why the flight arrived late?
9. You were right to resign.

10   I think there should be a law against it.

108

1   One never knows what's best for one's children these days, does one?

2   The long waiting list made it difficult for us to get a flight.

3   We had better go through this exercise again.

4   We'll have to get the piano tuned.

5   I wasn't allowed to stay up late when I was young.

6   He put his keys on a key-ring so as not to lose them.

7   The accountants are the only people who know what the real situation is.

8   It's time you settled the matter once and for all.

9   I'd rather she answered the letter herself.

10   It's the first time I've ever played squash.

109

1   He died as a result of a heart attack.

2   The situation is not the same as it was three years ago.

3   The robbers are thought to have used this car to make their escape.

4   Little is known about his plans for the future.

5   Unusual though his attitude appears at first sight, it is quite understandable.

6   I like all Mozart's operas, but the one I like best is 'Don Giovanni'.

7   So long did his speech last that everyone went to sleep.

8   It was decided that the money they had inherited should go to the poor.

9   What his future career is going to be is up to him, (his decision) (for him to decide).

10   It was with regret that he said goodbye to them.

Turn down: plier (snap); renverser, retourner (cartes)
réduire (feu, son), rejeter, refuser (travail)
────── USE OF ENGLISH ──────
dévaluer (money)

Section 4: Rephrasing

up down out to -
Turn dotu = doit

110

1 I was wondering when you would **turn up**. You're late.
2 He **turned down** the job because they didn't offer him enough money.
3 We thought the party would be boring, but it **turned out** better than we had expected.
4 The factory **turns out** 100 cars a day.
5 He could not earn enough money as a teacher so he **turned to** journalism.
6 Thousands of people **turned up** to see the procession, in spite of the bad weather.
7 Don't waste any more time trying to find it. It will **turn up** somewhere.
8 He was **turned out** of his cottage for not paying the rent.

111

1 It's typical **of him to forget your address**.
2 The difference **between us is** that I am not very interested in making money.
3 I've earned **more** than £100 this week.
4 I'll take legal action against you if **you don't pay the rent by next Monday**.
5 Alex and his sister are very much **alike**.
6 The tickets didn't cost **as much as** I had expected.
7 They have **similar** attitudes.
8 The house was not really **worth as much as** he paid for it.
9 It was **such a tiring journey** that we were all exhausted by the time we arrived.
10 The conditions you have been offered are the same **as those offered** me.

112

1 He has such a strange accent that I can't **make out** what he is saying.
2 He was too ill to go to the party, so we bought him a toy to **make up for** it.
3 Bad service does not **make for** good relations between companies and their customers.
4 He is not as honest as he **makes out**.
5 He spends the evenings **making up** stories for the children.
6 How many stamps do you need to **make up** the set?
7 The prisoners are believed to be **making for** London.
8 The sign was so far away that I couldn't **make out** what it said.
9 He **made over** all his property to his son.
10 I was very upset when we quarrelled and

I'm happy that we've **made it up**.

113

1 They have **made a complaint** to the management.
2 Now you will have to **make a choice**.
3 They have **made** me **an offer** of the job.
4 I hope you will **make a success of** what you're doing.
5 The police **are making enquiries** into the matter.
6 I'm not going to **make excuses for** his behaviour.
7 I think you **have made a mistake**.
8 The Minister **made a speech** on television.
9 I'd like to **make use of** this idea, if you don't mind.
10 He **made a journey** across the Sahara Desert.
11 **Make haste**! We'll be late.
12 You shouldn't **make fun of** people who are disabled.

114

1 The moment **she came in she switched** on the light.
2 It's **very kind of you to** take so much trouble.
3 The children **are easy to keep** under control.
4 We seem to be incapable **of making progress** without destroying things.
5 Do you mind having to work **on your** own?
6 **There's no** point **in arguing** about things you can't change.
7 Who's **in** charge **of** the sales department?
8 He makes inspections of the factory **at regular** intervals.
9 I am sure I can count on **your working** together.
10 I think the proposal would be worth **considering**.

115

1 The meeting was nearly over when he **brought up** the problem of the new salary scales.
2 It won't be easy to **bring** him **round** to our way of thinking.
3 We hope to **bring out** your book before Christmas.
4 It's the best thing that has happened in women's fashion since they **brought in** the mini-skirt.

5 His kindness gradually **brought about** a change in her attitude.

6 Her parents died when she was young and she was **brought up** by her aunt.

7 Throw some water on her face. Perhaps that will **bring** her **round**.

8 He was caught in the rain last night. That must have **brought on** his cold.

116 1 He's likely **to arrive late**.

2 She is regarded **as** the greatest actress in the world.

3 They have been accustomed to problems of that kind for **a long time**.

4 He **is very** fond **of** apples.

5 My opinion **of what he is saying is that it is** a lot of nonsense.

6 They **all sent** their kindest regards.

7 Many people **do not** know what has been achieved.

8 The shops are **within easy** reach.

9 At some country parks, you may **have to pay** an admission fee.

10 However, it only **costs** £1.

117 1 I **came across** this old diary in my desk.

2 Look! The crocuses and all the other spring flowers have **come out**.

3 Do you think this question will **come up** at the next meeting?

4 How on earth did that **come about**? It seems strange.

5 He has **come in for** a lot of criticism because of his policy.

6 I don't know if this experiment will **come off**, but it's worth trying.

7 We seem to have **come up against** an insoluble problem.

8 I can't understand what **came over** you for you to behave so rudely.

9 I was very disappointed in the film, which did not **come up to** our expectations.

10 He **came into** a fortune when his aunt died.

118 1 **Have** you **succeeded in solving** the problem yet?

2 **Did** he **account for** the machine **breaking down**?

3 All I am asking you to do is **to reply to** my question.

4 Several people **have applied for** the job.

5 Many people **do not know what** has been achieved.

6 I can't **let you** park here.

7 What time do you expect the plane **to arrive in** London?

8 Can you **explain to me** how it is done?

9 **Describe** it.

10 **It didn't appeal to me** very much.

119 1 What was the reason **for** the delay?

2 She can't **have left** the baby alone in the house.

3 Did he explain **why he had behaved like that**?

4 He may **not have understood** what he was supposed to do.

5 They **were** probably surprised that you rang them in the middle of the night.

6 I don't think he's **well** enough to be moved from the hospital.

7 The Government aims to provide these people **with special cars**.

8 Special cars **are going to be provided for** handicapped drivers.

9 He spends **a lot of money on** his stamp collection.

10 It took **him two hours to do** the shopping.

120 1 As time **went on**, he got used to his new surroundings.

2 She has **gone through** a great deal in the past year.

3 Why is there such a crowd outside? What's **going on**?

4 Milk **goes off** very quickly in hot weather.

5 I've decided to **go in for** the Proficiency examination.

6 Please **go on**. I'm sorry I interrupted you.

7 He thanked them for inviting him, and **went on to say** how much he had enjoyed the evening.

8 There's not enough food to **go round**.

9 You should not have **gone back on** your promise.

10 Your tie **goes** very well **with** your suit.

11 No one saw the thieves' faces. All we have **to go on** is the number of the car.

12 The Government threatened to raise taxes, but did not have the courage to **go through with** such an unpopular measure.

121 1 We **convinced** him **not to resign/that he should not resign**.

2 If that noise goes on, **it'll drive me** mad.

3 This sort of action **will lead to** trouble.

4 Did you **enjoy yourself** at the party?

5 We eventually **made them** give us back the money.

6 I don't think **I have enough money** to buy a new television.

7 He **finds it difficult to** make ends meet.

8 I have always **considered him to be** an honest person.

9 I **suggested that he shouldn't** take any medicine without consulting the doctor.

10 Would you **advise** people **to take** these cold cures?

122 1 He spoke to her kindly **so as not** to alarm her.

2 They have locked the door to prevent **the cat getting out**.

3 They built a high wall so that **the prisoners couldn't escape**.

4 The thief wore gloves to avoid **leaving fingerprints**.

5 He sent them to university so that **they would have a good education**.

6 They must **have been enjoying themselves**, because they were laughing and singing.

7 I **only realised** that I should have got out **when** the train had left the station.

8 They **didn't seem to understand** the difficulties involved.

9 You were not **to** blame for the accident.

10 The tickets **have already been posted** to your address.

123 1 I won't **put up with** your insults any longer.

2 The meeting has been **put off** for a week because the boss is away.

3 She **put herself out** to make everybody feel at home.

4 I was lucky you were able to **put** me **up** for the night.

5 His opponent's remarks **put** him **off** and he played badly.

6 He **puts aside** £5 every week towards his summer holiday.

7 The air crash was **put down to** engine failure.

8 When I accused him he **put on** an innocent expression.

9 He has **put** his house **up** for sale.

10 Could you **put** me **through** to your sales office, please?

124 1 Neither he **nor his wife knows** how much it cost.

2 Every **student is expected** to register before the beginning of term.

3 **Their success** was due to their hard work.

4 We **haven't heard** from Sheila recently.

5 They should seek legal advice instead **of taking** the law into their own hands.

6 You ought **to have taken** your medicine after breakfast.

7 Why don't you **ask the bank to lend** you the money?

8 He has lived here since **he was born**.

9 It's strange that none of the newspapers referred **to it**.

10 It's strange that it **wasn't mentioned in** the newspapers.

125 1 He **stood in for** the leading actor, who was ill.

2 The painting is so good that it **stands out** from the others in the exhibition.

3 If you are not prepared to **stand up for** yourself, how can you expect us to help you?

4 The letters UNO **stand for** 'the United Nations Organisation'.

5 These components are expected to **stand up to** great pressure.

6 I will **stand by** the agreement.

7 Do you expect me to **stand by** and do nothing when I see a friend being attacked?

8 I'm not prepared to **stand for** any more insults from you.

9 When he heard that the President had decided to seek re-election, he **stood down**.

10 We **stand for** a fair day's pay for a fair day's work.

126 1 The floods **resulted in** the dam collapsing.

2 The collapse of the dam **resulted from** the floods .

3 They were against the plan because they thought it would **cost too much**.

4 The question of dam safety has once again **been raised** because of the recent accident in Brazil.

5 His warnings **arise from** the research he has carried out.

6 I am glad to hear he **has recovered from** his illness.

7 It is a pity we **didn't succeed in contacting** him before he left the country.

8 The Prime Minister **commented on** it in his speech.

9 He has **substituted for** another actor, who was not available.

10 I was afraid he would **set fire to** the house with his experiments.

127 1 There **was no one** there.

2 No **changes have been made to** the plans since our last meeting.

3 There **is no one who** works harder than he does.

4 He had **too much to do** to pay any attention to me.

5 He doesn't **speak quickly enough** to sound convincing in the part.

6 They arrived so **late that we weren't** able to

make use of them.

7 The law has not yet been **put into** effect.

8 Most dam failures take **place** soon after construction or much later.

9 Under the new law, local authorities have been put **in charge of** dams.

10 Do you think she is as **tall as me**?

128 1 I won't **take up** any more of your time.

2 I know you're upset at missing the train, but that's no reason to **take it out on** the porter. It's not his fault.

3 When I'm too old to play tennis, I'll **take up** golf.

4 You can see from his nose that he **takes after** his father.

5 Flight 123 to Paris will **take off** in five minutes.

6 They have been buying shares in the hope of **taking over** the firm.

7 I've afraid you've been **taken in**. These pearls are not genuine.

8 He **took off** the Prime Minister perfectly on television last night.

9 The children have **taken to** their new teacher.

10 I have received your report and will **take up** the matter with the department concerned.

129 1 I wouldn't **take any notice** of them if I were you.

2 Where did the accident **take place**?

3 It's wonderful to hear that she has agreed to **take part** in the ceremony.

4 These problems must also be **taken into account**.

5 Why were you **taken aback** by what he said?

6 **Take care of** yourself!

7 As the police refused to listen to their complaints, they decided to **take the law into their own hands**.

8 The thieves obviously **took advantage of** your absence to get into the flat.

9 He **takes it for granted** that I will help him whenever he is in trouble.

10 He didn't mean to upset you. You mustn't **take it to heart**.

130 1 For many years, Hollywood owed **much of its success to the western**.

2 The television companies not only **bought westerns from Hollywood, but also created their own series**.

3 **Few** westerns were made in the 1970s, and they were neither **very good nor very successful**.

4 Film-makers were no **longer interested in**

westerns when they ceased to be profitable.

5 The crucial factors are **those of** technique.

6 The audience likes to take **an active part** in deciding what films should be made.

7 He doesn't **live** in this neighbourhood **any longer**.

8 The success of a film depends on the reaction of the audience, rather **than on its quality**.

9 We had **better leave** now.

10 Up **to a point**, I agree with you.

131 1 It is one thing to plan a new town, and another to **carry** the plan **out**.

2 He **carried on** working although he was tired.

3 He **carries on** as if he were the owner of the place.

4 He lost his place in the middle of his speech, but **carried** it **off** so well that no one noticed.

5 He **carried** the project **through** in spite of the problems.

132 1 Now that I **think about** it, aren't you the young man who gave me a lift home last Sunday?

2 We are **thinking of** going to Italy for our summer holidays.

3 I can't say 'Yes' or 'No' to the plan now. I must have time to **think** it **over**.

4 **Think of** what would happen if the level of the water in the river rose three metres in a single night!

5 I'll **think** your proposal **over** and let you have my decision tomorrow.

133 1 Michael was **the only one who** helped me.

2 Sarah **was the only one who** passed the examination.

3 Michael and Sarah **are the only acquaintances of hers** I know.

4 Do you still refuse **to help us**?

5 One **has to keep one's wits about one in this sort of situation, doesn't one**?

6 It's **the time it will take to get there that** worries me.

7 He sounds **as if he knows** what he's talking about.

8 Judging from those black clouds over there, it looks as **if it's going to** rain.

9 It was **in Edinburgh that we took them**.

10 That has never occurred **to me** before.

134 1 I'm **looking for** my pen. Have you seen it anywhere?

2 I **look forward to** meeting you again.

3 I'll **look after** the children while you're out.

4 We **look upon** this invention as one of the

most important in modern times.

5 I must stay in tomorrow. Some people are coming to **look over** the house.

6 I'll **look into** the matter, Madam, and find out what has happened.

7 I have **looked up to** him since I was a small boy.

8 She **looks down on** us because she belongs to an exclusive club.

9 I couldn't just stand there, **looking on**, when I saw him attacking the girl.

10 Don't **look to** him for help.

135 1 I **suggested that he should** go and see a doctor.

2 It **reminded me of** my childhood.

3 I **object to paying** more for it than it is worth.

4 I'**d rather walk** if you don't mind.

5 I **couldn't face seeing** that film again.

6 I **am sorry I told** her about it.

7 Would you **object to** my bringing a friend with me?

8 I **couldn't help interrupting** him.

9 He **is not used to getting up** so early.

10 I **couldn't stand working** for a man like that.

136 1 I'm afraid the books still **haven't arrived**.

2 He doesn't like working while he **is on holiday**.

3 The first performance was good, but the second was better **still**.

4 If **we don't leave soon, we'll be late**.

5 He would **rather walk than go by car**.

6 I wish **I had known you were in town last week**.

7 She suggested **that I should go and see the doctor**.

8 Should **you need any attention during the night, please ring this bell**.

9 Were **you to leave the company now, you would find it very difficult to get another job**.

10 I wish **they wouldn't put records on** at this time of night. TO BE

137 1 It's obvious that he **is out for** promotion from the way he speaks to the boss.

2 I **am off** to Bangkok tomorrow.

3 We must have a chat about it as soon as the conference **is over**.

4 Tonight's concert **is off** because of the illness of the soloist.

5 He **is not in** at the moment. I'll let you know as soon as he returns.

6 If I **am still up when** you come home, I'll

make you some coffee.

7 What'**s up**? You look upset.

8 Oh, dear, we **are out of** butter. I forgot to buy some.

9 What's **on** television tonight?

10 Those children **are** always **up to** something.

138 1 I hardly **ever pay** any attention to what he says.

2 Let's **not** throw away all the work we have done.

3 You should **get your hair cut**.

4 'You can't imagine **what a fuss he** made', she said.

5 I don't think he was **responsible for** the mistakes that have been made.

6 I doubt if the changes will have **much effect on** us.

7 This weekend people are heading for the coast **in large numbers**.

8 The company's policy does not **make sense**.

9 What is the **point of arguing** when nothing can be done about it?

10 It is doubtful **whether the experiment is of any value**.

139 (1) making (8) made (15) make
(2) made (9) do (16) do
(3) do (10) make(s) (17) making
(4) make (11) doing (18) do
(5) do (12) do (19) making
(6) make (13) make (20) do
(7) makes (14) make (21) make

140 1 If there **were no farmers**, the landscape could not be maintained.

2 Whether the situation **will remain unchanged in the future** is not entirely clear.

3 No one **knows whether it will be possible to create other jobs** that will not destroy agriculture.

4 Her husband does not **work nearly as hard as she does**.

5 The conditions make **it very difficult to cultivate anything**.

6 He explained **to us that this was** the best way of doing it.

7 My wife reminded **me to ring my aunt that evening**.

8 He offered **to give** me a hand with my luggage.

9 He apologised **for not having** contacted me before.

10 He warned me **that there had been** a lot of accidents there.

SET

141
1. They **set off for** London early in the morning.
2. He **set out** to prove he was a good workman.
3. We have **set up** a branch office in Manchester.
4. I must **set about** getting the dinner ready.
5. The thief broke the electric circuit and **set off** the alarm.
6. The rings were **set out** in the jeweller's window.
7. Every month I **set aside** some money for my old age.
8. The wallpaper is bright, and **sets** the carpet **off**.
9. He was **set upon** by a gang of youths.
10. Winter seems to be **setting in**.

142
1. As **I was too tired to walk any further**, I took a taxi.
2. There's no reason for **you to** be upset about it.
3. She insisted **on being taken to see** the manager immediately.
4. I tried to convince him **that he should act** with caution in view of the situation.
5. They searched the neighbourhood **for** the thieves.
6. They felt that they could **have made more** money from the collection.
7. Since **there was** no further business, the meeting broke up at 10 o'clock.
8. Of course it **belongs to** me.
9. I hope you don't object **to my saying this**.
10. You should set **an example to** your students.

WORK

143
1. If we sell 20 machines for £100,000, that **works out at** £5,000 each.
2. We have **worked out** a system for improving the delivery of materials.
3. The play gradually **worked up to** a climax.
4. Everything **worked out** according to plan.
5. We're still **working out** a solution to the problem.

144
1. He **convinced** the jury **that he was innocent.**/ He **convinced** the jury **of** his innocence.
2. Can't you **convince** him **that he should try** again?
3. They have **replaced** the old glass bottles **with** plastic ones.
4. Who is going to **substitute for you** while you are away?
5. He **inherited a lot of money from** his uncle.
6. I **demand to see** the manager.

7. I **demand that the manager should come down** immediately.
8. He **asked her to marry him**.
9. I don't think you can **rely on** computers to solve all your problems.
10. A mistake of this kind could **result in** the wrong person **being** arrested.

145
1. As **she was a nurse**, Mary was able to help the victims of the accident.
2. As a result **of the heavy rain, the river** burst its banks.
3. Herbert was **the only one who didn't like** the play.
4. The cat jumped on the table, and in **doing so**, scattered the cups everywhere.
5. I like all fruit, but I like apples **best of** all.
6. Nothing **will satisfy him except the truth**.
7. He never listens, **however often** you tell him.
8. Anyone **who believes that** must be out of his mind.
9. He was deserted by all of them, without **anyone to help** him.
10. What **gave you** the impression that I was planning to resign?

146
1. I have **given up** smoking several times, but I always start again.
2. My windows **give on to** the square.
3. He swore he had nothing to do with the crime, but his fingerprints **gave** him **away**.
4. I'm not going to **give up** as long as I have any chance of winning.
5. The food for the voyage would have **given out** if they have not rationed it.
6. When I opened the bottle, it **gave off** a peculiar smell.
7. I will not **give in** to threats of violence.
8. It was **given out** that the Minister would be coming to the reception.
9. He has **given up** his job and retired to the country.
10. His life was **given up** to idle pleasures.

147
1. He finds **it difficult to maintain** his concentration.
2. He encouraged **the children to** get to the top.
3. His poor eyesight made it **more difficult for him to study**.
4. No one **has ever thought** that education and freedom could have conflicting aims.
5. What is wrong **with letting him choose** his own career?
6. It is **accepted that he is** an expert on the subject.

7 Both **segregation according to ability and on class lines are thought** to be bad.
8 The school is reputed **to have** high academic standards.
9 The maximum choice should be allowed, **unless it has** an adverse effect on the system.
10 He is **known to be** interested in buying the house. *TO DO*

148
1 It has **nothing to do with** my affairs.
2 It is a bad law and the Government should **do away with** it.
3 The dress **does up** at the back.
4 We are going to have the living room **done up**.
5 The baker's is shut, so I'm afraid we'll have to **do without** bread this evening.

149
1 The fire **did a lot of damage** to the house.
2 The dog won't **do you any harm**.
3 He asked too much for **doing repairs** to the car.
4 I would always be happy to **do you a service**.
5 To **do him justice**, I don't think he really meant to deceive you.

150
1 I always enjoyed **visiting** the old town.
2 It was decided **that they would set up a different form of administration**.
3 **In other** places, the problems are quite different.
4 There ought **to be** a law against it.
5 In personal terms, London owes **a lot of its wealth to the surrounding counties**.
6 They should **have consulted** the people before they put this law into effect.
7 I'm not in the **mood to listen to** your complaints this morning.
8 I appealed **to him not to do** anything so foolish.
9 In my view, the preservation **of this building is worthwhile**.
10 Commuters **find the underground** very convenient.

151
1 Building a new bridge will **call for** a large sum of money.
2 She gave him back his engagement ring and **called off** the wedding.
3 He was willing to help but his services were not **called for**.
4 He was **called up** the day war broke out.
5 He **called upon** them to resist oppression.

152
1 **Keep off** the grass!
2 They **kept up** a lively correspondence for several years.

3 You will have to **keep in with** the boss if you want to make progress in this firm.
4 I wish you wouldn't walk so fast. I can't **keep up with** you.
5 The department has been closed down, but the workers have been **kept on**.

153
1 **Unless you help me**, I cannot do it.
2 **They are entitled** to demand redundancy payments.
3 I hope that we can **work on** this project **together**.
4 **Describe it to** me.
5 **They cannot be made** to accept it against their will.
6 You will have to **make a choice**, one way or the other.
7 Have you **made an application** to the university for a grant?
8 Have you **submitted your application** to the university for a grant?
9 Some critics **attribute it to** Rembrandt.
10 The Queen cannot take the side of any political party **in case she is** defeated with it.

154
1 Although I **have seen** the film already, I don't mind seeing it again.
2 By the time he retires at Christmas, he **will have worked for** the firm for 40 years.
3 We **have been** friends since we were at school together.
4 I think he played very well considering that he **has been ill** for several months.
5 By the time he **had made up his** mind what to have, everyone else was half-way through the first course.
6 When he was at school, he is said **to have been** an excellent student.
7 I've been abroad for seven years, so it's a long time since we **last met**.
8 Don't interrupt me! I **know what** I'm talking about!
9 When you **have finished** the washing-up, will you dust the dining-room, please?
10 We'll still be working while they **are enjoying** themselves on holiday.

155
1 We must order some more before we **run out**.
2 I **ran into** your brother in the street yesterday.
3 I'm not prepared to listen while you **run down** my best friend.
4 Don't **run away with the idea** that the job will be easy.
5 There's nothing seriously wrong with me.

I'm just **run down**, and in need of a rest.

6 Let's **run over** the main points of the article again.

7 Unfortunately, her dog was **run over** and killed.

8 I'm afraid we can't **run to** such an expensive holiday.

9 My driving licence **runs out** next week.

10 I've never **run up against** such an unpleasant man.

156
1 **Whenever I pass** that house I think of Uncle James.

2 I must **protest at** this method of questioning.

3 His sudden resignation has **given rise to** speculation.

4 We **arrived at** the station after midnight.

5 He called on the mayor **to pay his respects**.

6 It's a long time since you **paid us a visit**.

7 I **hardly ever** see him these days.

8 **Have you heard from** Mary recently?

9 There **isn't any** sugar **left**.

10 The police have **called off** their search for the missing children.

157
1 If I had known that it would make him angry, **I would not have asked** that question.

2 **If I don't see you** before you go on holiday, have a good time!

3 I wish you **could have seen** his face when he opened the present.

4 I wish they **wouldn't make** such a noise every night. I can't sleep!

5 She would have passed the exam if she **had worked** harder.

6 Had I not lost your address, **I would have sent it** to you.

7 If only **I had known you were** coming! I would have made a cake.

8 Should anyone **call** while I'm out, please take a message.

9 If I **won** the lottery, I would buy a new house.

10 We would be grateful if you **would send it** by return of post.

158
1 Let's **break off** for a while and have some tea.

2 We can **break down** the process into four stages, which will make it easier to understand.

3 My car **broke down** and I had to walk.

4 The war **broke out** without warning.

5 The meeting **broke up** at 10.00., and everyone went home.

6 She **broke down** when she heard the terrible news.

7 The burglars **broke into** the house and stole the television.

8 'You've no right to say that!' he **broke out**.

9 School **breaks up** three days before Christmas.

10 The police **broke up** the crowd of demonstrators.

159
1 I noticed two people **coming towards** me.

2 She is afraid to go out at night **in case she is** robbed.

3 Volunteers are being accepted in the army, **however young they are**.

4 The experts filmed people's behaviour on one crossing **of this kind**.

5 We **are likely to** hear a great deal about this in a few years' time.

6 Walking sounds **such a** complicated skill when the experts discuss it.

7 This won't **put** dedicated walkers **off**.

8 **No sooner had I come in than** the phone rang.

9 You **gave** him **sensible advice**.

10 I **disagree with** that suggestion.

160
1 Not until I had read the book again **did I understand** its true meaning.

2 I had a wonderful time at the party, and **so did** my wife.

3 Seldom, since I began my career, **have I had** the opportunity of working with such truly professional people.

4 She says Mrs Brown wasn't happy about the divorce. Neither **was her husband**.

5 Not only **do they come** late, but they don't even apologise!

6 Neither the Prince **nor the Princess rides** a bicycle.

7 Only after a great effort **did they succeed** in carrying the boxes upstairs.

8 Only the **wearer knows** if the shoes really fit her.

9 Under no circumstances **will I agree** to your marrying that man.

10 Rarely **do children take** any notice of their fathers when they say things like that!

161
1 Attendance at cinemas has **fallen off** in recent years.

2 Its a good thing we have another speaker to **fall back on**.

3 He applied for a number of jobs but they all **fell through**.

4 Everything **fell out** according to plan.

5 I **fell in love with** her as soon as I saw her.

ON – up – over – down.
out of – away – at – on f
on

6   They have **fallen behind** with the payments, so the company have reclaimed the television set.

7   I never expected them to **fall out**.

8   He finally **fell in with** my suggestion.

9   Do you think they will **fall for** it?

10   The support he had been counting on **fell away** in the week before the election.

162

1   **How do you react** when you see a flag-seller?

2   A friend of hers **gave her the** idea.

3   **Changes have been made in** our methods in recent years.

4   The flags were sold **to help** the blind.

5   This week, washing powder is being sold **at half price**.

6   I **would rather you didn't** come home so late.

7   **Would you mind helping** me, please?

8   He **fell asleep** as soon as he got into bed.

9   On our way to Norway, we'll **break our journey** for a few days in Amsterdam.

10   The Queen **was the person who** introduced flag-days to Britain.

163

1   The house is beautiful. It **must have cost** him a lot of money.

2   I **shouldn't have spoken** to you like that.

3   You had **better take** your umbrella.

4   You **can't have** done. He is in Australia.

5   I'd rather you **told the truth**, instead of telling me lies.

6   I **could speak** French when I was ten years old.

7   If you go to the library, they **will be** able to give you the information you're looking for.

8   He **might have missed** his train, for example.

9   He spoke so softly that I **had to ask** him to repeat the question.

10   You **will have** to be more careful!

164

TO GET

1   He is very intelligent and sure to **get on** in life.

2   We're trying to **get up** a football team to play against the next village.

3   I've **got over** my illness now and feel much better.

4   He **doesn't get on very well** with the people who work with him.

5   This terrible weather **gets me down**.

6   I ran after the thief but unfortunately he **got away**.

7   You said you would help me to wash up. Don't try to **get out of** it.

8   He is so charming that he can insult people

and **get away with** it.

9   I know what you're **getting at** but I'm not sure that you're right.

10   He's **getting on for** eighty (years old).

165

1   That whining voice of his **gets on my nerves**.

2   We mustn't **let** the situation **get out of control**. *To get out of hand*

3   It's about time you **got rid of** that old overcoat.

4   He's a clever businessman. It's not easy to **get the better of** him. *To defeat*

5   He borrowed a lot of money and **got into debt**.

6   The result of the argument was in doubt for some time but eventually we **got the upper hand**.

7   How did you **get it into your head** that it wasn't true? *To start to believe sth*

8   He found the job difficult at first, but he soon **got into his stride**.

9   In the fight he **got the worst of it**.

10   He has a bad temper, so don't **get on the wrong side of him**.

166   *To have*

1   Who **did you borrow** the money **from**?

2   **What is your explanation** for the loss of the money?

3   I'll help you, **provided that** you help me in return.

4   He is **in debt**.

5   **One** must look after **one's** own interests in this world.

6   Haven't they **explained it to you**?

7   How much did **you pay for it**?

8   I **find** it very **attractive**.

9   **It doesn't matter if** he comes or not.

10   **You needn't have** done all this by yourself.

167

1   You may have imagined we were old friends from the way we were talking, but as **a matter of fact**, we first met a week ago.

2   Of course we could sell the shares, but **on the other** hand there is something to be said for holding on to them.

3   I'm not altogether convinced by what you say – **in other** words, I think you're making a mistake.

4   We may eventually be justified in making a bid for the company, but **for the time** being, I think we should let things take their course.

5   **In the first** place, it is obviously to our financial advantage.

6   I wish I could share your optimism about the project, but **to tell you the** truth, I don't think it will succeed.

7 I don't really agree with what you say, although I support your ideas **to a certain** extent.

8 The performance was not perfect, but **on the** whole it was a reasonable attempt at a difficult play.

9 Take the car to the garage and get some petrol, and **in the** meantime, I'll go to the post office.

10 How can you possibly vote for such a man when you've told me over **and over again** that you can't stand him?

168

1 I don't **have any objection** to what you have proposed.

2 He has certainly **had an influence on** the course of events.

3 I must admit that my poor health has **had an effect on** me.

4 I don't know how he could have **had the heart** to drown the kitten.

5 **I had a long talk with** him.

6 I didn't interrupt them, because I saw they were **having** a serious conversation.

7 They **have** no interests **in common**.

8 I don't know how he **had the nerve** to say it.

9 You **have no right** to criticise me.

10 Did you **have a good time** at the party?

169

1 **I thought I might** find you here.

2 He obviously **had something on his mind**.

3 I tried to **persuade him not to do** anything so foolish.

4 He **has a tendency to worry** about unimportant details.

5 They are not really **very alike**.

6 They have very few interests **in common**.

7 How did you **expect me to know** what you were planning?

8 I have known him **since I was born**.

9 I was **on the point of** giving them up for lost when they arrived.

10 I **would hardly be able to** ask her for money.

170

1 I must **have/get my eyes** tested.

2 He's always had to catch the 7 o'clock train to work, so he**'s had to get** up early.

3 Let's go out and enjoy **ourselves**.

4 He was so funny that I couldn't help **laughing**.

5 We searched for the children all night, but it was not until dawn **that we found them**.

6 I'm tired. It's time we **went to** bed.

7 They locked the door to prevent **anyone from getting** in.

8 Neither Mr Smith nor Mrs Smith **knew**

where their daughter was.

9 I wonder why **we haven't heard** from John recently.

10 Incredible **though it is**, the story I'm going to tell you is absolutely true.

171

1 Will you **see to** this customer, please, Miss Jones?

2 **See** them **out**, will you?

3 He pretended to be a rich businessman, but we **saw through** him.

4 We're going to the airport to **see** them **off**.

5 I must **see about** the dinner.

172

1 There are two things to be discussed which were **held over** from the last meeting.

2 The train was **held up** because of fog.

3 Do you think the rain will **hold off** until we get home?

4 I don't **hold with** letting children do just what they like.

5 They **held out** for three days before the enemy broke through their defences.

6 The Minister said he could not **hold out** much hope of an early end to the strike.

173

1 A number of candidates **have submitted applications** to the Council.

2 One notice-board **is enough** to provide the information.

3 The improvements please **both** the workers **and** the management. **Both** the workers **and** the management are pleased with the improvements.

4 The railway has **never** given **such a good** service.

5 We are **as little** to blame **as** anyone else.

6 They **are ignorant of** the true facts.

7 Do you think you can **confide in** him?

8 The Prime Minister has been **informed**.

9 The crowd was estimated **to be over** a hundred thousand.

10 It took the jury a long time **to arrive at** a verdict.

174

1 She **apologised for not having** dealt with my request earlier, and said she would handle it straight away.

2 The doctor **advised him to** take a month's holiday because he needed a rest.

3 He said he would **not make up** his mind without consulting his wife.

4 He kindly **offered** me a lift to the station, and of course I accepted.

5 Thank you for **explaining to us how** the machine works. We are very grateful.

6 The detective **accused him of** stealing the money.

7   He said there was no proof that he had been involved, and **denied having** (had) anything to do with the affair.

8   It was a good thing you **reminded me to** post the pools coupon.

9   I saw the children playing near the quarry and **warned them not to** do so, because they could easily fall in.

10 It was clear that we were not going to reach agreement, so Sally **suggested that we should** put off a decision until the next meeting.

175   1   I knew nothing about it, and John will **bear out** what I have been saying.

2   The days **close in** in November.

3   I was talking to a friend, but the operator **cut us off**.

4   Unless we can prevent people from hunting these animals, they will **die out**.

5   Have you **drawn up** a list of points for us to discuss at the conference?

6   I don't think the possibility of our refusing had **entered into** their calculations.

7   My mother would have come to the wedding, but she didn't **feel up to making** the journey.

8   **Hang on to** your ticket! You'll need it later.

9   The shelf fell on his head and **knocked him out**.

10 This is the price **laid down** by the manufacturers.

11 You can rely on me. I won't **let** you **down**.

12 I doubt if the family will ever **live it down**.

13 Unfortunately, the play did not **live up to** our expectations.

14 He was frequently interrupted at the beginning of his speech, but once the police arrived, the meeting **passed off** without further incident.

15 We have spent a lot of money on the hotel so we hope it will **pay off**.

16 The train **picked up** speed as we left the station.

17 He agreed to lecture here next year, but I couldn't **pin** him **down** to a firm date.

18 There is a rumour that a number of ministers are going to be replaced, but the official spokesman is **playing** it **down**.

19 The thieves have **pulled off** one of the most daring robberies of the century.

20 His lecture was mainly about 'Hamlet', but he also **touched on** 'Macbeth'.

176   1   What **appeals to me** about Constable's work is its straightforwardness.

2   He did not **think it necessary** to add anything to what he had said before.

3   He **takes it for granted** that we will all support him.

4   **Is he aware of** the change in the situation?

5   I agree with you **up to a point**.

6   They are **short of money** at the moment.

7   His style of painting is **out of date**.

8   I'm afraid the book you are looking for is **out of stock**.

9   The rebels were **put to death**.

10 This example **brings** the exercise **to an end**.

177   1   I **have been working** so hard all morning that I feel worn out.

2   You needn't worry about the operation. You'll be asleep while the doctors **are operating on you**.

3   If we hadn't taken our umbrellas, we **would have got wet**.

4   I can't drive a car yet, but I **will be able to** when I have passed the test.

5   Should anyone **make you** a better offer, we'd be grateful if you'd let us know.

6   I wish you **wouldn't talk** while I'm working. It's very irritating.

7   I **was on the point of ringing** her when she rang me instead.

8   Of course he needn't have told you about it. He **could have kept** silent.

9   It's a pity you weren't there. You **should have heard** what he said when I told him the news.

10 I'm sorry, but I don't know **what you're talking** about. Are you sure you dialled the right number?

Section 5: Selective Cloze

The answers given below are for the most part the only acceptable possibilities, but there may be cases where alternatives not included here could fit in satisfactorily. Marks should only be awarded on such occasions, however, if the word makes sense in combination with other words, including blanks filled, in the same sentence; the alternative shoud be rejected in cases where it fills the gap correctly in isolation but does not make sense in the context as a whole. In this connection, words that are grammatically correct but in fact distort the meaning of the passage as a whole, (e.g. where *less* is used to fill the gap instead of *more*, which is correct) must also be rejected.

178
(1) the
(2) his
(3) on
(4) writing
(5) who
(6) makes
(7) as
(8) There
(9) much
(10) as

179
(1) whose
(2) among
(3) in
(4) in
(5) in
(6) whose
(7) at
(8) between
(9) who
(10) in
(11) up
(12) to
(13) at
(14) where
(15) that
(16) in
(17) without
(18) which
(19) from
(20) which

180
(1) According
(2) for
(3) hand
(4) of
(5) spite
(6) make
(7) matters
(8) either
(9) what
(10) In
(11) practice, fact
(12) work
(13) anything
(14) other
(15) as
(16) much
(17) how, whether
(18) circumstances
(19) rather
(20) at
(Note that such answers as 'appeals' (7) and 'much' (13), while grammatically possible, do not really convey the meaning of the passage as a whole.)

181
(1) place
(2) little
(3) made
(4) what
(5) must, should
(6) as, so
(7) on
(8) small
(9) two
(10) on
(11) than
(12) ago
(13) nothing, little
(14) an
(15) called, entitled
(16) there
(17) over
(18) every
(19) expected
(20) in

182
(1) It
(2) for
(3) with
(4) as
(5) unless
(6) by
(7) led
(8) first(ly)
(9) made
(10) unable
(11) only
(12) from
(13) in
(14) one
(15) being
(16) course
(17) without
(18) than
(19) at
(20) as

183
(1) sort, kind
(2) likely
(3) ask
(4) like
(5) There
(6) Whatever
(7) worth
(8) why
(9) hand
(10) one
(11) rising, increasing, growing
(12) at
(13) seems, appears
(14) so
(15) as
(16) very, so, extremely
(17) those
(18) Apart
(19) keeping, making
(20) let

184
(1) course
(2) for
(3) improve
(4) though, if, although
(5) make
(6) use, good
(7) choose, read, get
(8) across
(9) what
(10) without
(11) glance
(12) for
(13) rather
(14) unless
(15) ago
(16) as
(17) how
(18) which
(19) instead
(20) well, easily

185
(1) carried
(2) either
(3) few (or two, three, etc.)
(4) shows, indicates, says
(5) second, latter
(6) number, series
(7) may
(8) for
(9) put
(10) in
(11) sooner
(12) no
(13) due
(14) Until
(15) seldom, rarely
(16) even
(17) Furthermore, Besides
(18) although, though
(19) making, having
(20) in

186
(1) during, in
(2) Few
(3) or
(4) on
(5) which
(6) Unlike
(7) provided, showed
(8) one
(9) As
(10) longer
(11) like
(12) made
(13) less
(14) lost
(15) in
(16) on
(17) with
(18) puts
(19) themselves
(20) any

187

(1) while, although
(2) less
(3) far
(4) other
(5) capable
(6) cannot
(7) from
(8) on
(9) found
(10) for
(11) sets, gives
(12) like
(13) getting
(14) said, reported
(15) with
(16) order
(17) its
(18) getting, reaching
(19) himself
(20) wish

188

(1) rather
(2) as
(3) many, most
(4) similar
(5) All
(6) deal, cope
(7) where
(8) so
(9) being
(10) in
(11) from
(12) one
(13) in
(14) make
(15) since
(16) below
(17) which
(18) case, event
(19) looking
(20) thinking

189

(1) though
(2) as
(3) responsible
(4) Up
(5) yet
(6) on
(7) any
(8) by
(9) in
(10) once
(11) ever, good
(12) were, was
(13) make
(14) use, point, advantage
(15) so
(16) which
(17) difficult
(18) done
(19) There
(20) from

190

(1) least
(2) a, every
(3) make
(4) few
(5) stand
(6) job
(7) do
(8) view
(9) being
(10) afraid, frightened
(11) as
(12) to
(13) capable
(14) which
(15) without
(16) thanks
(17) cared
(18) kinds, types, sorts
(19) must, should
(20) part

191

(1) grew
(2) which
(3) one, anyone
(4) allowed, permitted
(5) had
(6) becoming
(7) for
(8) while
(9) fond
(10) whose
(11) like
(12) for
(13) last, 82!
(14) much
(15) nearly
(16) made
(17) from
(18) What
(19) mind
(20) on

192

(1) but, although, though
(2) should, could
(3) as
(4) let
(5) whom
(6) such
(7) in
(8) several, many
(9) every
(10) making
(11) one
(12) much
(13) order
(14) come
(15) Instead
(16) should
(17) in
(18) nothing
(19) make
(20) dressed

193

(1) on, entitled
(2) to
(3) as
(4) between
(5) on
(6) as
(7) every
(8) which
(9) above
(10) from
(11) given, allowed
(12) on
(13) which
(14) another
(15) teaching
(16) with
(17) would
(18) likely
(19) better
(20) point

194

(1) there
(2) as
(3) in
(4) up
(5) would, should
(6) favour
(7) pay
(8) their
(9) little
(10) with
(11) longer
(12) becomes
(13) arises
(14) doubt
(15) to
(16) in
(17) having
(18) ago
(19) rise
(20) own

195

(1) there
(2) in
(3) since, as, because
(4) looking, glancing
(5) newspapers
(6) same
(7) explaining
(8) copies
(9) worth
(10) at
(11) being
(12) between
(13) claim, promise
(14) to
(15) at
(16) birth
(17) every
(18) on
(19) forecast
(20) tells

196

(1) have
(2) most
(3) until, till
(4) search
(5) part
(6) make
(7) by
(8) worst
(9) those
(10) at, towards, near
(11) set
(12) whom
(13) Even
(14) few
(15) where
(16) still
(17) being
(18) though
(19) ever
(20) on

197

(1) as
(2) that, one
(3) able, going
(4) towards
(5) own
(6) walker, pedestrian
(7) otherwise
(8) too
(9) splits, breaks
(10) let
(11) doing
(12) holding
(13) each
(14) most
(15) turn, reach
(16) for
(17) make
(18) together
(19) along, on
(20) at

198

(1) How
(2) on
(3) Or
(4) Whichever
(5) no
(6) their
(7) when
(8) result
(9) being
(10) many
(11) to
(12) a, every, each
(13) any
(14) kind, type, sort, nature
(15) at
(16) This
(17) took
(18) given
(19) cost
(20) sale

199

(1) come	(8) used, tended	(14) place
(2) read	(9) grounds	(15) build
(3) which	(10) stronger,	(16) capable
(4) amount,	bigger,	(17) as
come	larger	(18) in
(5) one	(11) above	(19) more
(6) taking	(12) no	(20) whose
(7) whether	(13) out	

200

(1) being	(8) involved	(15) whose
(2) made	(9) few	(16) suffered
(3) of, aged	(10) drive	(17) second
(4) far	(11) leads	(18) at
(5) shining	(12) whom	(19) his
(6) still	(13) as	(20) such, these
(7) worn, needed	(14) losing	

201

(1) least	(10) longer	(16) from
(2) about, going	(11) able	(17) with
(3) way	(12) what	(18) at
(4) luck	(13) run	(19) better
(5) which	(14) thanks,	(20) ever
(6) grateful	owing, due	
(7) says, claims	(15) over, nearly,	
(8) on	almost, about	
(9) As		

202

(1) Unlike	(8) from	(15) terms
(2) little	(9) have	(16) so
(3) On	(10) as	(17) find
(4) spite	(11) give	(18) extent
(5) allowing,	(12) enough	(19) owes
permitting	(13) after	(20) earn
(6) have	(14) little,	
(7) in, seeing	nothing	

Test Papers

The scoring system adopted in the Cambridge Proficiency examination, depending as it does on computer-processed correlation with Papers 1 and 2, does not give a clear indication of the marks to be assigned to the different sections of the test papers that follow, which imitate the form of the examination. It is, however, justifiable to assume that something very close to the marking system adopted below, which will be clear for teachers to follow, applies in the examination itself. The pretesting results for the first 50 questions in the papers are given, my aim being to provide papers of equal difficulty where 32/50 (64%) should be considered equal to Cambridge standard. In marking Section B of the paper, teachers should bear in mind that only answers coming very close to those suggested should be awarded both marks for the first 15 questions, and that in correcting the summary, 13/20 should be considered as good enough for a Cambridge pass, 15/20 a B level pass, and 17/20 an A level, virtually equivalent to intelligent native-speaker performance.

Section A contains 50 questions, each counting one point, with no half-marks awarded. Section B (questions) contains 15 questions, each counting two points, one of which should be awarded for an answer demonstrating a clear understanding of the question, and the second only if the answer is complete, and resembles the suggested answer given. Section B (summary) should be marked out of 20 on the lines suggested above, and assessed according to the suggestions given. The total mark should be 100, where 64 per cent represents pass level, 72 per cent a pass at B level, and 80 per cent a pass at A level. Marks between 60 and 64 should be considered marginal passes. While there is unlikely to be much difference between scores from one paper to another, it is clear that an accumulated average score for the three papers will be more reliable than the result obtained by an individual student on any one of them.

Test Paper 1

Section A: Statistical analysis

Average score in pretesting: 33·1/50 (66·2%)
Estimated Cambridge level: 33
Discrimination analysis: 0·43

173

Answers:

1

(1)	what	(8)	making	(15)	mistake
(2)	That	(9)	as	(16)	belongs
(3)	lays	(10)	place	(17)	how
(4)	act	(11)	either	(18)	but
(5)	of	(12)	top	(19)	brought
(6)	those	(13)	deal, cope	(20)	few
(7)	one	(14)	rid		

2 a) I wish I had written down her address.

b) She dropped the milk jug and, in doing so, spilt the milk on the carpet.

c) Under no circumstances will I sign a binding contract.

d) He must not be told (must not hear) about it, whatever happens.

e) There's no reason for them to object, as far as I can see.

f) Let's not leave them behind.

g) I'm not bothered about it. Harold is the one (the man, the person) who's getting upset.

h) He never went back to Farley without being reminded of his happy childhood there.

i) It was unkind of him to say it was my fault.

j) He may not have seen the note you left on the table.

3 a) I have been looking (searching) (trying to find) you everywhere. (NOTE: The Past Continuous forms, 'was looking', etc., are also acceptable.)

b) When you have taken (gone in for) (been present at) as many examinations . . . (And other reasonable verbs in the right tense.)

c) If you hadn't spoken to her so rudely, . . .

d) He couldn't have done.

e) I'm sorry to have kept you waiting such a long time.

f) Only when I had read the message a second time did I realise (understand) what it meant.

g) To tell the truth, I don't think . . .

h) . . . but I doubt if he is capable of doing it well.

i) . . . it's time I was going (I went) home.

j) . . . whether he likes it or not (whether he is listening or not). (Or any other acceptable verb in the right form in context.)

4 a) He's lived here all his life.

b) Did you succeed in finishing the job?

c) I take it for granted you will be at the meeting tonight.

d) The new plan cannot be put into effect immediately.

e) Did he give any reason why he behaved like that? *or* Did he give any reason for behaving like that/for his behaviour?

f) His father did not approve of what he had done.

g) There's no point in losing your temper.

h) You shouldn't pay any attention to what she says.

i) I don't think there will be enough food to go round.

j) These problems must also be taken into consideration.

Section B

Suggested answers: (NOTE: I have not insisted on complete sentences here so as not to distort the marking system.)

5 a) Something that results indirectly from the situation.

b) Because fewer roads will be built and some of the money saved can be spent on schemes helping pedestrians.

c) Creating shopping precincts in the centres of new towns or blitzed cities.

d) Trade obtained from customers who stopped their cars on the way along the street.

e) Because they were afraid that they would lose the trade provided by shoppers in cars.

f) The idea that 'traffic-free streets must be totally free at all times of all traffic'. It has proved impossible to achieve this in Chichester.

g) 'It' refers to 'foot-streets'. (NOTE: Strictly speaking, the author should have written 'them', but the idea is clear.)

h) 'It' refers to London Street in Norwich.

i) They were convinced by the fact that trade did not decrease during the time when the street was closed to traffic (because of the sewer works).

j) Because it slows down the traffic, as a policeman would do if he were standing there, and acts as a kind of traffic control.

k) It is a good example of the installation of 'complete rear servicing without excessive cost or damage or delay'.

l) The phrase means that the effort and expense involved would not be justified by the advantages gained.

m) They were given confidence by the way in which the design of the area (suggested it was a pedestrian area and) caused lorries and vans to respect it.

o) It means that the lorries and vans had no right to be there, and were only allowed to be there as a concession.

p) The summary should make the following points:

1 At first there was a great deal of opposition to pedestrian shopping streets because shopkeepers were afraid that they would lose their trade.

2 Planners also slowed the process down by insisting that such streets should be free of traffic at all times.

3 The streets began to become more common when traders realised that customers enjoyed being able to look in the shops without worrying about cars, and when councils were either able to provide rear servicing cheaply or made rules that only allowed lorries and vans into the area on condition that they respected the rights of pedestrians. (97 words)

In effect, there are five points, and there is no need to cite examples of where the different systems proved successful.

Two marks should be given for the mention of each of the points mentioned, and the remaining ten should be allotted according to the standard of English and organisation of the paragraph.

Test Paper 2

Section A: Statistical analysis

Average score in pretesting: 33·4/50 (66·8%)
Estimated Cambridge level: 33
Discrimination analysis: 0·44

Answers:

1 (1) such   (8) look   (15) According
   (2) an, any   (9) as   (16) as
   (3) opposite   (10) which   (17) so
   (4) to   (11) taking   (18) able
   (5) that   (12) both, all (19) like
   (6) speaking   (13) whether   (20) do
   (7) as   (14) place

(NOTE: Some alternatives of variable validity – e.g. free, empowered – are possible for 18, which I leave to teachers' discretion.)

2 a) . . . in case any of them were prejudiced against him.
   b) Because of his illness (the fact that he was ill), he wasn't able to take part.
   c) She had (put) a new coat on.
   d) It was thanks to her hard work that we succeeded.
   e) It was not until last Wednesday that they had (some) news of his whereabouts.
   f) He said: 'You should have looked where you were going.'
   g) You had better leave now, before the rain starts.
   h) His honesty, more than anything else (more than his other qualities), is what I admire most about him.
   i) Susan hasn't written to us (hasn't rung us) (hasn't been in contact with us) recently.
   j) Only when there was no hope of victory did they surrender.

3 a) . . . how she gets her work done (how she is able to get her work done). (Also, variations with 'manages to', 'succeeds in'.)
   b) I wish I had taken (followed) (listened to) your advice.
   c) You needn't have done all the washing-up by yourself . . .
   d) . . . I'd rather have stayed (remained) at home. (NOTE: Other verbs may be acceptable here, provided the right form is used.)
   e) . . . in spite of all the changes that had taken place since his childhood.
   f) . . . I have never seen (heard, etc.) anything like that before.
   g) Had I grown up (been brought up) in such terrible conditions . . .
   h) . . . You should have paid attention to what I was saying.
   i) No sooner had the bell rung than they all rushed out of class. (NOTE: Other situations may be valid here – 'had the teacher spoken to them than . . .', etc.)
   j) He's not used (accustomed) to working at night . . .

4 a) I can hardly understand it.
   b) I am afraid of nothing (not afraid of anything). (NOTE: Although a little unusual – Nothing can make me afraid.')
   c) The court found him not guilty on all counts (. . . decided he was not guilty . . .).
   d) They described it as the best performance they had ever seen.
   e) I hope you don't object to me (my) talking to you like this.
   f) I'm going to put you in charge of this department.
   g) You've worked very well, so I'm going to give you a rise in salary.
   h) Why did you take offence at what he said? (Or, such elaborate paraphrases as 'What was the reason for you (your) taking offence at what he said?')
   i) We look forward (will look forward) to seeing you next Monday.
   j) They have replaced the old glass bottles with plastic ones. (Or, a passive sentence, 'The old glass bottles have been replaced . . .')

Section B

Suggested answers:

5 a) It means singing as loudly as it can or using the whole range of its repertoire in song.
   b) The daily battle for survival, (which resembles a sword-fight).

c) The oscines produce a number of complicated melodies, while other birds make simple call notes.

d) Because 'there is a seasonal correlation between the time they begin singing' and the time when they choose their territory and attract a mate.

e) 'Proclaiming territorial ownership' and 'attracting a mate'.

f) The phrase means that when a bird recognises the song of one of its own species, it knows that the other bird may try to take over its territory; 'it' refers to 'the song of his own species'.

g) The problem is that it would not be necessary for a bird to have such a complex repertoire of songs if it only intended to convey the simple message, 'Keep out' (and so there must be another reason for it).

h) It means 'getting used to one's surroundings' – (in this case, to a new territory).

i) The writer's research indicates that great tits 'habituate more rapidly to repetitive playback of a single song' and so a repertoire of songs may be intended to prevent other birds from habituating.

j) It means 'looks for different places to establish its home' (just as a shopper goes to different shops to compare prices, etc. before making a decision).

k) A repeated song suggests to a bird that there are not many birds in the area and so it is a good place to settle.

l) 'A low density area' is one where there are not many birds.

m) 'The territory holder' is the bird already established in the area.

n) The writer suggests that birds have a repertoire of songs in order to suggest to new arrivals that there are more birds in the area than there really are, and so discourage them from settling there.

o) It would be possible to prove his idea correct by comparing the reaction of birds settling in an area to recordings of song repertoires and others of single song types. (If the birds were discouraged by the recordings of repertoires and not by the others his theory would be correct.)

p) The summary should make the following points:

1 Song birds differ from other birds in being able to produce a repertoire of complicated melodies.

2 Because they begin singing at the time when they establish territories and mate, most people assume that they sing to prevent other birds from entering their territory.

3 The writer argues that it would not be necessary for them to use a complex repertoire

simply to tell other birds of the same species to keep out.

4 Since birds habituate more easily to a repeated song than a repertoire, his theory is that the repertoire suggests a greater concentration of birds, and so discourages newcomers from settling. (99 words).

Test Paper 3

Section A: Statistical analysis

Average score in pretesting: 32·6/50 (65·2%)
Estimated Cambridge level: 33
Discrimination analysis: 0·49

Answers:

1
(1) their	(9) audience	(16) if, though
(2) no	(10) or	(17) why
(3) have, get	(11) make	(18) such
(4) listening	(12) prevent	(19) anything
(5) which	(13) another	(20) say,
(6) on	(14) in	contribute,
(7) in	(15) most, only	offer
(8) front		

2
a) Unless he pays the rent by Saturday, I'll throw him out.

b) He may not have been working here long, but he's already impressed the manager.

c) The thieves are thought to have hidden the money near here.

d) Nothing less than the full amount will satisfy him.

e) I'll never forget what a terrible state she was in.

f) There was no one for him to talk to.

g) Should she feel worse during the night, give her these tablets.

h) I don't know what gave you the idea (what put it into your head) that I'm rich.

i) Such famous conductors as Toscanini and von Karajan have brought their orchestras here.

j) But for my affection for you, I would have hit him.

3
a) I'll ring you as soon as I get back (return) (have got back) (have returned) from my holiday.

b) Everything that could have gone wrong did go wrong.

c) . . .No, I'd rather you did it now.

d) It's the first time she has ever arrived (come) late.

e) . . .I will have done (answered) hundreds of examples like this.

f) . . .in case it gets colder later on.

g) . . .Oh, so you haven't heard from her since then.'

h) If only I had known (been told) you were coming! . . .

i) It was such a funny story that we couldn't stop laughing.

j) The doctor suggested that he should give up smoking, . . . (suggested to him that . . .) (NOTE: suggested his giving up smoking – but it sounds very odd.)

4 a) I insist on knowing what happened/I insist that you should tell me what happened.

b) You shouldn't let them take advantage of you.

c) It doesn't matter to me whether we go or not/Whether we go or not doesn't matter to me.

d) It's not my fault.

e) He is considered (to be) the world's leading authority on the subject.

f) The difference between us is that I'm due to retire next year.

g) I might have imagined (known) I would find you here.

h) They have very little in common (very few interests in common).

i) The play did not live up to our expectations.

j) I'm afraid that book is out of stock at the moment.

Section B

Suggested answers:

5 a) They suggested Antarctica is a special case because only twelve countries were invited to participate, whereas the sea and outer space are considered to be the responsibility of all countries.

b) The twelve countries participating in the meetings to discuss Antarctica. They are privileged because no other countries were invited.

c) It means that there are practical considerations involved, and Antarctica is not just a subject for learned, theoretical discussion.

d) The phrase means the food and other natural resources whose future depends on the twelve countries concerned.

e) Krill is important because it appears to be 'the world's largest single source of animal protein'.

f) It could create 'environmental hazards' because of the risks of oil spills occurring in seas where icebergs and other natural hazards make navigation difficult.

g) 'This' refers to 'the biological decomposition of oil'.

h) 'Spills' are escapes of oil from tankers. They would be particularly dangerous in the Antarctic because the ice would prevent them from spreading and make it difficult to clear up the pollution, and the low temperatures would slow down the decomposition of the oil, or stop it altogether.

i) 'Food chain' means the process by which one species feeds on another, and is fed on in turn, so producing a chain.

j) The gap is formed by the comparison of the krill eaten by whales before and the krill eaten now, when there are fewer whales. It is assumed that man could fill it by eating the krill no longer eaten by whales.

k) Antarctica provides scientists with a 'unique scientific laboratory', because it is undisturbed. Its exploitation would threaten research by changing the conditions, and it would also be more difficult for scientists to operate freely.

l) The rules made by the exploiting companies preventing people from travelling across the areas being exploited.

m) Next to them, very close to the areas being exploited.

n) They are likely to discourage them from travelling freely and conducting their research and to try to prevent them from spreading information freely about the area.

o) It means an integral part. (Secrecy is accepted as being automatically associated with commercial exploration.)

p) The summary should make the following points:

1 Exploiting the natural resources of Antarctica involves enviromental hazards, with consequent effects on the ecology of the area and possibly on world weather conditions.

2 Oil spills from tankers are likely in seas where icebergs make navigation difficult. The ice would prevent spills from spreading and decomposing. Apart from upsetting the ecological balance of the area, this could affect the climate elsewhere.

3 Exploitation of the food supplies in the Antarctic would have a dangerous effect on other species, and we do not know how it would be affected by a change in present conditions. (91 words)

(The question is concerned with ecology and therefore does not require any reference to the effect on scientific research.)

1 although ✓

2 less 3 simile 4 other 5 dated 6 nere

7 on 8 on 9 landed 10 for

11 giv 12 ~~testify~~ likes 13 getting 14 said

15 ✓ it 16 ~~able~~ 17 the 18 reading

20 ✓ ish